For Theory

For Theory

Althusser and the Politics of Time

Natalia Romé

FOREWORD BY WARREN MONTAG

ROWMAN & LITTLEFIELD
Lanham • Boulder • New York • London

Published by Rowman & Littlefield
An imprint of The Rowman & Littlefield Publishing Group, Inc.
4501 Forbes Boulevard, Suite 200, Lanham, Maryland 20706
https://rowman.com

6 Tinworth Street, London SE11 5AL, United Kingdom

Copyright © 2021 by The Rowman & Littlefield Publishing Group, Inc.

All rights reserved. No part of this book may be reproduced in any form or by any electronic or mechanical means, including information storage and retrieval systems, without written permission from the publisher, except by a reviewer who may quote passages in a review.

British Library Cataloguing in Publication Information Available

Library of Congress Cataloging-in-Publication Data
Names: Romé, Natalia, author.
Title: For theory : Althusser and the politics of time / Natalia Romé ; foreword by Warren Montag.
Description: Lanham : Rowman & Littlefield, [2021] | Includes bibliographical references and index.
Identifiers: LCCN 2020051587 (print) | LCCN 2020051588 (ebook) | ISBN 9781538147641 (hardcover) | ISBN 9781538147658 (epub)
Subjects: LCSH: Althusser, Louis, 1918-1990. | Theory (Philosophy)
Classification: LCC B2430.A474 R66 2021 (print) | LCC B2430.A474 (ebook) | DDC 194—dc23
LC record available at https://lccn.loc.gov/v
LC ebook record available at https://lccn.loc.gov/2020051588

*A las Madres y las Abuelas de Plaza de Mayo.
A las mujeres de Calama.
A las caminadoras de la memoria, porque nos enseñaron a vivir en estado de búsqueda.
A ellas y a la revolución feminista de las hijas de sus hijas.*

*To the Madres and Abuelas de Plaza de Mayo.
To the women of the Calama desert.
To the memory walkers, because they taught us how to live in a state of searching.
To them and to the feminist revolution of the daughters of her daughters.*

Contents

Foreword: Natalia Romé: Theory from the Outside   ix
   Warren Montag

Acknowledgments   xix

Introduction: Althusser *y nosotrxs*   1

Part I: Conjuncture

1   Against Theoretical Reformism: Materialism of the Imaginary, the Unconscious, and the Class Struggle   9

2   Against Humanism and Denunciation of Alienation   67

3   Against Neo-Anarchism: Toward a Radicalization of Social Reproduction Theory, within Plural Temporality and Overdetermination   93

Part II: For Theory

4   No Theoretical Thinking without Political Thought; No Political Thinking without Theory   127

5   Political Desire of the True: No Future without Marx   153

References   171

Index   181

About the Author   185

Foreword

Natalia Romé: Theory from the Outside

Warren Montag

Natalia Romé's *For Theory* is not just another book on theory. As the title suggests, it is both an argument for the need to pursue theory, to move toward theory, and for the necessity of taking the side of theory against its diverse critics. For reasons that will become clear shortly, the critics that concern her are not those who assert that we, globally, have passed into the epoch of post-theory, as if, according to a historicism of a linear succession of distinct epochs, the moment of its necessity has passed, yielding to a new moment marked by the elimination of (the need for) theory. Romé is well known in the Hispanophone world, and increasingly beyond, as a specialist in the work of Louis Althusser and it would be difficult to find a philosopher less inclined to accept analyses that proclaim "the end of" x and the inauguration of the time of "post-x," than Althusser. Romé is well aware that such declarations have a performative rather than descriptive function—that is, they are formulated with the aim of bringing about the state of fact that they pretend to describe. Moreover, the more frequent such declarations are, the less effective they become. Marxism has been pronounced dead so many times that it now appears immortal, its periodic retreats the surest sign that it is preparing a renewed assault, while those who insist that it is dead are understood to be expressing nothing more than their wish that it were. If this is true of Marxism, what is to be said about theory?

When critics, primarily in the United States, argue that the time of theory is over, the theory to which they refer is nearly always what is called French

Theory, organized around a pantheon consisting of Lacan, Foucault, Derrida, and, yes, Althusser, thought to be united by bonds too obvious to require any demonstration. What Romé means when she argues for theory, however, is something quite different from the Anglo-American construct, even when she refers to Lacan or Derrida: for her, the problem is to understand the precise relation of theory to practice, and more specifically, following Althusser, the nature of the unity of theory and practice that he regarded as central to Marxism. Further, unlike most scholars concerned with Althusser's work in the Anglo-American world, she has never been content simply to offer yet another commentary on or interpretation of Althusser; instead of simply thinking about Althusser as if his work in its totality belongs to the past, or forms a closed system that can simply be applied to some aspect of social reality, she attempts to think with him, in his idiom, and with the concepts (in their various stages of incompletion and unevenness) that he continued to produce throughout his life. Her concern with theory begins with and in Althusser's repeated attempts to grasp exactly what we mean when we speak of theory—that is, and this is important, we who are Marxists who, as in Marx's final thesis on Feuerbach, seek to understand the world in order to change it. The problem for her is not to prove that theory is still alive and well, but to specify its relation to practice and to politics. There is no outside of theory that in turn cannot be understood as existing outside of practice; the two are consubstantial. As the case of post-theory shows, the argument against theory must itself take a theoretical form, a case of one tendency in theory attempting to gain the advantage over an opposing tendency by disguising itself as non-theory. The criticisms of Althusser by Rancière and Thompson, as Romé points out, are examples of the uses of this disguise. Further, for Romé, the idea that it would somehow be possible to dispense with theory—let alone the question of the relation between theory and practice—is a luxury denied to those whose struggles are waged outside of Europe and North America, struggles whose existence no one would think to deny, and this is what gives Romé's book its urgency.

How does theory serve the process of changing the world? If it is the case that, as Althusser once argued, "in principle, true ideas always serve the people; false ideas always serve the enemies of the people," theory's role is to draw a line of demarcation between the true and the false as established by practice and in doing so, make true ideas visible and available (Althusser 1971, 8). In reality, of course, these actions are not separate steps in a chronological process, but simultaneous: theory accompanies practice and cannot exist without it. The question for Althusser was how theory accomplished the task of differentiation and demarcation that unites it with practice. Here, we confront what is singularly Althusserian: the unending quest for an adequate concept of theory, unending because it is grounded in a perpetual (re)theorization of theory, a quest that doomed to failure every attempt to define "Althusserianism." In the early 1960s, Althusser confided to Franca Madonia that he often invented concepts "on the spot" and at the last minute, in response to the urgent necessities he encountered without warning as he opened a path through the field of philosophy—that is, in the course of his own theoretical practice (to cite one of those very "improvised" concepts) (Althusser 1998, 756). If Hegel could speak of the patience of the concept, as it slowly and painstakingly worked its way through the trials necessary to the achievement of its end, Althusser's conceptual itinerary was marked by impatience: concepts tended to appear, only suddenly to disappear without comment, except perhaps later, in the body of self-criticism (not simply the *Éléments d'autocritique*, but his *soutenance*, published in English as "Is It Simple to Be a Marxist in Philosophy" [Althusser, 1990], and other works written in the latter half of the 1970s) to which he increasingly devoted himself after 1968. A significant number, however, vanished so soon after they appeared that they escaped the notice of many of his readers and indeed appeared to have been forgotten by Althusser himself. He left behind a trail littered with abandoned concepts, treated like vehicles fit only to transport him through certain kinds of terrain and not others. Even in the case of concepts that seem to have been preserved—if not throughout his work, at least through a relatively long period, such as "ideology"—we find that what persists is the word rather than the concept. The notion of *ideology* captured in the phrase "Ideological State Apparatuses" is not the same as that outlined in "Marxism and Humanism" (in *For Marx*) and is in fact defined in opposition to it. Althusser's relentless need to create new concepts, marked or unmarked as such, creates significant difficulties for readers attempting to grasp his work as a whole, confronting them with a series of discontinuous theoretical moments that can neither be understood as entirely separate nor as a progressive, linear sequence. To understand this, as Romé does, frees us to examine Althusser's concepts one by one without assuming that they were abandoned in favor of better concepts (or, for that matter, worse ones), considering them both in the light of his work in all its complexity and combined and uneven development and in the light of the present whose struggles may illuminate notions that heretofore remained unseen.

Romé thus rejects the assumptions that underlie the two most common ways of confronting the discontinuities and breaks characteristic of Althusser's writing: (1) the attempt to discover the hidden unity and continuity beneath its apparent diversity, as if he sought different ways of saying the same thing from "Contradiction and Overdetermination" to the *Underground Current of the Materialism of the Encounter*; and (2) the idea that Althusser's concepts were abandoned by necessity, each superseded by a superior concept, as if the late Althusser invalidates the earlier, and aleatory materialism represents a resolution of the problems associated with the notion of overdetermination. Instead, she takes certain of his concepts in their specific incompleteness, not to apply them as if they were finished, as was common in the 1980s, but to put them into practice, to test them and modify them in the light of the results. Moreover, she is too perceptive a reader to grant validity to Althusser's retrospective judgments, as if against everything he taught, his authorship conferred on him the authority to determine the meaning and effects of his texts and as if his exercises in self-criticism were not themselves texts susceptible, like any other, to a symptomatic reading. She is too Althusserian not to see the parapraxes at work his self-critical texts and not to understand the extent to which the effectivity of his concepts varies with the conjuncture in which they are put to work. Much of her book can be seen as an extended search through the conceptual pileup (*carambolage*) Althusser left behind to recover what, in the light of the present, Romé judges most useful to the work of shifting the balance of forces in theory and in practice on which the established order rests.

Of these concepts, one of the most important for any consideration of theory is that of reading. I refer here not simply to the concept, one of Althusser's most fruitful, of symptomatic reading, but just as importantly to his theorization of the act of reading in the work that followed *Reading Capital*—in particular, *Philosophy and the Spontaneous Philosophy of the Scientists* and *Lenin and Philosophy* (written in the period 1967–1968). While his discussion of *Reading Capital* focused on the text, the discrepancies, and lacunae that Althusser argued were symptoms of its unresolved conflicts, the discussions of philosophy that followed described the activity of reading itself. To read philosophical or theoretical texts as a materialist (*en materialiste*), he argued, was to draw lines of demarcation within them, the effect of which was to make visible the fractures and points of conflict that are the effects of the great struggles that spill over into the most carefully argued texts—for the simple reason that these texts participate in the conflicts they claim merely to observe or ignore. If it seems clear that the activity of symptomatic reading overlaps with reading *en materialiste*—in that for both, the conflictuality of philosophical and theoretical texts is their condition of intelligibility—Althusser did not specify their relation, leaving them isolated from each other and in certain ways from his larger theoretical and political project.

That said, Romé does not simply take ideas Althusser forged in different historical conjunctures in the heat of different battles and apply them readymade in her readings of theoretical texts, including and especially those of Althusser. If we can say that Romé appropriates some of Althusser's concepts for her own purposes, we must expand the meaning of the adjective "own." In a manner very similar to Althusser himself, who argued that a communist never thinks alone, and whose every text (including those produced in the last decade of his life) was the product of lengthy debate and discussion with the community of thought that took shape around him, Romé is above all a participant in a collective process of developing these concepts, of testing and refining them. Her appropriation is a collective appropriation, or an expropriation that distributes the means of theoretical production (forces and relations) to meet the needs of those engaged in struggle—both the process of gathering the intelligence necessary to fend off or attack a relentless enemy, and the production of knowledge from the raw material it provides. We might recall the fact that the notion of Ideological State Apparatuses was a modification of the Marxist theory of ideology in response to the experiences of the mass struggles of May 1968 that made the material existence of ideology visible and undeniable. In putting it this way, I do not mean to diminish the power and singularity of her work, but on the contrary to say that these qualities are the effects (the "Romé effect," to cite Althusser's "The Philosophical Conjuncture") of the collective practice of theory of which she is a part (Althusser 2003, 17).

The Anglo-American reader will undoubtedly find this way of speaking about theory strange: we remain captives of the individualization characteristic of what Foucault called the author-function, no matter what we think, or think we think. Nor should we be too quick to dismiss this feeling of strangeness: it is the objective effect of the fact that the productivity of Romé's work is determined in part by the place and time in which she writes and thinks. She brings to this field of inquiry the perspective of those shaped by the theoretical and practical preoccupations and concerns of the beginning of the twenty-first century, quite distinct from those, especially of the moment of

1968–1969, who left their imprint on all the great works in French and Italian written in anticipation of or response to the events of that time. Althusser did not live to witness the moment the end of history was proclaimed—and with it the triumph of liberalism and capitalism—nor the moment, not long after, the end of history itself ended and gave way to the epoch of war, economic crisis, and the slow-but-now-accelerating collapse of liberal democracy. Romé seeks to show, however, that a number of his ideas are singularly useful in the present conjuncture, on the condition that they are properly modified to confront the specific difficulties facing us now.

What sets hers apart from countless other studies devoted to theory—perhaps more than the historical moment in which, after all, many such studies have been produced—is the specific position or place she occupies and from which she speaks. Nearly fifty years ago, Althusser returned to Machiavelli's assertion that "just as those who sketch landscapes place themselves down in the plain to consider the nature of mountains and high places and to consider the nature of low places place themselves high atop mountains, similarly, to know well the nature of peoples one needs to be prince, and to know well the nature of princes one needs to be of the people. one must be of the people to know the prince"(Machiavelli 1964, 3). For Althusser, the precise configuration of conflicting forces, their nature and composition, and the relations of subjection and exploitation coextensive with them that define a given society at a given time cannot be known from a position of neutrality and objectivity—that is, from a position outside of the conflict. Instead, he argues that in a necessarily conflictual reality, such as a society, "one cannot see everything from everywhere; the essence of this conflictual reality can only be discovered on the condition that one occupies certain positions and not others in the conflict itself" (Althusser 1991, 21). To understand capitalism and capital, he argued, one must occupy the place of the very proletariat that capital seeks to exploit, the place of its adversary, the object of its strategy and tactics, and thus the position from which the struggle it wages may be seen and felt.

Let us take Althusser's argument one step further and say that the ultimate "conflictual reality" in Althusser's sense is the global order as a whole, a society of societies that is anything but an organic whole. Natalia Romé writes from a very specific and, indeed, singular place in this conflictual reality, one from which I would argue many things can be seen that are invisible to those situated in North America or Europe: Argentina, and in a broader sense the Southern Cone of Latin America, where, in a condensed and displaced form, some of the greatest dramas of the latter half of the twentieth century were played out. The Cuban revolution marked the beginning of a radicalization throughout Latin America and nowhere was it realized with greater intensity than in the Southern Cone by the end of the 1960s. The revolutionary wave that brought Unidad Popular to power in 1971 in Chile was preceded in 1969 by the insurrectionary general strike in Argentina known as the *Cordobazo*, followed by mass mobilizations of industrial workers and students, as well as by armed struggle on a mass scale. Nothing showed the magnitude of this radicalization and the extent of the threat it presented to the capitalist order (national and international) than the ferocity of the repression that came with the military regime installed in early 1976 at the urging and with the full support of the US government. In what was clearly an attempt to physically annihilate a generation of leftists, at least 30,000 radical workers, intellectuals, and students were killed, many more tortured and imprisoned, while others were forced into exile. I have elsewhere called this "absolute terror"—that is, terror without limits, emanating from both inside and outside the state, in the face of which law is meaningless and only force matters. In this condition where the only security lies in resistance, there can be no constitutional illusions and no highest court to appeal to. It is the last instance whose arrival can never be definitively ruled out and for which every revolutionary, as both Machiavelli and Lenin maintained, must prepare.

Terror was followed, with barely a respite, by destitution—perhaps nothing more than another kind of terror. Once again Argentina served as the example, this time of what can happen to those who disobey their European and North American creditors. By the end of the 1990s, more than a decade of neoliberal reforms, privatization, and severe austerity made possible by the years of repression and increasingly overseen by the IMF (International Monetary Fund), led to large-scale unemployment and general immiseration. By the end of 2001, the nation faced economic collapse, food shortages, and the disappearance of basic social services. The result was a large-scale revolt that took the form of the self-organized *piquetero* movement whose name derived from the tactic of using pickets to block transportation routes and access points. This was accompanied by workers' occupations of shuttered factories and enterprises and the creation of neighborhood *assembleas* to take up the administrative and social welfare tasks abandoned by the state. Moreover, neoliberal reforms shifted burdens of care to the family and eliminated jobs often occupied by women, in essence forcing them back into the home and aggravating existing gender inequality. This led to a what has been called a feminization of the resistance, where women often occupied leadership positions. From these experiences, a powerful women's movement arose that today is capable of powerful mass mobilizations. This movement is often called spontaneous, which is also to say that, in it, practice preceded theory; from Althusser's perspective, however, the theory of the movement that took shape between 1998 and 2002 existed, but "in the practical state," immanent in the actions and practices of the masses in their revolt.

Of course, the great struggles of the decade preceding the military coup of 1976, necessarily gave rise to debates, often fierce, over questions of strategy, based in turn on an analysis of the conjuncture, as well as of the disposition of class forces proper to Argentina. Far from leading to a dismissal of theory—and of Althusser—the necessity of debating and deciding tactics and strategy meant instead that "the reading of Althusser was undertaken with great intensity," not only in the universities (where the left was very strong), but also in the organizations of the left themselves (Ortega Reyna and Pacheco 2019, 10, my translation). In Argentina, the drift of the Communist Party to the right, above all after 1966 with the installation of the Onganía dictatorship, insured a period of fierce debate in the Party, at the very moment Althusser's students left the Parti communiste Français (PCF), citing its revisionist character. The mass radicalization that followed the *Cordobazo* and the launching of mass armed struggle only intensified the sense of the urgency of theoretical labor. Journals such as *Pasado y Presente* and *Los Libros*, from the late 1960s to the mid-1970s, published translations of Althusser's work and featured frequent discussions of the development of his ideas (Starcembaun 2011; 2017). The concepts Althusser proposed and that seemed so puzzling or objectionable to many readers in the Anglo-American world— above all, the notions of class struggle in theory, the theoretical conjuncture, and the act of drawing lines of demarcation in theor— made perfect sense as an extension of struggle into a realm that few were disposed to consider an ideal realm, outside the conflictual plane of material reality.

In fact, at the same time, Althusser and his students regarded the Cuban revolution and the process of radicalization it initiated throughout Latin America as extremely important. In 1965, the journal organized by a group of Althusser's students, *Cahiers Marxistes-Léninistes*, devoted its fifth issue to the theme *Amérique latine. Problèmes de stratégie revolutionnaire*. It featured a debate between Regis Debray and Étienne Balibar on the question of underdevelopment as it was posed by the Cuban experience. Within a little more than a year, Debray joined Che Guevara's ill-fated attempt to organize a guerilla army in Bolivia, where he was arrested and imprisoned, becoming the subject of an international campaign. Althusser corresponded with him during this time and aided in the effort to secure Debray's freedom. Sometime later Balibar visited Cuba for an extended period, where, as Jaime Ortega has shown, intellectuals passionately engaged with Althusser's work in the first decade following the revolution. Further, Marta Harnecker from Chile and Emilio de Ípola from Argentina studied with Althusser in Paris in the 1960s and played an important role in the dissemination of Althusser's positions throughout Latin America. Even in the last decade of his life, Althusser retained a vivid interest in Latin America, where he felt he had a large and sympathetic audience, and valued his friendships with Mexican philosopher Fernanda Navarro and Argentine philosopher Mauricio Malamud that only began in 1984.

While Romé's orientation to Althusser, understood in the Argentine context, is hardly unusual, the same cannot be said about the objectives of *For Theory*. Very much in the spirit of Althusser, she engages in a kind of provocation, a bending of the stick, a thinking in extremes. To *"faire bouger les choses,"* she proposes a rehabilitation not only of the notion of theoretical practice, but with certain qualifications, even of "theoreticism" itself, arguing "that the problem of the articulation of political practice and theoretical practice is already inscribed—and enacted—within the early development of the category of *overdetermination*, with which Althusser pursues the materialist figure of Marxist dialectics, even in its most 'theoreticist' formula: the definition of philosophy as the *theory of theoretical practice*" (chapter 4 of this volume). Romé highlights what in fact has been ignored even by those who have read Althusser's self-critical remarks on these questions (which few of his critics did): the elliptical and evasive character of his rejection of the definition of philosophy as the Theory of theoretical practices, together with his only partial rejection of the category of "theoretical practice" itself (it fails to distinguish philosophy from the sciences). He does not explain the conditional nature of his critique of the notion of theoretical practice—that is, he does not explain how it could be used in a way that is not "speculative-rationalist." As for the Theory of theoretical practices, which represents the high point of the theoreticist tendency: it suggests the "primacy of theory over practice; the one-sided insistence on theory" (Althusser 1976, 124). Romé to my knowledge is the first to note the paradoxes inherent in these self-criticisms, starting with the notion of theoretical practice that, if anything, extends the realm of practice to theory itself in that it asks us to understand that there can be no theory that does not have a practical and material existence. It undoubtedly bears a certain relation to what Foucault would call the mutual immanence of power and knowledge around the time of Althusser's self-criticism, but which already exists "in the practical state" in *L'histoire de la folie* (1960). Romé argues that the notion of theoretical practice, contrary to Althusser's self-criticism, prevents even the notion of the Theory of theoretical practices from establishing the primacy of theory over practice: "Althusser's so-called 'theoreticist deviation,' far from constructing a pantheoreticism or a hypertrophied formalism, allows to point out the *limits* of theory and, consequently, opens up the road to the possibility of thinking a materialist philosophy in its full right; that means, one that attempts to make history thinkable without subsuming it to its own logic. We place the nerve of this movement in the concept of overdetermination that, by being proposed as a key to the intellection of a conjuncture, lays down the limits to the *intelligible* in the *conjunctural*" (chapter 4 of this volume).

Romé performs a symptomatic reading of Althusser and most spectacularly of his own self-critical texts, drawing lines of demarcation within them that make visible what, although present to us, remained unseen and overlooked in the texts he wrote before 1968. The questions she raises in her examination of Althusser are not simply "theoretical," because as she shows, the theoretical is always united with the practical, a fact that most intellectuals are quick to deny, but which Althusser openly acknowledged. Romé introduces us to an Althusser unlike the others we have encountered: the structuralist, the aleatory materialist, the Stalinist, and the anti-Marxist. Hers is unlike the others because it consists of the addition of what Althusser rejected, salvaged from the heap of unfinished concepts he left behind, and added to the sum of Althussers we know to produce a new Althusser—an Althusser who is more than Althusser, Althusser beyond Althusser, moving outside of himself to become himself, the most authentically Althusserian theory there is: theory from the outside.

Acknowledgments

No one thinks alone. This book is the result of many years of shared readings, discussions, and conversations with a wide range of researchers, political activists, and university students. It is also the result of the work carried out within Argentinian public university, with its complexity and economic difficulties, but also its deep democratizing work. To those who participate daily in these spaces, my gratitude and recognition.

Especially to those who shaped an ethic of reading against time. To Emilio de Ípola, for his tireless lucidity and generosity. To Susana Murillo, for her passion. And particularly, to my dear mentor, Sergio Caletti, in memoriam.

To my friends and comrades in debates and struggles, Carolina Collazo, Carolina Ré, Laura Figueiredo, Ingrid Sarchman, Martina Sosa, and Silvia Hernández. To Mariana Gainza, Mara Glozman, Elena Mancinelli, Julia Expósito, and Gisela Catanzaro. With all of them, many of the questions that animate this book were woven. For their dedicated readings, for the shared writings, but especially for the perseverance on the way toward a materialistic, popular, and Latin American feminism.

To Ramiro Parodi, Carlos Britos, Ricardo Terriles, Mariana Zugarramurdi, Manolo Rodríguez, Marcelo Starcembaun, Marcelo Rodríguez Arraigada, Roque Farrán, Martín Cortés, Diego Lanciote, Ezequiel Nepomiachi, Sebastián Ackerman, Leandro Viterbo, Ernesto Schtivelband, Paula Morel, Didier Contadini, Jaime Ortega Reyna, Victor Hugo Pacheco, and Pedro Karczmarczyk, for being part of a body of thought and friendship. And to my companions of Proyecto Comunidad, because without political intelligence, no critical theory is possible.

To Vittorio Morfino, Agon Hamza, Warren Montag, Étienne Balibar, Anthony Faramelli, Stefano Pippa, Cindy Zeiger, David Pavón Cuellar, Rodrigo Gonsalves, and Danilo Martuscelli, for encouraging me in various ways in this writing and for the generosity of their readings of preliminary versions.

To Ignacio Riel-Schies and Lourdes Cruz for their seriousness and commitment in taking care of the translation and editing of the manuscripts. To Frankie Mace, Scarlet Furness, Naomi Mindlin, Janice Braunstein, and Dhara Snowden of Rowman and Littlefield for their generosity and professionalism.

To the Facultad de Ciencias Sociales and the Instituto de Investigaciones Gino Germani, Universidad de Buenos Aires, where I carry out most of my research and teaching tasks. To the Faculty of Arts, Universidad Nacional de La Plata and to the Popular Music School of Madres de Plaza de Mayo, where I have found other ways of thinking and production. To the editors of *Crisis and Critique, Continental Thought and Theory*, and the *Revista de Filosofía de la Universidad de Costa Rica*, and the volume *Ensaios sobre mortos-vivos*, where I published some preliminary fragments of this book.

Finally, to Marila Terzaghi and Juan Carlos Romé for their unconditional support and example. To my brothers and sisters.

To Martín Unzué, because there is not a single word in this book that is not due to his company, his lucidity, and his love. To Camila, Iñaki, and Maite, for the music and the laughter.

Introduction

Althusser y nosotrxs

When, in 1983, Argentina began the long road of reconstruction and reparation after a fierce civil-military dictatorship that implemented, with the connivance of international powers and the financing of large corporations, a systematic plan of political persecution, extermination, and destruction of all forms of social organization, the world had changed.

It took almost twenty years of post-dictatorship to evaluate the effects of the profound breakdown of the productive matrix; the destruction of the structures of workers' organization and of the bonds of solidarity between popular sectors, peasants, university students, and professional middle classes; and the breakdown of economic sovereignty and the subordination to the financial logic of public and private debt. The shock was so intense that it took a long time for Argentinian society to interpret the root causes of this, which was presented as an event of inconceivable violence and cruelty, despite the fact that some voices had clearly warned of the political-economic project that was forthcoming.

In this sense, the writer and journalist Rodolfo Walsh, in "Open Letter from a Writer to the Military Junta," published in 1977, shortly before being kidnapped, tortured and killed, said:

> Fifteen thousand disappeared people, ten thousand prisoners, four thousand casualties, and tens of thousands in exile: these are the raw numbers of this terror....

> Nevertheless, these events, which have shaken the conscience of the civilized world, are not the ones that have brought the greatest suffering upon the Argentine people, nor are they the worst human rights violations that you have committed. This government's economic policy is the place to look not only for the explanation of your crimes, but also for an even greater atrocity that is leading millions of human beings into planned misery.
>
> Over the course of one year, you have decreased the real wages of workers by 40 percent, reduced their contribution to domestic income by 30 percent, and raised the number of hours per day required for a worker to put in to cover his cost of living from six to eighteen, thereby reviving forms of forced labor that cannot even be found in the last remnants of colonialism. (Walsh, 1977)

Some years ago, in the chapter "The Construction of Consent," David Harvey pointed this out very clearly:

> How was neoliberalization accomplished, and by whom? The answer in countries such as Chile and Argentina in the 1970s was as simple as it was swift, brutal, and sure: a military coup backed by the traditional upper classes (as well as by the US government), followed by the fierce repression of all solidarities created within the labor and urban social movements which had so threatened their power. (Harvey 2005, 39)

Therefore, as Martin Unzué (2012) remarks, it is not a minor fact that after the coup by the Chilean socialist, Salvador Allende, in September 1973, and before the coup in Argentina, in 1976, two key figures of the neoliberal mainstream, Alfred Von Hayek in 1974 and Milton Friedman in 1976 received the Nobel Prize in Economics (2012, 7). Nor is the presence of Chicago School theorists as advisors to the dictator Augusto Pinochet a mere detail.

As the 2019 demonstrations of mass exhaustion in Chile have shown, the formally restored democracies, after long years of destruction, have been pregnant with dictatorship. Accordingly, Silvia Schwarzböck (2015) states that during the restoration of "democracy" in Argentina, a post-dictatorial mode of life coexists and blends into all areas of life, characterized by aesthetic exacerbation, explicit fictionalization, and a capacity of making unimaginable any form of life that is not right-wing. Post-dictatorship is what remains of the dictatorship, after its victory disguised as defeat. As an aesthetic concept, it is characterized by the overabundance of discourse—of "isms" that are known not to be true but can replace the insistence on the unspeakable. It is found in the aestheticization of our own defeat and in the lack of analysis of the victory of others. The post-dictatorship is a regime of *absolute representation*—an intellectual culture in the light of day and in the open air (Schwarzböck 2015, 2).

We, the generations born and raised during dictatorial and post-dictatorial 1980s in academic institutions, and even in certain areas of cultural life, let Foucault, Derrida, Deleuze, Williams, Hall, and Gramsci pass through the filter of post-dictatorship. The condition was this: that no one would talk about class struggle anymore and, especially, that the civic-military dictatorship could no longer be thought of as the dictatorship of capital. The modality would no longer be censorship but, rather, over-information, the infinite pluralization of discourses. In this new scene, where almost everything passed, some authors' writings didn't. Althusser's writings did not; his political prose and theoretical conceptualization did not lend itself to the processes of indoctrination, museumization, or aestheticization to which many others thinkers were subjected. Althusser did not pass and his absence—or his extremely caricatured presence—left the mark of something lost.

This is the truth of a case: the Argentinian case constitutes the concrete national-regional conjuncture in which the debates covered in the following pages take shape. Argentina is only just one case, but how else can historical truths be read, if not in the eternity of universal-singular "cases"?

Just as the recognition of the theoretical references of neoliberalism is global, so is the silencing of others. As Étienne Balibar has written, the violent reaction unleashed against Althusserian theory was part of the general theoretical and political operation of reducing Marxism to a dead and perished theory, consisting of denying that, in the 1960s and 1970s—for a moment that was *eternal*—Marxism was more than dogmatic repetitions. It seems that it was necessary to make us forget that there was intellectual activity and productivity and that theoretical and political events took place within it, so that Marxist—and especially Communist—intellectuals would appear in retrospect, and at any cost, as naïve victims, scoundrels, or impostors (Balibar 1993).

Why did the elimination of the Marxist component drag along with it that one who had been the incarnation of the heresy? What reasons explain the twinning, against the figure of Althusser, of the antithetical arguments of the defenders of the Marxist orthodoxy and the referents of the vanguard of the fin-de-siècle post-Marxism?

During the Venice Colloquium, organized in 1977 by *Il Manifesto*, Louis Althusser proclaimed the "crisis of Marxism." Against the dogmatic reaction of the official position, but also confronting the optimism of delegating the future of Marxism to the pure spontaneity of workers' and popular movements, he called for operating a theoretical and political distance in order to discover the meaning and scope of the so-called "crisis of Marxism" (1978b, 242–53). He questioned the idea of Marxist theory as a complete entity, a belief in which usually converges both those who consider that everything of itself has already been given and those who suppose it to be infinite and totally immune to the siege of the dominant ideology. He repeated frequently that the rupture that gave rise to Marxist theory is a battle with no end.

Inscribed in the conjuncture of Third World revolts, movements of the New Left, feminist, and anti-imperialist struggles, in the 1970s, the "crisis of Marxism" still presented the promise of an *open question*. Toward the 1980s, the operation of primitivization of Marx and theoretical Marxisms was massively consolidated—not only within the theoretical *mainstream*, but also among a wide portion of critical theories. With perseverant but isolated exceptions, its reduction to a dead body of already solved issues, the object of historiography or exegetical investigation, prevailed for decades over the active production of theory and analysis of conjuncture. The most interesting efforts of critical thought went through long detours into other territories, at a distance from Marxism—such as feminist and queer studies, the field of Spinozian philosophy, the theory of discourse and the critique of political philosophy. But Marx's heritage was a task that very few have the courage to read in the terms of an *enigma* (cf. Derrida 1993).

In South America, between the end of the last century and the beginning of the new one, the ravages caused by the failure of the information society utopia began to offer the opportunity for a meeting between critical thinking and popular desires for emancipation; some of them were articulated in political experiences and in a new kind of popular government and grew from massive movements. Within this context, a series of encounters took place between the old Marxist intellectuals who had returned from exile (or from silence, which is almost the same) and the new generations who were more eager for questions than answers. A renewed Marxist reading was growing—heterodox, plebeian, and controversial—forged in the heat of new questions but nourished by long-term traditions. The suspended promise of the Althusserian opening of Marxism regained relevance and allowed us to formulate, once again, the critical questions—of feminism, anti-imperialism, the injustices and sufferings generated by late capitalism in the form of discourses on self-exploitation, technological transparency, compulsive happiness, and uninterrupted consumerism.

The writings gathered in this volume are the product of that collective process.

Not only Althusser's writings, but also a wider Althusserian problematic that goes beyond Althusser himself and involves many names contradictorily connected and many forgotten "Marxist" fragments of still well-known "non-Marxist" philosophies, returned as a sort of compass. This was not because a revealed truth could be found in it, but because the violence of its silencing—suddenly repressed in the 1970s after a greatly successful diffusion—could be read as a *symptom* of the impoverishment of left thinking when, for one reason or another, it gradually abandoned the question of the imbrication of specific social and subjective concrete processes and the broader horizon of historical transformation.

As Warren Montag—one of the most brilliant readers of Althusserian theory—often insists, [1] perhaps we are in better position to understand the magnitude of Althusserian philosophical intervention while the increasing confluence of many isolated efforts happen (Navarro [1988] 1998; de Ípola 2007; Rodríguez Arraigada and Borques 2010; Caletti and Romé 2011; Montag 2013; Morfino 2014a; Hamza 2016; Popovitch 2017; Ortega and Pacheco 2019; Sotiris 2020; and others). Within the field of Althusserian studies, theoretical production has taken up a new impulse to unfold those insufficiently explored but extremely fruitful areas of the Marxist tradition, such as plural temporality studies (Morfino and Thomas 2017; Collazo et al. 2020, among others), research on transindividual materialism (cf. Morfino 2014; Kelly and Vardoulakis 2018; Balibar 2018; Read 2015), a left-wing tendency in Psychoanalysis (Badiou 1982; Laclau 1985; Stavrakakis 2007; Pavón Cuellar 2010) and the efforts of exploring the links between ideological-discursive conjunctures and class struggle (cf. Žižek 1989, 2002; Butler 2006). These developments matched those driven by political processes of massive scope—among which feminism, especially that of the *social reproduction theory* (Vogel 1983; Barret 1989; Brenner and Ramas 1989; Arruzza, Bhattacharya and Fraser 2019) and the heritage of *Latin-American anti-imperialist* thought (Aricó 1982; Echeverría 1994, Zavaleta Mercado 2009; Murillo 2008; García Linera 2009; Casullo 2007; Grüner 2010; Cortés 2015) are of the most interest. With deep differences and unequal degrees of development, these traditions express a common concern for recovering the ability to read the contradictions of the situation, while a majority of the critique of late capitalism is still produced within a false dichotomy between nihilistic and desperately enthusiastic tendencies, in which the image of the end of history and politics is imposed with equal force.

Because there is currently no safeguard against the melancholy of defeat, it is necessary to insist on the need to understand the tendencies of late capitalism precisely as *tendencies* of a conjuncture—that is, as contradictory processes that give shape to the complex fabric of social reality in a precarious state of regular but unguaranteed duration. Althusserian theory looked toward these specific materialist dialectics, with the guide of the category of *overdetermination*, to open the structural relations of a given order to the intelligence of its conjunctural consistency—that is to say, its contradictory and complex system of forces. This has substantive consequences: if a structure, read in the critique of its contradictory reproduction, can be taken as a *conjuncture*, then, those analyses of the current situation reduced to the given evidence of a totalized noncontradictory present, contemporary to itself, are practical denials of the political thinking. The reactionary cliché of "the end of history" expands itself to the imaginary operation that modulates the experience of an impoverished time that lies in every attempt to explain reality by turning some of its parts into its final cause. When critical thinking replicates that simplification which is the typical mechanism of dominant ideology, it is no further from idealism than the most vulgar economicism. The persistence of the old Althusserian so-called "theoreticism" finds today the renewed opportunity to support the development of the critique of this operation of simplification of the complex temporality of a conjuncture. The overdetermined complexity of the conjuncture, which lies as an assembly of times, connecting archaic memories with emancipatory desire, is today the field of a crucial dispute and, therefore, the essential task of the kind of theory we need.

NOTE

1. Among many books and essays, Montag's book *Althusser and His Contemporaries* (2013) is one of the most erudite analysis of the philosophical influences and controversies that lay in Althusser's oeuvre.

Part I

Conjuncture

Chapter One

Against Theoretical Reformism

Materialism of the Imaginary, the Unconscious, and the Class Struggle

Among his manuscripts, Louis Althusser left a ninety-page essay titled *Que faire?* ([MS 1978] 2018b), presumably written in 1978, in which he critically revised the Eurocommunist tendency within the Parti communiste Français (PCF), conceived as an identity between the end and the means and as a poor response to the crisis of communist thought and the popular *demands* of democratization in the USSR. Such a response risks being an empty proclamation that lacks a "concrete analysis of the concrete situation," not only of the class struggle of the countries concerned but of the whole world, capitalist imperialism, and "socialist countries included" (Althusser [MS 1978] 2018b, 130, 131, my translation).

In the prime of the global neoliberalization process (Harvey 2005), Althusser admonishes that the crisis of the international communist movement and, more broadly, leftist thought, is intertwined in a reformist tendency that will ultimately contribute to it.[1] The abandonment by the PCF of the crucial concept of class dictatorship and the introduction of some watchwords ("*lutter contre les saisies*"; "*pas à pas, pierre a pierre*"; "*la union de la gauche est le ciment*")[2] —tending to mark the line toward a "union of the people of France," founded by the union of the left (Althusser 2018a, 40–43), far from providing some kind of shelter from the fledgling antidemocratic tendencies[3] —leads to the risk of debasing the very concept of democracy. In a series of interventions published in *Le Monde* during the month of April of 1978,[4]

Althusser rightly discusses the *strategic* imposition of unity slogans as a top-down decision within the party. Against this idea, he proposes a popular unity, forged within masses in the experience of real antagonism, as a "primacy of combat" over the "primacy of contract" between leaders (1978). Whereas in the essay titled *Que faire?* ([MS 1978] 2018b), he focuses on the political consequences of a poor understanding of the link between *strategy* and *theory*. He warns that a slogan derived from a political line that does not take objective "conditions" seriously—however fair it may be in formal terms—cannot replace the analysis of the *concrete situation* without which no strategy is possible ([MS 1978] 2018b, 44). The crucial point is, for Althusser, an inadequate conception of the relationship between theory and concrete analysis and its replacement by an empiricist idea of the "application" of a theory to a series of observables.

Accordingly, this writing suggests the pregnancy of a certain Gramscian deviation in the transit toward Eurocommunist reformism ([MS 1978] 2018b, 88). This influence, usually recognized in Togliatti's positions, for example, is here read by Althusser in a series of expressions present in the public speeches of the PCF members, such as Marchais and Laurent (Althusser [MS 1978] 2018b, 101–2); also and more generally, in an inappropriate implementation of the Gramscian idea of "war of position" to the European reality of the 1970s; but especially, in the gravitation of a historicist conception of theory: one which operates *in a practical state* in the notion of "application" of theory to the concrete. The very idea of "applying" a theory (even if it were a good one) to the "visible concrete" cannot offer as a result any analysis of the concrete situation, but an "absolute philosophy" that is supposed to already contain the truth of any conjuncture. This tendency, is both empiricist and historicist because it does not problematize its own concept of historical time (and therefore, historical totality), and this impacts the way of conceiving the relation between theory and strategy. This is what Althusser recognizes in the recall of Gramsci within the Eurocommunist position and what he sees at work in the way the French PCF pretends to offer a political line lacking a rigorous reading of its conjuncture.[5]

In this context, the PCF's official strategy, which dispenses with a concrete analysis of the situation, strengthens theoretical errors and political risks. Some traces of idealism in Gramsci's thinking are now reinforced in the Eurocommunist reading: the idealistic approach to the concept of "concrete" that can be traced, according to Althusser, in Gramsci's theory of hegemony becomes in the PCF's discourses a foundation for a verticalist and reformist strategy. What Althusser poses is that a philosophical problem (the definition of *concrete*) that impacts both the theory of history (the concept of historical totality) and of political thought (the way of conceiving a "situation" or *conjuncture*) has consequences in the party's strategy and in its way of confusing the necessary analysis of the concrete situation with an inadequate "application" of abstract concepts to a set of observable ones.

Accordingly, Althusser recognizes a series of shifts that operate around the concept of *hegemony*, which overflies the idealistic Eurocommunist strategy, by associating the notion of "historical block" with the idea of a "concrete universal ethics," coined by Hegel, to replace the *historical* unity with an *ethical* unity, taking the conjuncture for the social totality, which should instead be conceived as its *ideological effect:* the "society effect." The interpretation of economic exploitation as a mere component of "civil society," coupled with a (corresponding) neglect of the "force" component in its conception of the state under the theory of "state *as* hegemony" (Althusser [MS 1978] 2018b, 135), tends toward a simplification of the heterogeneous elements of the historical concrete that lead to the replacement of the concept of class struggle with that of "a struggle of hegemonies" and to a partial dissolution of the materiality of the state (the part of *force*) within the question about the hegemony of the dominant class ([MS 1978] 2018b, 136).

The interest of the analysis offered by Althusser stems less from what he may elucidate of Gramsci's thought—whose consequences should be qualified by the considerations that Althusser himself proposes in other writings and even evaluated in relation to Gramsci's influence on his thinking beyond what he can recognize (cf. Morfino 2019b)—than from what it shows us about the Althusserian intervention itself and its critical commitment to its own conjuncture. If such intervention turns out to be more audible today than in the 1960s and 1970s, it is because the consequences of the theoretico-political torsion that Althusser denounced in the intellectual field that was his own, as understood by some of his colleagues and disciples may today be read more bluntly.[6]

Althusser insisted on signaling that the idealist turn in the communist intelligence, which, shrouded as a supposedly ethical affirmation, abandoned the question of the historical determinations of the conjuncture (that of the long agony of imperialism that foreshadows the coming barbarity).

Que faire? ([MS 1978] 2018b) suggests in a perhaps more explicit and "political" way, an idea that is at the beginning of the Althusserian reading of Marx since *Pour Marx* (cf. Althusser 2005)—that there is a kind of solidarity between the diverse tendencies that simplify the *overdetermined* complexity of the social totality and the *plural and noncontemporary* condition of historical time, and the tendencies to capture the strategic thought of the left by the capitalist class struggle in the ideological field. This solidarity can change its emphasis but constitutes the same operation of simplification of the concrete under the form of an idealistic abstraction: it is read as a "historicist" and "humanist" tendency in the 1960s, but it becomes, with the Eurocommunism first and the consecration of the social democracies later, a *reformist* abstraction.

"Reformist" is, in this context, the simplification of the concept of historical time in the hypertrophy of an "Absolute Present," which is the State regime of temporality. This implies a tendency to abandon the concepts of social formation and historical totality—both irreducible to a unique political temporality—under the subordination of that of the "historical block," and involves the flattening of two distinct levels: that one of the structural stability of the dominant forces and that of the imaginary eventfulness of politics, under the historicist guise of permanent change, "without a fixed point" (Althusser [MS 1978] 2018b, 66–67). "Change" may be another one of the images in whose name an impoverished conception of *time* operates, rendering unthinkable the *immanent exteriority* that constitutes any dominance and erasing the theoretical function of the concept of *class struggle*. This amounts to the simplification of the complex temporality of the concrete formations and a displacement toward a contemporary and homogenous conception of historical time in the shape of a *spiritual concrete* of the universal ethical unity.

Reformism is not here the name of a kind of "moderate" standpoint between revolutionary or integrated political standpoints; it consists, in a *theoretical operation* of a series of idealist reductions worked on the set of differential practices articulated in a social totality—economic, ideological, theoretical, political—and their homogenization in a single abstract conception of practice: the (philosophical) idea of political *praxis*.[7] Among these reductions we can see the displacement from the relational notion of political practice to an ideological conception of politics and the reduction of a necessary complex reality of state with the Idea of state—or with state's ideology. The problem is not per se the "strategic" option of fighting within state structures but the lack of a materialist conception of state, and therefore of political struggle and history that impoverishes any possible strategy. The claim against "reformism" is not about a mere and obtuse insistence on a nostalgic image of Revolution but about the need to develop strategic positions based in *theoretical* production and *realist* and rigorous analysis of the concrete situation.

THE THEORY OF IDEOLOGY AS A CRITIQUE OF IDEOLOGICAL ABSOLUTE PRESENT

Many of these ideas had been anticipated in other passages of Althusser's writings and 1960s courses at the *École Normale Supérieure* and can especially be found in the class notes published as *Politique et Histoire, de Machiavel à Marx* (2006b). It can be seen, there, that Hegel's theory of the state as the "reality" of the Ethical Idea—*die Wirklichkeit der sittlichen Idee*—developed in his Grundlinien der Philosophie des Rechts (Hegel [1821] 1955, §237), constitutes the prehistory of Althusser's theory of ideology; because his theory of *Ideological State Apparatuses* emerges from a break with the Hegelian theory of the state and, more precisely, with his idea of the state as an incarnation of the Absolute (cf. Romé 2020; 2011a, 133–40). The emergence of Ideological State Apparatuses as the unseen in the visual field of Hegelian historicism grounds the problem of the relationship between the time and philosophical discourse as part of the question regarding a materialist theory of history.

The identity reconciled in the Absolute Knowledge is, from a materialist perspective, the ideological *identification* between philosophy and history.

> It is well known that Hegel defined time as "*der daseiende Begriff*," i.e., as the concept in its immediate empirical existence. (Althusser and Balibar 1970, 93)

> Two essential characteristics of Hegelian historical time can be isolated: its homogeneous continuity and its contemporaneity. . . .
> . . . The fact that the relation between the social totality and its historical existence is a relation with an immediate existence implies that this relation is itself immediate. In other words: the structure of historical existence is such that all the elements of the whole always co-exist in one and the same time, one and the same present, and are therefore contemporaneous with one another in one and the same present. . . . It is clear that it is the specific structure of the social totality . . . , a "spiritual" unity, if we can express in this way the type of unity possessed by an expressive totality, i.e., a totality all of whose parts are so many "total parts," each expressing the others, and each expressing the social totality that contains them, because each in itself contains in the imme-

diate form of its expression the essence of the totality itself. (Althusser and Balibar 1970, 94)

The Hegelian whole, says Althusser, supposes a type of unity in which each element of the whole, whether a material or economic determination, a political institution, or a religious, artistic, or philosophical form, is never anything more than "the presence of the concept with itself at a historically determined moment." In this sense, the copresence of the elements with one another, and of each element with the whole, is based "on a *de jure* preliminary presence: the total presence of the concept in all the determinations of its existence." There, the formula according to which nothing can run ahead of its time, means that the present constitutes the absolute horizon of all knowing, "since all knowing can never be anything but the existence in knowing of the internal principle of the whole." This historicism, as Althusser stresses, despises real political practices: "no Hegelian politics is possible strictly speaking, and in fact there has never been a Hegelian politician" (Althusser and Balibar 1970, 95).

In the Hegelian *Vorlesungen über die Philosophie der Weltgeschichte* (1837), the account of history is contemporaneous to the historical fact; it is a "common internal foundation" which makes them both manifest at once, because the history of the state lives in the memory of the individuals, to the extent that they are *possessed* by it (Hegel [1837] 1967, 141). A materialist rupture with the *contemporaneity* based on this "common foundation" makes visible the *ideological efficacy* constitutive of the state's power and reveals itself as a *material dispositive*: the staging of a *scene* for the production of evidence that places in the same narrative temporality *some* subjects for *a* state.

A symptomatic reading of the Hegelian historicist philosophy of the state can bring out what it shows without seeing itself: the simultaneous need for a materialistic concept of historical time in rupture with the idealist notion of time on which the efficacy of state power rests; and the need for a materialistic theory of ideology that allows us to think of the mechanism of state power in terms of a *theory of identifications*.

That is why for Althusser the critique of ideology as a criticism of the contemporaneity between history and philosophical discourse, inaugurated by Marx in 1845, is, in another sense, Freud's too. In the context of a break with the so-called Philosophies of Consciousness, Althusser's first references to Freud are related to history and, more precisely, to an overdetermined conception of the dialectics that question the concept of *contemporaneous time* as well as every concentric *topique* (be that of conscience or that of social totality as a spiritual unity).

> We have known, since Freud, that the time of the unconscious cannot be confused with the time of biography. On the contrary, the concept of the time of the unconscious must be constructed in order to obtain an understanding of certain biographical traits. In exactly the same way, it is essential to construct the concepts of the different historical times which are never given in the ideological obviousness of the continuity of time (which need only be suitably divided into a good periodization to obtain the time of history), but must be constructed out of the differential nature and differential articulation of their objects in the structure of the whole. (Althusser and Balibar 1970, 103)

Thus considered, the detour through psychoanalysis allows him to critically recover the Hegelian idea of the state deeply connected with the homogeneous and contemporary conception of time, in order to recognize the core of its *ideological function* and conceptualize one dimension of the power of the state in the materialist terms of a complex of apparatuses of which it consists, along with its subjects, while *narrating a common history*. The materialist theory of history, which involves a theory of the ideological materiality (apparatuses) of the state and the mechanism of identification (interpellation) in which Marx and Freud find themselves, requires a question about concrete existence. This question acts in a "practical state" in the political thinking that conceives the present in a materialistic way—that is to say, interrogating the "conditions" of the concrete situation of the conjuncture.

> When Lenin said that: "the soul of Marxism is the concrete analysis of the concrete situation'; when Marx, Engels, Lenin, Stalin, Mao explain that "everything depends on the conditions," when Lenin describes the peculiar "circumstances" of Russia in 1917 [. . .] they are appealing to a concept that might appear to be empirical: the "conditions," which are simultaneously the existing conditions and the conditions of existence of the phenomenon under consideration. Now this concept is essential to Marxism, precisely because is not an empirical concept: a statement about what exists. . . . On the contrary, it is a theoretical concept with it bases on the very essence of the object: the ever-pre-given complex whole. In fact, these conditions are no more than the very existence of the whole in a determinate situation, the "current situation" of the politician. That is the complex relation of reciprocal conditions of exis-

tence between the articulations of the structure of the whole. (Althusser 2005, 206–7)

"Conditions" has the status of a concept that can be weighed with rigor in real political struggle. Political thinking and practice have put Marxist dialectics proper into action, writes Althusser in 1963 (2005, 175). The product of this intuition is the introduction of the Freudian notion of *overdetermination* that takes shape as a concept of materialist dialectics, in the framework of the effort to think of history in terms of complex processes of material articulation in which the points of rupture—or reproduction—are conceived in terms of the *condensation* of material forces, whether imaginary or not (2005, 88–106). *Overdetermination* is the concept of structural causality (cf. Morfino 2017)—structure of structures—that allows us to think of those "conditions," simultaneously, as existing conditions and conditions of existence—that is, lodging in each one of them the present existence of the whole, not by an expressive bond with the "Truth," but as seat of the "displacements" and "condensations" that constitute the complex and real condition of the whole. The reference to the work of "condensation" and "displacement" as an activity inherent in all "formation" and as its marks in the conjuncture, is explicitly read by Althusser in Mao and Lenin (cf. 2005), but it makes evident the trace of his interest in Freud, who recognizes in *Die Traumdeutung* (1899) those operations in the work of the dream as a mechanism of ciphering its formations.

After this brief digression, we can return to the question of state power and affirm that a materialistic theory of history, based on an adequate concept of time that seriously considers the *complexity of the concrete* and avoids the idea of the present as the immediate expression of a "spiritual unit," can offer the ground for a positive theory of state power in its ideological effectiveness, as an "external" material force and as a "subjective" affection. Althusser finds it again in Machiavelli's political thought in the measure that he introduces the question of real political practices in the core of historical (tendential) laws.

Althusser finds in Machiavelli's discourse a singular theoretical dispositive. Machiavelli's political thinking—as Lenin's—operates at an "internal distance" in the fabric of theoretical thought. The relationship between an objective legality of history and the political problem (What is to be done?), which is always that of the position of a singular and contingent "case," is inscribed in Machiavelli's writing in a way that leaves its mark on the conceptuality of his thought—to the point of disrupting epistemological relations and challenging all logic of inductive universalization—within the framework of a rejection of expressive causality. That is why Althusser finds himself able to say about Machiavelli's writing something similar to what he says about Lenin's: that his thought is philosophical—in a materialist sense—*because* it is political. This is his way of conceiving the materialist position, whereby history is not a "generalization" of empirical cases, nor is each case the "expression" of an abstract history; it will be developed by Althusser in a 1985 paper, also posthumously edited. It is about establishing, as precisely as possible, the question of a materialistic apodicticity in terms of a *tendential* necessity, supported by generic invariants, which operates both in Marx and in Freud and whose antecedents Althusser recognizes in Machiavelli and Spinoza.[8]

From this "objectivity," open to the intelligence of the singular, it is possible to think the *tendential* legality of history as a reading of the "exceptionality" of the cases. The Machiavellian theory is, in this framework, "political" because it is "partisan" thought, immanent to political practices. From the materialist position in which Spinozian philosophy and Machiavellian theory converge with Marxist developments and psychoanalysis, the problem of state power becomes thinkable, while it allows us to distinguish its internal differences. Mainly, the difference and break with the ideological identification, between the legality of the material historical processes in their concrete tendencies and the deployment of the philosophical idea, open the possibility of problematizing from a materialistic and realistic position, the conception of the state as the materiality of the Ethical Idea.

It is in this interstice that the political problem of the relationship between domination and struggle takes shape. It is this problem that is now developed as a theory of state power, in terms of the constitutively contradictory relationship of ideological and affective processes within which the state and "its" subjects are simultaneously configured: a theory of *identification* as the unconscious support of power, intersected at the same time by subjective experiences and affects and conflicting social tendencies of class struggle. This is suggested by Althusser in *Machiavel et nous* (cf. [MS 1966]), but strongly developed in *Que faire?*:

> Everything is already in Machiavelli, the theory of the state, and its two moments, "the beast" (the force) and the man (the consensus), although there is in him more than in Gramsci, since in his thinking the beast divides, being both lion (brutal force) and fox (ruse and fake) [*ruse et feinte*], and finally the fox is

nothing but the *virtù*, or capacity to use force and consensus (hegemony) at will, according to the exigencies of the conjuncture . . . . [T]his capacity of cunning is reduced in the end to the power to feign, to the power to pretend [*de faire semblant*]. (Althusser [MS 1978] 2018b, 106, my translation)

In this sense, Althusser says, Machiavelli goes beyond Gramsci by forcing the division strength/consensus that remains captive in the inward/outward scheme proper to the philosophies of consciousness on political theory. The price paid for his historicism is therefore an impoverishment of the complex reality of state power that withholds the primacy of force in ideological efficacy. This efficacy involves a dimension that is of the material order of force, *but produces its effects in the subjective experience of "interiority."*

The figure of the *fox*, which Althusser identifies as "psychic violence" ([MS 1978] 2018b, 110), allows us to point out the *unconscious efficacy* of the ideological instance. For Althusser reading Machiavelli, the Prince is not an empirical subject, but a *political strategy*: man-lion-fox, a "*topique* that has no center, that has no 'I' that may unify the three 'moments,' the three 'instances,' that is never 'man,' in other words, *moral subject, any more than being conditioned to seem one*" ([MS 1978] 2018b, 112, my translation, original emphasis).

The strength/consensus dichotomy does not let us acknowledge that which constitutes the key to political power: that force may be productive. And specially, it may be able to be part of a strategy, producing effects of hegemony, as a *materiality* that produces *psychic* effects based on a compulsion that is neither *brute* force nor *consensus*.

Foucault rightly pointed out that force is productive; Althusser is aware of that, but considers that Machiavelli says more, because when saying that force is productive, he points toward the *product*: force produces *ideology* ([MS 1978] 2018b, 109). And ideology is not only about obedience or autonomy, but also about *unconscious life* and *class struggle*. Ideology is, briefly, a contradictory, conflictive, and transindividual process that connects psychic life with historical tendencies in terms of overdeterminate causality.[9]

Machiavelli conceives of the "political education of citizens through their amalgam in the army" in the sense of a *psychic force*—which involves both unconscious and social relations—which is constitutive of state power (Althusser [MS 1978] 2018b 113). In order to account for its mechanism, Althusser speaks about the Prince's *semblance* as a mask or a unified *image* as the "State Ideology" ([MS 1978] 2018b, 106). Closer to force than morals, the imaginary logic of the figure of the fox consists in its "power to feign" (*pouvoir de feindre*). That imposture—or *representation*, according to Lefort ([MS 1978] 2018b, 110)—is consubstantial with the state, but only to the extent to which the image that sustains it is "recognized" by the people. The power of the state does not exist without the people *recognizing themselves in the image* of the Prince. State power is a *transferential* power in the psychoanalytical sense.

We find thus a *theory of identification* with psychoanalytic resonances, which supposes a complex materiality of "bodies," "images," "*semblants*," and "psychic violence," which evokes the Freudian development of military corps in *Massenpsychologie und Ich-Analyse* (1921), which is related to his theory of ideology as constitutive of state power and the conceptual importance that the function of *recognition* acquires within it. It is there where he discovers the paradoxical *retroactive temporality* in which the effects of hegemony are both the product and the condition for the birth of a new state (1921, 114).

Thus considered, state power is much more than a complex of ideological formations such as nationalism, or patriotism connected in a mechanical way to a set of recognizable institutions belonging to the Nation-State form; state power can be considered within the concrete situation, the ideological form of political struggle of supra-state forces, such as those developed from imperialism to neoliberalism, against the institutional form of the Social State.

TOWARD THE CONCEPT OF INTERPELLATION: ANTI-HUMANISM IN TERMS OF IDENTIFICATION

Since his essay, "*Marxisme et humanisme*," firstly published in 1964 (Althusser et al. 1965), Althusser evokes Marx's *Thesis VI* on *Feuerbach*, to recognize in humanist philosophical discourses the ideological structure of an *identification* organized on the ontological assumption of the expressive causality, which makes of every empirical subject the phenomenic expression of some abstract and essential attributes that seem to emanate from an ideal and universal figure of Subject (Althusser 2005, 227–28).[10] In *La querelle de l'humanisme* (Althusser 1995 [or 1967]), Althusser strongly criticizes Marx's thesis on Feuerbach for enshrining the search for "*l'essence de l'Homme*" instead of openly introducing the question—in materialistic terms—of the problem of the theory of society and the history of societies. This turns the thesis into a "dark and unintelligible" consideration (Althusser

1995, 470–72). But, what begins as a criticism of humanism, understood as a dominant ideological formation in the philosophical field and in that of the social and "human sciences," becomes, some years later, the matrix of the theory of interpellation that will allow Althusser to analyze the structure of the ideological mechanism. For Althusser, a double-specular-relationship is found in the ideological functioning of the subject's experience as *causa sui*. But, moreover, as the reading of the *Theses on Feuerbach* constitutes, as Balibar (1995) has underlined, texts of *transition* that give an account of the *processual* character of the *rupture*, the Althusserian reading of *Thesis VI* can be placed within its Spinozian and psychoanalytic roots. It supports his understanding of the process of subjectivation as a *transindividual* process, which functions on the basis of an exchange of the identity credentials of "the subjects" (which Althusser writes with a lowercase *s*) and their possibility of reciprocal recognition, in return for their subjection to a matrix of interpellation centered and sustained by a tautological figure—the unique Subject—identical to himself (written with a capital *S*). The supposed "intersubjective" play of recognition (which also operates as a condition of self-knowledge) is thus governed by a *thirdness* incarnated in the juridical and abstract figure that operates as a metaphysical guarantee of identity, providing their "evidence" of being to the subjects. Not coincidentally, Althusser decides to illustrate the ideological mechanism of the interpellation with the concentric structure of the religious discourse organized by the unspoken thesis of emanative causality.

As Althusser explains later in his *Éléments d'autocritique* (1974), God unfolds himself and sends his Son to Earth, as a simple subject abandoned by him—subject but Subject, man but God. God needs to "make himself" man, to show in a visible and tangible way to the subjects that if they are subjects, subjects to the Subject, it is to finally enter (on the day of Final Judgement) into the bosom of the Subject (Althusser 1974). This remarkable need for a split offers Althusser the structure of every ideology as a doubly specular, centered structure of identity guarantee and opens the path that connects the Spinozian legacy (where a critique of the anthropomorphic image of God leads to a materialist approach to the concrete efficacy of imaginary relations) with the Freudian theory of identification, within which psychic activity involves a kind of unfolding logic, where "ideas" can only be considered "causes" while constituted *nachträglich*, retroactively, as the effect of their material effects.[11]

Theological evocations may carry with them the price of a return to the problematic of consciousness, as Butler warns (1997, 112–31). But unlike Butler in her reading, Montag shows that as this problem is inescapable—even for Foucault, who abandons many of the notions in which it is embodied—the illusion of "escaping" it may lead us to new forms of consciousness interiorities. Against the fall into an idealism of the imaginary force of the law (under the identification between human law and divine law), suggested by Butler's reading of Althusserian concept of interpellation,[12] the concern for breaking the imaginary "interiority" of consciousness will take in Althusser's research, the form of a new, radicalized materialism of the imaginary rooted in the thesis of structural causality. As Butler proposes, Spinoza is there, a philosophical clue, but in a different way than the one she suggests.[13]

For Althusser, the (divine) investiture of the (juridical) law in the ideological functioning enables us to think about the overdetermined articulation of the ideological with the psychic and the social, without confusing either its specific structures or the concrete formations of its material existence. Far from the *critic of alienation*, in the sense of a Feuerbachian tradition of *Das Wesen des Christentums* (1841), the historical existence of ideology is conceived in the terms of concrete ideological formations that take shape within a transindividual material process but function as if they were the totalized space of subjective experience.

This brings us back to the theoretical anti-humanism that Althusser reads in *The German Ideology* (Marx and Engel 1939) as a triple movement: (1) the beginning of the proper materialistic problematic of history; (2) the break with the *theoretical* pretension of humanism, and (3) the understanding of humanism *as* an ideology.

This means that the materialist approach to the problem of ideology (on which the opening of the theoretical space of the materialist theory of history itself depends) requires moving beyond the *critique of alienation*. As Balibar (1995) argues, Feuerbach resolves the religious essence into the *human essence*, and shows that the idea of God is a synthesis of human perfections, personified and projected out of the world. Montag stresses that, for Feuerbach, "God is nothing less than the alienated essence of man" (2013, 135). And it is here where Althusserian reading of ideology places the materialist break with humanist idealism.

In an original reading, Balibar goes beyond the plain rejection of "essence," raised by Althusser in *La querelle de l'humanisme* (1967) and suggests a materialist reading of *Thesis VI*, in what he considers a very *peculiar non-metaphysical* "metaphysics": where "the human essence is no abstraction inherent in each single individual. In its reality it is the *ensemble* of social relations (in a sort of mixture of French and German, Marx writes *das Ensemble der gesellschaftlichen Verhaltniss*)" (1995, 27).

> To say that, "in its effective reality" (*in seiner Wirklichkeit*), the human essence is the ensemble of social relations . . . is to attempt radically to displace the way in which it has until now been understood not only where "man" is concerned, but also as regards "essence." . . .
>   . . . The point is to reject both of the positions (the *realist* and the *nominalist*) . . . : the one arguing that the genus or essence precedes the existence of individuals; the other that individuals are the primary reality, from which universals are "abstracted." For, amazingly, neither of these two positions is capable of thinking precisely what is essential in human existence: the multiple and active *relations* which individuals establish with each other (whether of language, labor, love, reproduction, domination, conflict etc.), and the fact that it is these relations which define what they have in common, the "genus." They define this because they constitute it at each moment in multiple forms. (Balibar 1995, 30)

Balibar underlines that the French term *ensemble* rejects both perspectives: that of *individualism* (the fiction of an individuality that could be defined in itself) and that of *organic* or *holistic* point of views (the primacy of a kind of whole considered as an indivisible contemporary unity of which individuals are merely the functional members).

As Althusser will develop in some of the essays compiled in *Pour Marx* (1965), it is the *overdetermined* consistency of the historical totality (understood as a complex ensemble of contradictory relations and unequal and articulated temporalities) that offers the way out of the humanist problem of consciousness as interiority, in which the psychology of the self, liberal political theory, and juridical philosophy confine themselves. But, by means of a displacement of the very question, from philosophical field to historical relations, this *overdetermined* consistency of the historical totality also enables the statement of a critique of ideology beyond that of a critique of alienation based on a humanist idealism. In this sense, the decentralized *topique* offered by the psychoanalytic theory of the unconscious that Althusser reads in the concept of *overdetermination* meets the Marxist problem of social reproduction, considered under the primacy of class struggle.

The materialistic break with the idealistic conception of historical totality as a spiritual whole (which assumes state as a universal ethical unity) and the problematization of the "theater of consciousness," open up the possibility of analyzing, in materialist terms, the structure where an "original" identity is the result of a splitting that involves a kind of temporal *disadjustment*, repressed in the fictional narrative time. This structure that Althusser calls with the unfortunate term "Ideology in general," is valid for every ideological formation. In morality, for example, the specular relationship is that of Duty—as the Subject—and moral consciences—as subjects—in juridical ideology; the Justice summons free and equal men—as subjects. In political ideology, the Subject varies and is less homogeneous; it can be the People, Homeland, the Interest of the Nation; Revolution, among others, and the subjects can be the citizens, the militants, the patriots.

An experience of "interiority" (*Erfahrung*) is built within the imaginary space articulated in these specular pairs, which function by means of denying the overdeterminate *thirdness* that govern these "inner" relations. This experience—which is not a knowledge, but instead functions with recognition (*reconnaissance*) and mis-recognition (*meconnaissance*)—points toward the material efficacy of ideologies. Because, as Warren Montag has clearly settled, the thesis of the material existence of ideology, connected with that of the individual interpellated as subject by Ideological State Apparatuses (Althusser 2013b), banishes the conceptual pretension of any image of "interiority": "There are only exteriorities, not only the materiality of actions and movements, but also the *materialities* of discourse, whether written, spoken, or silent and invisible but still material, still producing effects as only the material can" (Montag 2013, 154). It is in order to problematize the imaginary "interior" of the "activity of the mind," the "soul," or "consciousness" as philosophical categories, that this radical materialism of ideology is posed against the diverse humanist tendencies from political theory to epistemology, despite the commitment to a language of the "spiritual" that the very notion of "ideology" may carry with it. In this sense, Althusser's theory of ideology is inscribed within the Spinozian legacy to the extent that it develops the same battle:

> Against the entire liberal tradition from Hobbes (who was the immediate object of Spinoza's critique) to Kant (and beyond), which posits a human interiority free and separate from the laws (and forces) that govern the physical world as if it were "a kingdom within a kingdom . . . that has absolute power over its actions and is determine by no other source than itself," Spinoza argues that whatever decreases or limits the power of the body to act simulta-

neously decreases the power of the mind (mens) to think. (Montag 2013, 155; ellipsis in the original)

This kind of materialism that rises from the banishing of the liberal philosophical idea of interiority connects, according to Montag's reading, Althusser's theory of ideology with Foucault's *Discipline and Punish* ([1977] 1979), despite the efforts of its author to separate his thinking from that of Althusser. Moreover, in some respect, Foucault's statements could be considered.

A development of Althusser's materialist approach, to the extent that he manages to eradicate the very notion of "ideology," which still carries a sort of interiority image, connected with the notion of "ideas."[14] What in Althusserian terms is called "interpellation," in Foucault "must be conceived less as a hailing . . . than the permanent production of a hold over the body, the manufacturing of a soul not only around and on the surface of the body but in it, modifying its composition" (Montag 2013, 168). As a result of a construction, the "soul" becomes a "piece in the mastery that power exercises over the body" (Foucault [1977] 1979, 200). To answer the question about the nature of this instrument that allows the body to be controlled, Foucault, "like Althusser, is compelled to turn to allegory to represent the unrepresentable . . . . Here the subject is constituted . . . not by the policeman's order but by the imperturbable gaze of the prison watchtower, . . . the *Panopticon*" (Montag 2013, 169). Montag dialogues with Judith Butler, who has pointed out that "this normative ideal inculcated, as it were, into the prisoner is a kind of psychic identity, or what Foucault will call a 'soul.' Because the soul is an imprisoning effect, Foucault claims that the prisoner is subjected 'in a more fundamental way' than by the spatial captivity of the prison" (Butler 1997, 85). But Montag discusses with Butler, in as much as he considers that the Foucaultian architectural allegory restores the same dilemma of conscience with which Althusser deals:

> It is precisely in the process of making visible, the process that assures the fabrication of docile bodies, that the soul is born and that something like subjectivity, interiority, or consciousness takes shape. . . . What Foucault has described is nothing less than the genesis of consciousness. (Montag 2013, 169)

The *Panopticon*, Montag concludes, "is the figure of an anonymous and unknowable subject who creates its subjects, whose souls are born in fear and trembling. . . . [T]he language of consciousness and its illusions is not as easy to escape as one might have thought" (2013, 170). Foucault's developments take up again the Althusserian theory of interpellation and even carry with them his dilemmas. However, as we read in the reference above,[15] Althusser chooses to insist on the notion of *ideology* despite the fact that its abandonment, as Montag says, could mean a deepening, in a materialistic sense, of his theory. Probably this is because the special ambiguity it carries allows him to sustain his materialistic bet within the encounter between psychoanalysis and Marxism. The main effort is directed toward thinking out the problem of power and subjection, making room *at the same time* for the concept of the unconscious and the concept of class struggle. On the one hand, as Butler has pointed out, "*psyche*, which includes the unconscious, is very different from the subject: the psyche is precisely what exceeds the imprisoning effects of the discursive demand to inhabit a coherent identity, to become a coherent subject" (Butler 1997, 86). On the other hand, as Althusser underlines in his discussion with Gramsci, the explanation of domination and power is inseparable from a theory of class struggle and material exploitation. That is to say, it must be conceived within a decentered *topique* capable of resituating the scheme subject-state power among an overdeterminate materialist causality. This involves an ethical approach to desire, as Butler says, "a willingness *not* to be—a critical desubjectivation—in order to expose the law as less powerful than it seems" (1997, 130); but also, and beyond Butler, it requires a theory capable of thinking of the objective weakness of state power—from the *point of view of reproduction*, which claims the consideration of the transindividual ever-pre-given complex whole—in order to move forward from the *critique of alienation*.

In this way, Althusser takes his analysis to extremes that have not been yet fully explored: interrogating material force to the edges of the unconscious—as he reads in Machiavelli—while interrogating the conditions of emancipation beyond the problem of autonomy, toward the transindividual potency of transformation of the material order (the complex ensemble of relations that sustains the given forms of power) that is irreducible to the scheme of the relation of interiority between *the* state or *the* law and *its* subjects.

Notably, Butler sees the trace of the Althusserian theoretical program: to inscribe the dilemma of the retroactive temporality as nongenetic temporality formation of the ideological subject (that connects the psychic dimensions with the power relations) in the frame of a question for the social reproduction (of a social formation). But she does not manage to formulate it completely, because she reduces the problem of reproduction of the complex *ensemble* of a social formation to a restrictive conception of the technical reproduction of labor.[16] As Balibar has pointed out, without a question about the complex material *ensemble* within which identification is forged, the theoretical space remain "interior" to the humanist scheme of theory of alienation (cf. 1995).

IDENTIFICATION: FORCE AND FANTASY

In general terms, if the concept of interpellation related to the Althusserian theory of ideology seems to have offered everything it had to give, it is because of this. To some extent, the reductionism of some critics lies in the limitations derived from producing a "regional" cut of Althusser's theory of ideology, limited to a few texts—or even fragments of them as is the case of the mentioned article, extracted from a much larger and more complex unpublished volume *Sur la reproduction* (2011), firstly published in 1995. It is therefore necessary to note that many of the elements of the Althusserian theory of ideology have only just begun to be known with the posthumous edition of a large number of manuscripts. But beyond the problem of access to his writings, there is a theoretical reason for affirming that within the framework of his main theses, it is not possible to develop a honest reading of the problem of ideology without taking into consideration the complexity of its inscription in the complex social totality conceived from a decentered *topique* and a noncontemporary concept of time, both of which point toward the Freudian category of *overdetermination*.

The recovery of this complexity supposes the consideration of the double status (ontic and ontological) of psychoanalysis in Althusser's writings: the double inscription of the topical consistency of materialism, as a critique of idealistic *metaphysics*, in relation to the philosophical problem of historical causality; and as a *theory* of the unconscious, in relation to the theoretical problem of ideological efficacy at the subjective level and in relation to the functioning of power.

In relation to the latter, the gravitation of psychoanalysis enriches the theoretical development of the interpellation, opening up the possibility of a consideration of the link between ideology and politics beyond the pure logic of domination. As Butler (1997) has remarkably shown, it allows the specific temporality of the *aporia* of subjection to be thought of, under the idea of the constitutive division of the subject conceived as the processual result of a temporal gap.

> In *The Psychic Life of Power*, Judith Butler adds a supplementary logic to her remarkable analysis of this radically aporetic dialectic of "subjection" as a differential of subordination (*assujetissement*) and subjectivation without symmetry or reversal, a paradox she calls, a bit mischievously, the discursive turn (or return), which is both situated on the scene of subjectivation and constitutive of this scene. All structuralists lend themselves to it precisely to the extent that they reject the facilities of metalanguage. But it was Louis Althusser, in his essay "Ideology and Ideological State Apparatuses," who gave it what we can call its pure form: there is no "subject" who does not name him—or herself, or rather, whom theory does not stage as naming him—or herself and thus becoming a subject and being subjected in the moment and gesture of emergence from what is not yet a subject (a "pre-subject": in Althusser' s terminology, the individual) and thereby becomes always already the subject. There is no structural constitution of the subject that is not, if not an image and resemblance of the Creator like the metaphysical subject, at least the performance or ironic enactment of a linguistic *causa sui*. Previously, if only to remark its *aporia*, I called this presentation or reinscription of the limit on the basis of its own unpresentability: unassignable difference, violence, or radical passivity, and also the *Thing*, the death mask, the primitive scene of interpellation (Balibar 2003, 17)

There are passages and emphases in Althusser's own writings that contribute to a reductionist reading of subjection, in the sense of a fully effective symbolic mandate without internal division. This reading would imply a blind structure, whose play would be reduced to a *combinatory logic*, a structure with no point of heterogeneity. Despite the insistence of Althusser himself on distinguishing his approach on *combination* from that of *combinatory*, (cf. Althusser 1974) this seems to be the reading of Butler, among others.[17] But that who has most recently contributed to reinforcing a hypothetical dissonance between the Althusserian theory of ideology and psychoanalysis, is Slavoj Žižek (1997).[18] His circumscription of the Althusserian theory of ideology to the idea of a radically external ritual—materialized in the Ideological State Apparatuses leads to a consideration of the function of fantasy disconnected from the desires of the subject and reduced to a kind of mechanical social materiality (1997, 6).

According to Žižek, the weak point of the Althusserian theory is that he or his school never managed to clarify the link between state apparatus and ideological interpellation: Althusser conceives ideological interpellation in terms of a symbolic machine by which ideology is "internalized" into the ideological experience of Meaning and Truth. He does not contemplate that this "internalization" by structural necessity is never fully achieved, that there is always a residue, a remainder, a stain of traumatic and meaningless irrationality attached to it.[19] That remainder that is incommensurable with the Symbolic, radically heterogeneous to it, is what, far from hindering the full submission of the subject to the ideological mandate, is, in Žižek's opinion, it's condition: there is, in his terms, a nonintegrated "plus" of meaningless traumatism that gives the law its unconditional authority. This is what, reading Lacan, he calls *jouissense, jouissance-in-sense*, and that he understands to be the psychic condition of possibility of ideology (Žižek 1997).

This thesis assumes two guiding ideas: that the Althusserian theory of ideology does not contemplate the affective (meaningless) dimension of the functioning of the interpellation, reducing it to a pure blind machine that produces a full mandate, and that this affective dimension is the "nucleus" of truth of the ideological functioning, the condition of possibility of the historical and social efficacy of ideology. Against this double consideration, it can be affirmed that the development on the problem of state power within the readings of Machiavelli and Freud exposes Althusser's concern for the unconscious, affective dimension. But unlike Žižek, it is conceived as a plain *material force* articulated in the structure of ideological interpellation, where the distinction *interior/exterior* has no place at all. In this sense, Althusser's evocations of psychoanalytic concepts of original phantom, semblance, transference, among others, testify to this—but also, his efforts to conceptualize the type of link between psychic and ideological structures (Althusser 1993; Montag 2013; Morfino 2014a).

What the Althusserian theory does not accept and constitutes the main point of disagreement with the Žižekian approach, is the subsumption of the problem of the ideological in the specific psychic formations logic and the homogenization of their specific "materialities," whose (articulated) differentiation constitutes a key to the Althusserian conception of causality as is articulated in his " Trois notes sur la théorie des discours " (in Althusser 1993).[20] For Althusser, the problem of interpellation requires the distinction of psychic and sociohistorical dimensions that can neither be spatially distributed in inner and outer regions, nor juxtaposed. If this experience of space is part of the imaginary efficacy of the process of subjection, in strictly theoretical terms, it can't be a starting point. Moreover, Althusser's great materialistic effort consists of conceptualizing the type of causality capable of preserving the different levels without homogenizing their relative logics. Neither can class struggle explain subjective beliefs and experiences, nor can the structure of the libidinal economy explain the historical efficacy of ideological processes in their concrete conjunctural configurations. The materialist position requires a strong resistance to two principles of simplification that, not coincidentally, tend to function in tandem—those which confuse diverse structural levels and those which ontologize structural effects—in an impoverished interpretation of immanent causality.

The reading that Žižek makes of the problem of ideology in Althusser replicates the gesture of the old criticism to his pretended "theoreticism," which is based on excerpts of certain moments of his writing, as if the "regions" in the Marxist *topique* could be perfectly separated (*vide supra*). Consequently, a more serious misunderstanding arises: that of assuming that the problem of the relation of ideology with politics, in Althusser, is reduced to the subsumption of the latter in the former—that is to say, to the link between ideology and domination (in the sense of the reduction of politics into a theory of state power, it strength or weakness)—as it also seems to come out of the criticisms of Foucault and Butler.[21]

But the Althusserian theory is not a theory of the full efficacy of the Symbolic. Neither its conception of overdetermination that implies a plural temporality is reducible to an entirely symbolic status—as Ernesto Laclau and Chantal Mouffe (1985) have suggested—nor does its conception of the ideological subject deny the specific efficacy of unconscious affects for attachment. While it is true that there is no explicit theorization in his writings for what Žižek, evoking Lacan, identifies with the concept of *jouissance*, it can be said that its heterogeneous and eccentric place with respect to the symbolic-imaginary interpellation exists in a practical state in his developments. It takes place from the very moment in which Althusser follows the trace of the temporal misadjustment (*décalage*) in the narrative time of the subject's imaginary genesis and, in particular, he will try to positively analyze it in relation to the affective, *transferential* force that supports state power. Moreover, the premises of Althusserian heterogeneous materialism are more compatible with a complex conception of *jouissance,* irreducible to the *jouissence-in-sense* associated with the Simbolic and instead open to the relationship of *jouissence* with the Imaginary and with the Real, as it will be developed in Lacan's teaching from the mid-1960's.

Against the backdrop of this multiple reduction, a detail comes to light: the research on Machiavelli developed by Althusser during 1972–1986 (cf.

Althusser 1995), has an antecedent in a course given in 1962 (cf. Althusser 2006b). Althusser highlights, among the themes of the course given in 1962, the confluence of two main principles of Machiavelli's political thought: a theory of history (in which the cyclical temporality of state forms is interrupted by the question of the beginning of a new state) and a theory of human nature. Not a genetic anthropology or one of an ethical or religious nature, but a profane anthropology, which identifies man with desire. And this interest appears to be directly related to the problem of the foundation of state power, associated with the function of "appearance," violence, and affection in the relationship between the Prince and the People, among other questions. At that time, according to Negri, Althusser reaches the point of finding in Machiavelli the utopian limit of his thought, "the emptiness into which he immerses us and from which he always allows us to rise" (Negri, in Althusser 2004, 30, my translation).

In the interval of the decade between 1963 and 1972, the detour through psychoanalysis took place, including published texts, manuscripts, and correspondence, where the substantial Althusserian reading of Freud and Lacan was developed. This suggests that Althusser's interest for Machiavelli must be taken seriously when reviewing his theoretical connections with psychoanalysis, because there are, beyond the anecdote, enough theoretical references that cannot be ignored—both because of their forcefulness and because of the theoretical and political consequences they entail. It opens up the possibility of an approach to the problem of the articulation between ideological interpellation and unconscious economy that Žižek claims not to find in Althusser. But mainly, as the problematic is linked not only to a theory of human nature but also to its relation to the question of *historical time*, it gives opportunity to an interrogation of the problem of politics in terms of a contradictory and overdeterminate ontology of struggle—and not only in the reduced sense of pure (state) domination that, as it does not present material contradictions, seems to be closer to the humanist notion of alienation.

For Althusser, state power is not a unidirectional phenomenon, but based on a complex symbolic, imaginary, and affective play of transference and countertransference. So, what psychoanalysis brings is not only the clue to think about the affective attachment that constitutes an active dimension of state power, but also the relationship between affection and (political) struggle. Read from the Althusserian point of view, Žižek's critique of interpellation is on the side of philosophical idealism: first, because it makes psychic causality a metaphysics of historical life, and second, because in doing so, it restores the homogeneity and uniqueness of the discourse of the Philosophy of History in terms of Absolute Knowledge. With this, all of Althusser's effort to recover the real force of the concrete (in the Marx writings and in political struggles developed by Marxists) is silenced and disciplined.

Against this it is necessary to emphasize Althusser's insistence in thinking simultaneously of the object of Machiavellian thought and the relation of that thought with its object: "Machiavelli's thought is not exclusively a break with classic political science, but also perhaps a challenge to 'Theory'" (Negri 2004, 30, in Althusser 2004, my translation). It is there that psychoanalysis intervenes in its double worth, as a critique of metaphysics and as a theory of the unconscious, which allows the reading not only of the content of Machiavellian theory of power, but also of the political force of his Theory.[22]

In order to focus on this political inherence in Machiavellian thinking, Althusser brings to the scene the Freudian category of *Unheimlichkeit* to think of the politicity of the text in the sense of a force capable of disrupting the effect of interpellation (Althusser 1988). The Machiavellian *topique* (theoretical dispositive, the *dispositio* of its elements) calls us to an estrangement, operating at a distance in the "inner space of discourse," the precise place where other texts of political philosophy arouse identification, by means of telling the story of the Myth of Origin (cf. Althusser 2014).[23]

By inquiring about that "strange familiarity" in connection with the Freudian notion of *Unheimlichkeit*, Althusser reaches the problem of desire, *jouissence* and fantasy, chasing politics in the borders of ideological working within discourses (that is, in the contours of the ideological tendency of all discourses, including the one of Machiavelli and Althusser speaking of Machiavelli). And this is because the theory of ideology always demands a double struggle: on the one hand, against the constant siege of the ideological capture of theoretical relations and, at the same time, against the possibility of locating politics as immanent exteriority to a discursive device, opening it to political effectiveness and to the possibility of its theoretical transformation. This double front requires that every single step of theory must expose itself to a critical inquiry that is also, in last instance, a struggle and can be considered one of the motives Althusser had to prefer to keep the concept. Ideology not only refers to social or subjective processes, it simultaneously also refers to the inevitable weakness and finitude of every theoretical discourse.

In this sense, the ideological struggle is, Althusser writes, the resistance to "storytelling." The narrative device—as Butler (1997) insists—constitutes the paradigmatic *stage of the scene* where the evidence of Subject and the Meaning takes shape.²⁴ In other words, it is the field of the *phantom*. In this sense, it is worth remembering that, according to Lacan, Freud insists that the essential dimension that the field of fiction gives to our experience of the *Unheimlich* is that it allows us to see the function of the *phantom* (2004, 24).

The reader who first underlined this idea, in order to elaborate a materialist theory of discourse within an Althusserian scope, was Michel Pêcheux (Glozman 2016, 2020).²⁵ In *Les vérités de La Palice* (1975), by focusing the scenic operatory of fantasy, in "conscience theatre," he recognized very early the links between the temporal gap of subjection and Freudian theory of identification. The figure of interpellation has, for Pêcheux the advantage that

> the theatre of consciousness (I see, I think, I speak, I see you, I speak to you, etc.) is observed from behind the scenes, from the place where one can grasp the fact that the subject is spoken *of*, the subjet is spoken *to*, before the subject can say: "I speak." . . .
>
> The last, but not the least, advantage of his "little theoretical theatre" of interpellation, conceived as an illustrated critique of the theatre of consciousness, is that it designates, by the discrepancy in the formulation "individual"/ "subject," the paradox by which *the subject is called into existence*. (Pêcheux 1982, 105–6)

He concludes, by recalling Freud, to show that "the 'evidentness' of identity conceals the fact that it is the result of an identification-interpellation of the subject, whose alien origin is nevertheless '*strangely familiar*' to him" (Pêcheux 1982, 107). For him it is possible to regard the effect of the discrepancy between individual and subject performed in the temporal dislocation (*décalage*),²⁶ as a certain discursive modality that he calls "preconstructed." But this is not about any relation between subjectivity and language:

> [It is] *the subject as process* . . . *inside the non-subject constituted by the network o signifiers, in Lacan's sense: the subject is "caught" in this network*—"common nouns" and "proper names," "shifting" effects, syntactic constructions, etc.—*such that he results as "cause of himself*," in Spinoza's sense of the phrase. And it is precisely the existence of this contradiction (the production as a *result of a "cause of itself"*), and its motor role for the process of the signifier in interpellation-identification, which justifies me in saying that it is indeed a matter of a *process*, in so far as the "objects" which appear in it duplicate and divide to act on themselves as other than themselves. (Pêcheux 1982, 108)

The power of this mise-en-scène, the metaphorical effect that takes you right to the scene, thus depends on the implicit condition of the dislocation (*décalage*) of origins ("the zero point of subjectivities")—which is a temporal displacement, "from the present to the past," coupled with the double-specular relation that constitutes identification (Pêcheux 1982, 119)

This is the mechanism proper to the structure of any ideology unconsciously denied in the narration of a fictional story of the Origin, in which the "point of view creates the object" (Pêcheux 1982, 150) and that allows us to emphasize the profound connection between the genetical narrative temporality and fantasy, that Butler will rediscover two decades later. It is in relation to the Freudian notion of fantasies that Laplanche and Pontalis (1974) warn that, like collective myths, fantasies try to dramatize as a moment of emergence, as the origin of a story—the *original scene*—the origin of the subject.

In relation to this, Žižek himself emphasizes that all historicization, all symbolization must "represent" that gap that constitutes the transformation of the Real into history. In this sense, he argues, the psychoanalytic clinical experience bears witness to the ongoing struggle to secure entry into the realm of historicity (1997, 53). It is impossible not to recognize in this glossary the tacit evocation of the words of Althusser, who places the contingent temporality of the beginning—the "absolute prior question"—at the base of his definition of the unconscious "as a struggle for survival or a long forced march" (cf. 1996). It is curious because Žižek believes he finds his (and Lacan's) difference with Althusser right there, when he insists that the primordial decentering of the Lacanian subject is

> much more radical and elementary than the decentrement of the subject with regard to the "big Other," the symbolic order which is the external place of the subject's truth is the decentrement with regard to the traumatic Thing-*jouissence* which the subject can never "subjetivize," assume, integrate. *Jouissence* is that notorious *heimliche* which is simultaneously the most *unheimliche*, always already here, and precisely as such, always-already lost. (Žižek 1997, 49)

It is then difficult to assume that the Althusserian problematization of the Subject has stopped at the exterior of the symbolic machine. We note, instead, that Machiavelli's Althusserian reading places the problem of the link between command, desire, and fantasy in a way that makes room for the question of *jouissence*—if not as a concept, at least as a problem. In other words, that problematic is already operating in the Althusserian question about politics, as that contradictory place that exceeds the symbolic alienation of the subject.

Althusserian interpellation is not reducible to a *Symbolic machine*, nor is it based in any mechanistic causality. The interpellation of the individual as subject of his discourse is achieved by the identification with the discursive formation that dominates him, "this identification, which founds the (imaginary) unity of the subject, depends on the fact that the elements of *interdiscourse* . . . that constitute, in the subject's discourse, *the traces of what determines him*, are re-inscribed in the discourse of the subject himself; and his lays on the 'forgetting' of the dispositive of subjection itself, as the occlusion of the subjects cause" (Pêcheux 1982, 114). The concept of *interdiscourse* indicates the sort of *exteriority-in-discourse* that connects with that "exteriority" involved in the temporal *décalage* that operates by contradiction *"between* the familiar strangeness of this outside located before, elsewhere and independently *and* the identifiable, responsible subject, answerable for his actions (1982, 107).

Pêcheux's reading of interpellation shows that Althusserian theory thinks of the problem of the Real as a mismatch—that is, as an affective "remainder" that is not "substance" but *activity*. Žižek instead thinks of it as a pre-ontological "nucleus," a sort of metaphysical condition of material history. Althusserian theory of interpellation requires unconscious repression: the "exteriority" of this misadjustment with respect to the "theatre of consciousness" not only connects with that of the "discursive machinery," but also with that of its inconsistent articulation with the "familiar strangeness" that refers to another kind of "exteriority." And it is on this basis that the (phantasmatic) scenic consistency of the interpellation enforces the heuristic power of the theatrical metaphor and enables a critique of the Philosophies of Consciousness that is in solidarity with a critique of the Philosophy of History; both of which propose spaces of pure "interiority."

The level at which the fundamental disagreement between Althusser and Žižek is produced is not that which Žižek assumes. The strongest difference does not lie in the Lacanian concept of Real, which Žižek would take into account and Althusser would not, but in what Žižek *adds* to Lacan. We are referring to the consideration of *jouissance* as a traumatic "nucleus." This difference, which seems to be minor in the context of the remarkable closeness of the developments of Žižek to those of Althusser, is rooted in a considerable ontological divergence, which could be synthesized in the Hegel/Spinoza controversy, as Mariana Gainza has pointed out (2011, 250).

The Žižekian approach to the notion of *jouissance* as the ultimate substratum—which functions as a point of truth from which to deploy a political program—is different from the place assigned to that pulsional "remainder" in the Althusserian *topique*, in which the topology of overdetermination (which is not only symbolic) obliges us to resist all substantialization, including that of *jouissance*. In Althusser, as in Žižek, every "historicization" must "represent" (in a symptomatic way) the transformation of the Real into history (cf. Žižek 1997) but his effort is to avoid placing there the Truth of politics (and of history). In other words: where Žižek finds a new solidarity between Lacan and Hegel, Althusser clings to a (re)beginning of Marx, through Spinoza. The strictly real condition of Althusserian overdetermination demands the consideration of the political problem in a differentially articulated relationship with the ideological one—and immediately subsumed neither in it nor as its Essence—while, as Pêcheux stresses, it supposes another kind of "exteriority":

> The concept of *Ideology in general* makes it possible to think "man" as an "ideological animal," i.e., to think his specificity as *part of nature* in the Spinozist sense of the term: "History is an immense '*natural-human*' system in movement, and the motor of history is class struggle." Hence history once again—*that is*, the history of the class struggle, the reproduction/transformation of class relationships, with their corresponding infrastructural (economic) and superstructural (legalpolitical and ideological) characteristics: it is within this "naturalhuman" process of history that "Ideology is eternal" (omnihistorical)—a statement which recalls Freud's expression "the unconscious is eternal"; the reader will realize that these two categories do not meet here *by accident*. (Pêcheux 1982, 103–4)

This leads us to understand that the effectiveness of Machiavellian thought, as a confluence of a theory of man's nature and a theory of historical time, can only be measured if subsumption of one by the other is avoided.[27] Precisely, the heuristic value of the decentered *topique* of overdetermination consists of its capacity to bring into light the interstitial space "between" different instances. Of course, this is only possible within the framework of a complex consideration of structural causality: the immanent causality of a hierarchical combination—the concept of the *efficacy of the structure in its effects*, which Marx continually searched for within partially inadequate terms and figures such as *Verbindung, Gliederung, Darstellung* (cf. Morfino 2017).[28] Briefly, what separates Althusser from Žižek is not "the last Lacan" but the materialism *avant la lettre* of Spinoza.

Finally, the Spinozian reading of Machiavelli's theory of state power leads to a play of reenactments without a center or a "nucleus" of Truth, which indicate the unequal relationship of *transference* between the Prince and the People. The question is played out in the image of the Prince (and his "doubles") that demands him to pose as "the emptiness of a distance taken" with respect to himself, in control of his own passions—a pose that, as Althusser suggests in 1985 (Althusser 1997, 17), "we would say today of every transference and especially *countertransference* (for the countertransference not to be harmful, it must, while neutralizing it, anticipate transference)," offers the Spinozian scheme for an ethico-political strategy:

> The mastery of passions in Spinoza, far from being able to be interpreted as "intellectual" liberation of the negative efficacy of passions, on the contrary, consists in their subsumption united with the internal *displacement* of the "sad passions" into "joyous passions." Just as later in Freud no fantasy ever disappears, but—and this is the effect of the cure—is *displaced from a dominant position to a subordinate position*, so too in Spinoza no passion ever disappears. . . . It is here that one could bring together Spinoza with Freud. For this *conatus*, torn between sadness and joy, what is it here by anticipation if not the libido torn between the instincts of death and life, between the sadness of Thanatos and the joy of Eros? (Althusser 1997, 18–19)

Unlike the Žižekian image of a "nucleus," the notion of *décalage* positively takes up this unfolding of the ideological subject in the terms of a *contradiction* that assumes a *noncontemporary temporality* (cf. Glozman 2020). Balibar (2003) knew how to read that temporary dislocation that makes possible a subject as a constitutive tension of the interpellation (more visible in the French term *as[sujet]tissement*), thus allows thinking the subject in the place of a *contradiction* or internal tension in the very *topique* of the Other that sustains his identity. In this sense, he says that,

> The subjection of the subject [is] . . . [a] differential of subordination (*assujettissement*) and subjectivation, that is, of passivity and activity, perhaps of life and death, or metamorphosis and destruction. We have no unequivocal formula . . . to mark its turning point, which can appear in the form of extreme violence, or the appearance of what Lacan, following Freud, calls "the *Thing*" (*das Ding*), deindividualized and desubjectified, taking the place of the objects to which the will and desire of the subject are attached. We do, nonetheless,

have examples of its hallucinatory presence, or its over-presence (which is no longer a self-presence), in the "real" of individual or collective experience—that of *jouissance* or terror. (cf. Balibar 2003, 17)

He points out, with all the force of its ambivalence, the question of the subject within the problem of its emplacement (the "house" of the unconscious) as a temporal *décalage*, which involves a contradiction between the thesis that "the unconscious is the discourse of the Other" and the thesis of an "exteriority" in the "exterior" field of the Other. The *heimlich* in the *unheimlich*.

It can be said that the development of Althusser's theory of ideology, between the kind of "exteriority" implied in the figure of interpellation and the kind of "exteriority" posed in his readings of Machiavelli, is the productive development of that contradiction. In this sense, a political struggle for autonomy exhibits its aporetic condition in that it finds its place in the very "core" of heteronomy and unfolds its heterogeneity (and its resistance) as a kind of *immanence in exteriority* within the *naturalhuman* process of history.

DISCOURSE AND MATERIALISM OF THE IMAGINARY: FROM FOUCAULT TO PÊCHEUX AND SPINOZA

Pêcheux notices that linguistic theories have never ceased to encounter the question of "exteriority" in terms of "extra-linguistics" (such as situation, context, referent, speaker, enunciator, speaking subject, acts of language, power of words, etc.). But on the whole, for them as well as for historians, sociologists, political scientists, "the fact that there is language (and linguistically describable languages) was not explicitly related to the fact that there is ideology (and socio-historically assignable ideologies)" (Pêcheux 1984, 7, my translation). While, since 1960s, the progressive constitution of discourse analysis tends to transform this situation by thematizing the discursive object as a "theoretical frontier object" in effective contact with linguistic research on the one hand and sociohistorical research on the other. In this sense, Pêcheux writes,

> The need to take into account, in the analysis of discursivities, the theoretical positions and reading practices developed in M. Foucault has been one of the clearest recent signs of the revival of discourse analysis: the theoretical construction of intertextuality, and more generally of *interdiscourse*, has emerged as one of the crucial issues of this revival. . . . However, it remains clear that,

> unlike lexicometric treatments, for example, the current results produced by discourse analysis of historical material remain far too punctual and trivial to be of real heuristic interest to historians: most often, they only confirm or illustrate classical hypotheses "borrowed" from historians. (Pêcheux 1984, 7–17)

The question for the status of discourse as a problem of the theory of history is clearly formulated by Foucault in 1969, in terms of the status of the *document* in historiographical labor. When it ceases being an inert piece of matter on which to attempt to rebuild what was said or done, the image of history as memory falls to pieces; for a society, history is a certain mode to provide a status and elaboration to a mass of documents *from which it does not separate* (Foucault 1969, 4).[29]

Foucault discovers the solidarity between the transformation of the status of discursive materiality and the problematization of the concept of *historical time*. The classical postulates thus challenged are those of a *General History: the possibility of establishing a system of homogeneous relationships*—the one and only form of historicity between the diverse instances that subjects them to the same type of transformation (Foucault 1969, 17–18).

In keeping with the ideas of *Lire le Capital* (1968), Foucault places the "first moment" of this epistemological mutation in Marx and acknowledges the obstacles to grounding that discovery in the subject's foundational function: "as if we were afraid of thinking the *Other* in the time of our own thought" (Foucault 1969, 21). Time is conceived of in terms of totalization, and revolutions are never anything but a *raising of awareness* (Foucault 1972, 22).

It can be said that it is Althusser who, within Marxist tradition, takes on the task announced by Foucault of "thinking the Other in the time of our own thought itself" by breaking with the Hegelian idea of the State as an incarnation of the Absolute in history and by opening up a theory of State ideology as the effect of a double identification based on the materiality of bodies and apparatuses—which produces the experience of a temporal simplification that could be called *ideological*.

Consequently, Foucault can be considered an ally, but as Althusser points out in *Que faire?* ([MS 1978] 2018b), his theory leaves the problem of ideology vacant (*vide supra*). Foucault (1971) thinks of the relationship between materiality and discourse as *productivity of force*; discourse can be considered as the power that one wishes to own. Nonetheless, what Althusser suggests in this 1978 writing is that he lacks the necessary theoretical tools to go beyond a *descriptive* theory of power: (1) a theory of the *unconscious* that may account for the mechanisms of "psychic violence" in their specific materiality, and (2) a theory of *class struggle* that may account for historical violence in its specific materiality. That is to say, his theory is "descriptive" to the extent that it does not formulate the question of materialist causality in which the temporal gap in the process of subjection (cf. Butler 1997) and a pluralist concept of temporality (cf. Foucault 1969) converge.[30]

It is instead Michel Pêcheux who lays down the two theses that allow us to comprehend the problem of *ideology* adequately, within "the *naturalhuman process of history*."

> To take seriously the reference to historical materialism means to recognize the primacy of class struggle in relation to the existence of classes themselves, and that entails, with respect to the problem of ideology, the impossibility of any differential analysis (of a sociological or psycho-sociological nature) that attributes its own ideology to each "social group" before the ideologies enter into conflict, as each seeks to ensure its domination on the others. This also leads us to interrogate the notion of dominated ideology . . . in order to determine its characteristics given the primacy of class struggle.
>
> To take the reference to the psychoanalytic concept of the unconscious seriously means to recognize the primacy of the unconscious over consciousness; and that entails, speaking still of ideology, the impossibility of any psychologistic conception that produces a consciousness . . . . To conceive ideological processes according to the form of such a pedagogical trajectory (auto- or hetero-determined) is quite simply to reject in practice the consequences of Freudian materialism. (Pêcheux 2014, 1–2)

These theses trace the limits of the Foucaultian perspective. Avoiding the materialist interrogation of causality turns the proposition of the problem of discourse out to be insufficient to confront the idealist siege, and it may shift into a new universal dialectic that imagines having the property of producing its own matter. But the problem is not, as some economicist positions may argue, the mere introduction of the problem of discourse within Marxist materialism. What is at stake is the historical condition of the "discursive event" and the specific status of the discourse materiality, which, as Terriles and Hernández (2014) expose, results from a self-critical work in Pêcheux's theoretical and analytical production, where a critical dialogue with the ideas of Foucault and Althusser has an important role to play.[31] This concerns the mode of conceiving the concrete material forms under which "ideas" enter the struggle of history, and this compromises the positions assumed by the different theoretical currents concerning discursive processes.

In this sense, it is interesting to take up a lecture given by Pêcheux in 1977 (two years after of publishing with C. Fuchs, "Mises au point et perspectives à propos de l'analyse automatique du discours") in which he explores the link between theoretical discourses and politics, which allows us to think that the possibility of grasping the politicity inherent in discursive processes first requires an identification of the practical modalities in which political battles are fought in the history of theoretical ideas about language and discourse. In this sense, it is possible for Pêcheux to recognize a series of spontaneous philosophical statements about history that work overlappingly as foundations of linguistic traditions, and may have political consequences. It is a "veiled and contradictory relationship that language theories have with history" and, therefore, with the concept of class struggle—what obstructs to perform a theory of the historical materiality of discursive events (Pêcheux 1977, 183, my translation).

The *logical-formalist tendency* eliminates history (and class struggle),[32] as it conceives of the human Spirit as ahistorically transparent to itself, under the shape of a universal theory of ideas, while the *historicist* tendency in language theories conceives of history as a "series of differences, displacements, transformations."[33] If the former completely denies struggle, the latter "understands domination as a form of interiorization" and *subordinates division to unity*, to the extent that it conceives contradiction as the encounter of preexistent contraries. Following Althusser (1973), Pêcheux calls this empiricist approach to the class struggle subordinated to the preexistence of "classes": *reformism* (1977, 185).

The incipient field of the theory of discourse, insofar as it works with this "frontier object" between linguistics and history, allows us to problematize the theoretical (and ideological) commitments that intrude into language theories in the form of nontheoretically formulated questions about the "extralinguistic." In this sense, Pêcheux (1977) puts onstage the contributions of two theoreticians who, being non-Marxists, allow us to think of the relations between history and discourse in the terms of a "material fight for ideas." Between Spinoza's and Foucault's practical methods of reading, the theoretical destiny of that which is called discourse and the possibilities of its analysis are traced.

Comparing the contributions of Spinoza's *Tractatus Theologico-Politicus* with *L'archéologie du savoir*, Pêcheux shows that the main point of controversy lies in what he calls the *regime of materiality of the imaginary* that underlies the interpretative mode of each perspective.

Spinoza explains that very similar narratives can appear in different discourses, under disfigured and unrecognizable forms. "God has no style of his own" speaks of the same thing under different forms or can name different things with the same words (Pêcheux 1977, 190, my translation). Foucault, for his part, raises the question of unity and division of meaning in a different way:

> The affirmation that the Earth is round or that species evolve does not constitute the same statement before and after Copernicus, before and after Darwin, it is not for such simple formulations that the meaning of the word has changed; what changed is the relation of these affirmations to other propositions, their conditions of use and reinvestment, the field of experience, of possible verifications, of problems to be resolved, to which they can be referred. (Foucault 1972, 103)

Pêcheux concludes from this comparison that Spinoza is ahead of Foucault insofar as his practical method of reading allows us to think of the historical condition of discursive transformation (that is, the material existence of an ideology) in the form of a unity in division, a unity that is only realized as a struggle of opposites that sustains the claim to the true in the form of the contradictory.

Pêcheux's comparative analysis is based on the reading developed by Dominique Lecourt on *L'archéologie du savoir* (1970). Lecourt underlines the importance of the notion of "relationship" in "Sur *L'archéologie du savoir*," as a set of conjunctions of "coexistence, succession, mutual functioning, reciprocal determination, independent or correlative transformation," and recognizes the problem of its insufficiency—as the insufficiency of a *combinatorial* logic—to account for the properly historical character—that is, the *event* condition of the "discursive event" (1970, 68–87). The decisive problem of defining "the regime of materiality" of what he calls the discourse, and consequently of thinking of the history of this "discourse" in its materiality, is manifested there. The great contribution of *L'archéologie du savoir* lies in the introduction of the category "discursive practice" related to that of "subject positions." This constitutes the index of the materialistic background of his effort, which consists of not establishing any "discourse" outside the system of material relations that structure and constitute it (1970, 68–87).

However, the task remains trapped in the infertile distinction between discursive and nondiscursive practices. On the one hand, according to Lecourt, Foucault advances in recognizing that "discursive practice" is not *autonomous*, that the transformation and change of the relations that constitute it are not carried out through the play of a pure combinatory but that to understand them it is necessary to refer to *other* practices of different nature. With the function of the rule, Foucault tries *at the same time—that is, in its unity—* to think about the relations that structure the discursive practice, its effect of submission on the "subjects" that speak, and what he enigmatically calls the *embrayage* of one type of practice over another. This discovers a new determination of "discursive formation": it is structured *hierarchically*. In effect, there are guiding statements that designate what a certain discursive formation includes and what it excludes. That thesis will be of much worth for Pêcheux.

Foucault forced himself to think about what constitutes the regularity of the rule, what orders its hierarchical structure, what produces its mutations, what gives for every subject its imperative character. But in each of these points he encounters the same difficulty. He conceives of the need to refer the whole of this complex process to the same principle: *the articulation of discursive and nondiscursive practices*; but this principle, tirelessly repeated by Foucault, is not really thought through for Lecourt. Foucault's blind spot is his polemic with the Althusserian science/ideology distinction, which structures his theoretical effort to introduce the category of "knowledge." However, and despite the epistemological contributions that the task of developing a non-negative conceptualization of knowledge makes, Foucault neglects another inescapable dimension of the concept of ideology in the framework of the materialist theory of history: its relation to the overdetermined causality and therefore with the concepts of *contradiction* and *class struggle*.

Therefore, although he advances in the attempt to think of the differential unity of two histories (science and knowledge) and in recognizing the relative autonomy of knowledge (which for Lecourt is nothing more than the ideology thought of under the category of "knowledge," as a system of relations hierarchically structured and embodied in practices), he fails to enunciate the principle that would allow him to break out of the circle that leads him to the inadequate distinction between discursive and extra-discursive practices, for fear of falling back into economism. From there Lecourt deduces that, for having wanted to escape to the transcendental idealism, he falls into an empiricist mechanicism that is only the inverted form of the first one. What *L'archéologie* lacks is the "classist point of view" that Marx puts into play in his own method of reading Ricardo's theory. Not in the sense of a political theory of struggle, but in the sense of a theory of history within which the history of sciences (and knowledge or ideologies) must be placed. This involves not only the contents of a theory of discourse but also its "epistemological" fundaments. Marx's practical method of reading can be translated into a thesis that would have been of benefit to Foucault—that *diverse objects arise from the same discursive formation*[34] —but for that he should have accepted that practical ideologies (and knowledges, including his own field) are crisscrossed with class contradictions. By not doing so, *L'archéologie du savoir* is blind to the contradiction it displays.

Foucaultian method falls into an inability to think outside of his own theoretical discoursive, both in the form of the ideological siege and in the form of political struggle. History returns as the denied politicization of the theoretical discourse, its "unconscious" denial.

Pêcheux concludes, based in Lecourt's analysis, that the absence of the category of *contradiction* in Foucault's thinking is responsible for the return of notions such as *status, norm, institution, strategy, power,* and so on, which outline the materiality of the state power, without being able to think of the relationship of the concrete (discursive) formations of ideology and domination with class struggle. That is why Pêcheux acknowledges a more solid forerunner in Spinoza, for whom the materiality of discourse is contradictory.

This is possible for Spinoza, against what Butler (1997) may argue, posing precisely the theological question of God. Spinoza takes as his *materia prima* the theological position that, when interpreting the word of God, reads in it His thought and His will, and transforms this *materia prima* to the extent of characterizing it as an imaginary materiality determined by the material conditions of human existence. Thus, his work constitutes the outline of a materialistic theory of ideologies, under a rudimentary form but which contains the essential: the thesis according to which, the less one knows the causes, the more one is subject to them (Pêcheux 1977, 191). By criticizing religious ideology in the name of religious ideology, Spinoza shows that in itself (and in the discourse that realizes it), ideology may not be taken as a homogenous whole identical to itself. And it is from Spinoza that Pêcheux draws the idea that ideology does not exist except *under the (material) mode of division*: it does not concretely *exist* except within the contradiction that organizes its unity in itself and in the struggle of the contraries. This leads him to consider that the Foucaultian concept of *discursive formation* should be submitted to a Spinozian "rectification" to reach the decisive point of thinking about the specificity of ideologies in terms of their *divided unity*—that is, in materialist terms of the unequal contradiction "of two worlds in one," or to put it in Leninist terms, the one that divides into two (Pêcheux 1977, 195). Thus considered, the question of the *divided unity* could not be solved in terms of dispersion or plurality but in terms of a kind of complexity conceived as a relational *thirdness*: a relation of relations—the kind of "*non-metaphysical* metaphysics" implied in the term *ensemble*.

It is not possible to fully account for the material consistency of discourse if its historicity is not thought about from a materialist point of view; this means, in terms of its *contradictory (overdetermined) objectivity*. This is a crucial point to comprehend the bifurcation between the theories of discourse that embrace the constitutive problem of ideology and those that think about it as a secondary or subordinate question. And this allows us to point out that what is lost in this field, when the theory of ideology is blurred out, is precisely the relationship between discourse and history, in a complex materialistic sense.

Theoretical reformism in the field of discourse is the name of a consideration of historical change that dispenses with a transindividual and structurally contradictory objectivity. A space of interiority is reaffirmed to be at the heart of the discursive formation if its unity is not conceived of in its overdetermined condition (under the double primacy of the unconscious and contradiction). If it is not conceived in terms of an unequal, hierarchical, and contradictory articulation, as much as it may be proclaimed as a pluralist critique of any form of metaphysical unity, the notion of formation loses its historical condition because it turns into a category blind to the "ensemble system" that is its constitutive exterior: the "material objectivity" of the structure of subordination-inequality of the complex whole with the dominance of the ideological formations of a given social formation (cf. Pêcheux 1975). If the concept of discursive formation is blind to its contradictory unity, it is thus thought of as "interiority," for it acquires a structure isomorphic to the structure of consciousness, which exists in a temporality closed in on itself. A theory that enunciates such exteriority in terms of the relationship of a discursive totality with its symptom is not enough. Additionally, a theory of historical causality is necessary—that is, a complex conception of time and the concept of social totality capable of interrogating and conceptualizing the real consistency of that "exteriority" and the relations between it and the imaginary experience of "interiority" of the discursive formation. This necessary theory of historical causality is a theory capable of accounting for the objective *materiality of the imaginary*, which supposes the primacy of unconsciousness over conscience and the primacy of contradiction over contraries.

AGAINST REFORMISM (AND NEOLIBERALISM): UNCONSCIOUS AND CLASS STRUGGLE WITHIN DISCOURSE

Ironically, in 1978 Althusser denounces this *reformist* position in relation to the political strategy in his *Que faire?* in terms of the idea of "class consciousness." The visual operation that the image of "self-consciousness" constitutes, which is internal to the ideological field, takes on a new consistency when the field itself closes up and denies the complex *ensemble system* that rules over it: "We see only what we see, and this does not go far enough . . . [;] only, the rest is missing . . . [—]the rest, that is to say the whole *ensemble system* that governs the concrete forms and the concrete means of the bourgeois class in its antagonism toward the working class struggle, and which leads to this simple fact, which seems to go without saying" ([MS 1978] 2018b, 30, my translation).

The "proletarian point of view" may coincide (in a relation of interiority) with the "point of view of the State," in spite of believing its opposition to it or being its "alternative," if the construction of that perspective is produced as an identitarian experience, in a phenomenological relation to *its world*—as *contemporaneity* between facts and its narrations. This is what Althusser calls insistently: to tell oneself stories.

That is why he denounces the politicist temptation of historicism that enshrines "change" in abstract terms—not only because of the theoretical problems this carries along, on which he had insisted already in his criticism of historicism (cf. 1965), but also because of the political consequences he supposes this could have in the conjuncture of the late 1970s: "Forms of enlarged reproduction are by no means technical forms . . . . That our century is the century of speed is due to the needs of the bourgeois class struggle: to make capital circulate as quickly as possible to extract as much of surplus-value as possible" (Althusser [MS 1978] 2018b, 48, my translation).

In this context of accelerated change, commanded by the temporality of extended reproduction of capital at an unprecedented rate, materialist theory must acknowledge that the reasons for "change" are not to be found in what we simply "see" changing, and enunciating the historical condition of theory—submitting it to the temporality of its object—only strengthens the "absolute historicism" that lacks an outside and, therefore, is interior to ideology (Althusser [MS 1978] 2018b, 49, my translation).

These passages from *Que faire?* expose, with mastery and anticipation, some of the theoretical risks that form a unity with the dominant ideological tendencies. On one side, the fascination with what we "see change," as if that were in itself the "reason for change," leads to a technological fetishism that believes itself to be a critical diagnosis of the neoliberal conjuncture, a renewed form of "biopolitical" economism that consecrates the Absolute Power. On the other, there is the risk of the production of intelligibility schemes of the conjuncture that fall into a certain "politicist" optimism: a fetishism of popular *demands*, taken immediately as political, blind to the complex ensemble that reigns over concrete historical formations in the struggle of the bourgeois class in its antagonism toward the working-class struggle. This involves a diagnostic that hypostatizes the contingent aspects of the conjuncture, subsuming the structural ones in a kind of ontologization of a determinate (technical or political) practice.

Those same concerns organize Althusser's posthumous volume *Sur la reproduction* (2011), whose main part emerged in a frenzy of writing in the months after the events of 1968. There, Althusser warns of the *politicist deviation* that, under the generic term of "domination," simplifies the Marxist problem of the relationship between economic exploitation and the political and ideological class struggle. And he recognizes its mirrored image in the technological fetishism that confuses the *social* division of labor for a *technical* one. He saw then a double simplification looming over theory that flattened the conjuncture between the "neo-anarchist" denunciation of "power" and an "economicist or technocratic" fascination (2011, 68–69). When the climate of revolt would not allow the elicitation of the price the left would have to pay for unburdening itself of theoretical Marxism, Althusser would insist on the dependence of the vitality of Marxism on the rigorous development of what he called "the point of view of reproduction" based on a conception of *existence as duration*. Starting from the principle of the primacy of the relations of production over the productive forces, determinant to a *social formation*, the "point of view of reproduction" is indispensable in order to account for any *concrete situation*: where the capitalist relation of production—as a structural relation of dispossession and separation of the labor force from the means of production—is *abstract* with regard to the concrete and contradictory complex of relationships of production and superstructural formations in which its reproduction is given *as duration and, as such, existence* (2011, 68).

In a social formation, there is not a single intervening mode of production, but one functions in a *dominant* mode in an articulated whole, wherein residual or emerging relations of production strive, but are conditioned by its dominance, in a *complex and contradictory unity*. In this sense, the determined social formation is, in its objective unity, a contradictory and hierarchical combination of temporalities.

In a mode of production, understood as the unity of productive forces and relations of production, it is the *relations of production that play the dominant role* and not the productive forces. And relations of production are not to be confused with either "work" or with "property": the *social* division of labor is neither the technical division of labor nor the legal form of its organization (Althusser [MS 1969] 2011, 69).

These two theses situate the historical existence of a social formation as a complex *ensemble* of concrete relations in which it *lasts*. In this development we find the framework that sustains Pêcheux's thesis. His references to the French expression *ensemble* have the philosophical worth that Balibar (1993) discovers in Marx and develops in the terms of a *transindividual ontology*, underlining its double, material and imaginary, consistency. Milner (2002) suggests this with the aporetic expression of *tesei-objectivity*.[35] These statements, given the new dimensions starting from Pêcheux's work, lead us to think that the development of historical materialism requires a (materialist) theory of the discursive processes and formations, to the extent that a singular need may not be conceived of but as a *relation of relations* in which the imaginary is a part of the concrete materiality (Balibar 2018).

The Marxist historical totality itself supposes in its structure a double relationship (properly, a relation of relations), which exists only as overdetermined in its temporal complexity and contradictory materiality. On this terrain, the possibility opens up to think of the problem of ideology as an objective overdetermined complex of contradictory processes, and not only as a failed operation of domination or ideal universalization or as a sociological opposition between two "worlds"—a scheme irreducible to a single interpellation (which would constitute the inversion of a false criticism of the spiritual totality) or to the image of the plain subsumption of subjects in the technical logic of capital.

Les vérités de La Palice (Pêcheux 1975) lays out the consequences of these theses on the terrain of the problem of discourse. But, far from being a mere application, it advances the field of discourse in terms of a *theory of discursive processes* and develops the problem of historical temporality (which other theories abandon by abandoning the concept of ideology).

The development of his conception of the decentered and necessarily repressed determinations that produce the subject-effect as a cause of itself provides an account for the philosophical thickness (and political sense) of Althusser's intervention that reintroduces the so-called Philosophies of Suspicion (Marx, Nietzsche, Freud) in a genealogy that extends beyond the nineteenth century, including Spinoza in the perpetual battle against idealism—distinguishing itself from Foucault in this respect. His materialist reading of discourse based on the thesis of a constitutive forgetfulness (Pêcheux 1977) is the fiber that reunites what is only imaginarily experienced as separate: *discourse and decree* (Montag 2015).

As Montag shows, Pêcheux's reading of Althusserian theory of ideology allows us to recognize the gravitation of Spinoza's *Ethics* (cf. EIII, P2) in terms of what Montag calls his "theory of the *decree*" (*decretum*): as that which *compels* us to say certain words in a certain order while *allowing* us to say others and which arises from a "forgetting" (of words and phrases) that is itself forgotten and lived by the individual as the act of decreeing by himself what he says and what he does not say—in other words, a theory of the immanent cause of the distribution of memory and forgetting, which, being prior to the will of the individual, determines his decisions through the forgetting of its causes.[36] Key to this idea is the materialistic concept of *ritual*, in its enabling (rather than prescriptive) materiality and, as Pêcheux reads, in relation to the possibility of thinking about practical failures, false steps, mistakes, in the very heart of its reiteration, as a space for the *chance* of a deviation in its effects.[37]

Following this materialism and in the context of a question about the causality inherent in these processes, Pêcheux sets himself the task of elaborating a materialist theory of discursive processes able to account for the *necessary material* connection of repression and the unconscious with ideological subjection. The category of *overdetermination* constitutes the philosophical framework of his program to develop a *non-subjectivist theory of the subject*, based on a theory of identification and the *material efficacy of the imaginary*. "Necessary material" means that "discourse" does not *exist* except in concrete discursive *processes and formations*. The concept of discourse does not designate a discursive existence, but the atemporal mechanism of a *forgetting* (enabling/limiting) that supports mutual consistency between a signifying articulation and the subject-effect. If the concept of "discourse" is to be upheld, it is in order to name this *material inscription of a double forgetting as a mechanism of subjection*. In this sense "Trois notes sur la théorie des discours" (in Althusser 1993) holds a certain familiarity with Lacan's discourses theory developed in 1969–1970 (Lacan 1991).

The framework of the Spinozian theory of the *decree* to think of a materialism of discourse, allows Pêcheux to formulate more clearly the place of linguistics and to open psychoanalysis and Marxism to a dialogue between it, avoiding simultaneously the historicist and the formalist risk of effectively thinking of discourse as a "frontier object." In this sense, his insistence on conceptualizing *langue* as the *base* of diverse discursive formations should be understood within the project of searching for the immanent cause to different "discourses." Althusser denominated them: the discourse of science, of ideology, of aesthetics, and of unconscious (cf. Althusser 1993). For one thing, this means understanding *langue* as a structure, "indifferent" to history and, therefore, to the class struggle. This is how Pêcheux avoids coalescing the dimension of discursive practices and concrete formations into the structure of *langue*, to uphold the materialist causality that affirms the *immanence of the structure in its effects*, which is the condition of a theory of history as a *necessity of contingency* and as a temporal complex.

This is not about replacing the metaphysical and foundationalist image of a metalanguage with the equally metaphysical and foundationalist affirmation of its pure inexistence, in order to affirm a pluralist and relativist ontology of the contingency; it is about affirming the historical existence (*the presence of the absence* of metalanguage) in the contradictory and conflicting form of the class struggle that is fought on the discursive materiality. *Langue* is not a "metalanguage" (an over-structure or a Cause), but an *absent cause*—a structure that does not exist but in the contradictory complex of its effects. As Althusser points out, *langue* has no function because langue does not "exist" as such. Only discursive practices exist, to which *langue* provides the constitutive elements. Even before the *topique* of base-superstructure, what Althusser sets in motion, according to Montag (2015), is the rejection of any scheme that may imply an expressive causality, in order to substitute for it the concept of immanent causality inspired by Spinoza. *Langue* does not exist as the "discourse of discourses": it disappears in the irreducible plurality of discursive materialities. It is the complex of the *discursive forma-*

tions and *discursive processes* that constitute the concrete of a determinate (discursive) *conjuncture*. And this is because the *langue* only exists as discourses that only exist to the extent that they are embedded in the material existence of ritual practices assembled in a set of apparatuses that maintain complex relations of unequal articulation, juxtaposition, contradiction in which ideological formations are subordinated both to the subjective and random temporality of history (Montag 2015). This is why *langue* cannot ever be simply a system governed by rules whose expression follows a legal model. And it only exists as an absence, in the material process of a systematic repression of what Gadet and Pêcheux (1981, 51) will later call, following Jean-Claude Milner, *gaps* and *contradictions* that set this order against itself in a perpetual production of equivocity (Montag 2015, §17). *Metalanguage* is there the (imaginary) experience of the unity of *meaning*, the effect of *forgetting a forgetting* of the complex material *ensemble* of practices and rituals that determine it: an objective, contradictory *complex in dominance* of discursive formations in which the structural unity of *langue* exists. Pêcheux inaugurates a theoretical program that enables us to simultaneously think about historical time and the symbolic order, not only thinking about "the time of the *Other* in the time of our own thought" but also inscribing it within a theory of history in its heterogeneous and multiple materialities:

> *The signifiers* appear not as the pieces in an eternal symbolic game which determines them, *but as what has "alwaysalready" been detached from a meaning*: there is no naturalness about the signifier; what falls within the reach of the unconscious as a verbal signifier has "always-already" been detached from a discursive formation which supplied it with a sense for it to lose in the nonsense of the signifier. Note that this is by no means in contradiction with the supremacy of the signifier over the signified, so long as that supremacy is understood to act in the context of a discursive formation determined by its specific exterior, which, as has been seen, is radically occulted for the speaking subject that that discursive formation dominates (what I shall continue to call *forgetting no. I*), and this in conditions such that any access to that exterior by reformulation is prohibited him for constitutive reasons connected with the relationships of division-contradiction which traverse-organise the "complex whole of discursive formations" at a given historical moment. (Pêcheux 1982, 126)

TOWARD A THEORY OF SOCIAL REPRODUCTION: FORMATION AND DISCURSIVE PROCESSES AS *CONJUNCTURE*

As we have already pointed out following Lecourt when taking into account the peculiar method of reading of Marx, but also following Althusser's reading of Machiavelli, the "point of view of reproduction" names the analytic approach that might be, in a certain way, "partisan" (for being capable of reading structure in terms of the concrete "conditions" of the situation), and so is not to be confused with the *reformist* "point of view of the state" (which does not distinguish conjuncture and structure and presents the point of view of one part as the vision of the whole).[38] From this, Pêcheux elaborates an analytic of the concrete form of the conjuncture and the articulated and contradictory complexity of the temporalities that make it up.[39]

From the very definition of *social formation* as a temporal complex, the concept of *formation* gains theoretical weight in Althusser's *Sur la reproduction* (2011) by holding the distinction (and disproportion) between the concepts of social formation and mode of production and affirming that there is always more than one mode of production in any concrete historical formation. A *social formation is a tendentially unified temporal complex*. The diversity of social formations is not due to the existence of an indeterminate multiplicity of modes of production (which are no more than five or six in Marxist theory), but to the singularity of its hierarchical articulation in a complex totality of superstructural formations, overdetermined by this *combination*.

Therefore, it is not possible to account for this complexity if not producing a detour through *conjuncture* from the starting point of the ideological conditions of reproduction/transformation of relations of production. And this should be understood in two ways: (1) that of the *need for* a thought *of* the conjuncture, and (2) that of a *conjunctural practice of thought*. The Althusserian reading of Marx consists of, first of all, an enterprise of shaping a kind of theory capable of assuming that there is no way of naming the historical complexity without embracing the concrete existence of a singular situation; the main principle of that kind of theoretical thinking is what Althusser calls *overdetermination*.[40] As we have already introduced, Althusser returns in 1985 to this idea based on the Spinozist theory of the three genres of knowledge and proposes a kind of epistemology of Marxism and psychoanalysis as *clinical theories*: dispositives of knowledge whose laws do not constitute legal generalizations, but tendential ones, which aim to the singular (Althusser 1994).

This very idea of a "theoretical dispositive" appears in his reading of Machiavelli as a counter-mythical dispositive, a peculiar "theoretical dispositive." We find it also in Pêcheux, in his conception of the Marxist "experimental dispositive" as an "experimental science of history," articulated with the proletarian political practice: it is *experimental* (in the sense of *Experiment*) and not subjective because it breaks with the spontaneous political functioning of the subject-form that is *experience* (*Erfahrung*) (Pêcheux 1982).[41]

The structural approach to the functioning of concrete formations will allow us to acknowledge the "mechanism" that functions in the imaginary experience as a repetitive circle; but to acknowledge it at the same time as a *conjuncture* may preserve us against understanding the "eternality" of this mechanism of ideology "in general" as a *primary form* (because there is no *prima philosophia, nor God's eye*). Any analytic that does not distinguish structural and conjunctural approaches grants either the structures or the empirical subjects a metaphysical priority, simplifying temporal complexity. This kind of simplification that works in the experience of interiority is consecrated to the historicist reduction of history to Absolute Present, and, thus, can be considered the "point of view of the state," conceived as an ethical unity. Theoretically *reformism does not accede to the point of view of reproduction*, which is the assumption of the conjunctural conflictive consistency of the *Present*.

The theory of interpellation is a *clinical* theory in the sense of a reading of the concrete processes and formations in which it exists as its immanent structure, in as much as its ideological efficacy consists in the necessary repression of its constitutive "secondary order": the mythical restitution of the immediacy of the "world" (forgetting of having forgotten, as Montag says).

Although Pêcheux does not speak of a "discursive conjuncture," the idea acts in a practical mode in the concepts of *discursive process* and *discursive formation*. In order to keep the structural category of *langue* from colonizing the discursive formations and thereby reinstating the expressive causality that would turn them into "phenomena," he identifies the overdetermined action of *three structures* (the structure of *langue*, the social totality, and the psychic structure) in the discursive processes and formations. This implies that discursive materiality implies a very complex approach to the concrete of a *conjuncture* that should be considered within the development of the problem of *social reproduction*.

Thus, Pêcheux reintroduces the Althusserian idea of *conjuncture* at the heart of the problem of ideology and manages to comprehend the difference between the structural dimension of ideology—confusingly called "general ideology"—and the conjunctural dimension of historically determined ideological formations—called "particular ideologies" (Althusser [MS 1969] 2011, 209). The idea of a *dominant ideology*—better understood as "State Ideology" (Althusser [MS 1969] 2011, 92)—is no longer to be confused with the "Ideology in general," but comprehended as the imaginary effect where an articulated and contradictory material complex with a dominance over the ideological formations exists *as if it was "Ideology in general"*—that is, the structural ("eternal") mechanism immanent to those formations, stuck between tendencies and counter-tendencies with a dominance. This inscribes the theory of ideology within the framework of the problem of social reproduction—which Pêcheux emphasizes as "reproduction/transformation" to account for the nodally contradictory character of all social formation (cf. Pêcheux 2014). In relation to ideology, this means noticing the overdetermination of its conditions due to its relations with technology and politics:

> We may now take one more step in the study of the ideological conditions of the reproduction/transformation of the relations of production by saying that these contradictory conditions are constituted, at a given historical moment and for a given social formation, by the complex set of ISAs [Ideological State Apparatuses] that this social formation includes. We say complex, i.e., a set with relations of contradiction-unevenness-subordination among its "elements," and not a mere list of elements: indeed, it would be absurd to think that in a given conjuncture all the ISAs contribute equally to the reproduction of the relations of production and to their transformation. In fact, their "regional" properties—their "unquestioned" specialization into religion, knowledge, politics, etc.—condition their relative importance (the unevenness of their relations) inside the set of ISAs, and this in turn as a function of the state of the class struggle in the given social formation. (Pêcheux 2014, 5)

It is a question of rejecting the mechanical linearity that supposes that a mode of production generates its reproduction to make thinkable, instead, the immanent cause that makes thinkable the duration of a social formation as the process of a conflicting and unequal unit submitted to movements of encounter and struggle (cf. Montag 2015). Thus, theory of ideology discovers that the retroactive temporality of the state power meets the retroactivity of the subject, who is decreed as such through a double forgetfulness. It is the temporality of a *myth* that makes the narrative experience of existence possible.

The Pêcheutian theory of discursive processes is the theory of temporal processes necessarily repressed in the discursive formations, with the subject-effect as *causa sui*, which requires the double repression of the decentered—social and unconscious—determinations that constitute it. Thus, it reads the mutual consistency of the "evidences of the subject and meaning" that are at work in the discursive processes as operations of simplification of the complex historical temporality: double simplifications—simplification of the procedural complexity of the times articulated in the conjuncture that is lived as the "Absolute Present" and simplification of the temporality of the subjection processes in the retroactivity that enables the subjects' experience as if they were "always already" subjects, which Pêcheux describes as "metaphysical figures" of the type of *Münchausen* (Pêcheux 1982, 101–9).

The combination of these two orders of simplification is at the core of the imaginary scene identified as the "theater of consciousness," which the Althusserian concept of *interpellation* has the merit of exposing. In it, we once again find the relation between image and force as a relation between state power and (unconscious) "psychic violence." This figure, by means of which the theater of consciousness "is observed from behind the scenes," is associated, as Pêcheux stresses, "both with religion and with the police ('You, for whom I have shed this drop of my blood' / 'Hey, you there!')" (1982, 105). Interpellation, as a concept that exposes the *scenic* backdrop of consciousness, exposes the mechanism through which the experience of identity (*Erfahrung*) operates in a phenomenological space and a non-dialectical time, whose condition is the forgetting of the superstructural (overdetermined) bond between the unequal structured complex of (legal, ideological) apparatuses and the structures of certain discursive formations ("Hey, you . . . ," "You, for whom") and the divergent process of identification, whose result is a subject "identical to itself." The theatrical metaphor constitutes a strong claim in the effort to read the mutual consistency of eccentric (historical) determinations of ideology and the eccentric (unconscious) determinations of the *psyche*. Drawing on Brecht, Althusser uncovers the *topique* of the *phenomenological drama* that

> gave us tragedy, its conditions and its "dialectic," completely reflected in the speculative consciousness of a central character . . . . What is the ideology of a society or a period if it is not that society's or period's consciousness of itself,

that is, an immediate material which spontaneously implies, looks for and naturally finds its forms in the image of a consciousness of self living the totality of its world in the transparency of its own myths? (Althusser 2005, 144)

Every myth describes a spatial interiority and a non-dialectical temporality or a fake circular dialectic that produces an experience of its own situation under the dramatic-dialectical mode. Against this concentric topography, Marx's materialist principle of historical time warns us that "there is no dialectic of consciousness: no dialectic of consciousness which could reach reality itself by virtue of its own contradictions; in short, there can be no 'phenomenology' in the Hegelian sense" (Althusser 2005, 144).

It is no coincidence that the theatrical evocation and the reference to the structure of myth also meet in the genealogy of the Freudian concept of "original phantasies" (*Urphantasien*)—whose naturalist predecessor are the "original scenes" (*Urszenen*). As Marx did, Freud simultaneously inherited and challenged the epistemic distinction between the imaginary and the real, starting with the problem of *temporality*. Fantasies are "imaginary scripts" in which the subject finds itself present and in which it represents its origin (Laplanche and Pontalis 1974). As collective myths, fantasies attempt to provide a solution to the enigma of the origin (and its suspended temporality): they *stage* the moment of emergence of the individual as the *origin of a history*. It is so that they represent its Cause: they represent, in a displaced way—because of defensive processes—the realization of *an unconscious desire* (Laplanche and Pontalis 1974)—"Scenes" in which the subject is always present, including the primary scene (of its conception), from which it would seem to be excluded and in which it participates through the permutation of roles, attributions, and syntactic changes, like those Freud outlines in the neurotic's family romances (Rank 1909).

Fragments of *Family Romances* (Freud [1909] 1914) were integrated through quotations and paraphrases in the work of Otto Rank, *The Myth of the Birth of the Hero* (1909), which affirms that the manifestation of the intimate relationship that exists between dream and myth fully justifies the interpretation of myth as the dream of a people. "The child's self-behaves like the hero of the myth, and the hero should actually be always interpreted simply as a collective self" (cf. Freud 1914, 63–68).

Myth functions as a discursive dispositive that allows the identifying of the tautological effect of the *retroactive* temporality of interpellation, in whose paradox the subject is produced as if having *always already been a subject*, and the social order, as if derived from an anthropology: "The 'evidentness' of identity conceals the fact that it is the result of an identification-interpellation of the subject, whose alien origin is nevertheless 'strangely familiar' to him" (Pêcheux 1982, 107).

That said, what Pêcheux enables us to think and contributes substantially to the materialist approach to ideology is that the Freudian temporality of *estrangement in the experience of the sameness*, which consecrates the effect of the interpellation as the reunification of a *décalage*, finds its existence in the discursive materiality of the syntactic incrustation—called "preconstructed" (1982, 107)—a repressed temporal separation, distance, or gap in the phrase, between what is pretended to have been thought before, elsewhere, or independently and what is contained in the global affirmation of the phrase.⁴² This function is supported by another concept that is the core of the materiality of imaginary within this theory of discourse: the concept of "interdiscourse."

> By saying that the *ego*, i.e., the imaginary in the subject (the place in which is constituted for the subject his imaginary relationship to reality), cannot recognise its subordination, its subjection to the Other or to the Subject, because this subordination/subjection is realised precisely in the subject in the form of autonomy, I am thus not appealing to any "transcendence" (a real Other or Subject). I am merely repeating the terms that Lacan and Althusser respectively have given (deliberately adopting the travestied and "phantasmagoric" forms inherent in subjectivity) to the *natural and socio-historical process* by which the subject-effect is constituted-reproduced as an interior without an exterior, and that by the determination of the real ('exterior'), and specifically, I would add, of *interdiscourse* as real ('exterior'). (Pêcheux 1982, 113–14)

Pêcheux reaches thus the syntactic level of discursive formations to reinscribe the conflictive consistency of the imaginary materiality in their *dispositio*. And this is possible by rejecting the very idea of discourse as representing the real, by means of conceiving discourses as *parts* of the real "*natural and socio-historical process*."

Finally, Montag locates in the Spinozian background the ambivalence between *demand* and *decree*—which Freud was also aware of—in order to bring out the politicity that is inherent to discourse. In syntax, one finds "the paradoxical *retroactive temporality* in which the effects of hegemony are at the same time product and condition for the birth of a new State" (Pêcheux 1982, 65). On the one hand, the dimension of the *command* that any *demand* conceals is deactivated when its discursive form is made visible.

> To read the discursive form, reality, is for Pêcheux to reformulate it as command, thereby inscribing it in a scene of discipline and punishment: one cannot ignore a command without impunity. [. . .] [N]or does the command present itself as an act of both illocutionary and physical force: it is expressed in such phrases as "everyone knows that . . ." or "as anyone can see." [. . .] To formulate the command as command, to translate it into itself, is to disobey one of its most important orders: it is thus both the cause and effect of a shift in power relations. (Montag 2015, §29; unbracketed ellipsis in the original)

The possibility of reading in every demand a command offers the elements for a critical theory of social demands, we could say, that places Pêcheux at the antipodes of political spontaneity. But, at the same time, it opens a path to making politics thinkable: to the extent that any ritual is forced to come to pass, to repeat itself materially, it is—says Montag—exposed to "infelicities," "misstatements" that may be the *occasion* for something new: "*il n'ya cause que de ce qui cloche*" (2015, §12).

Pêcheux allows us to understand politics in the strong meaning of a radical transformation, without replacing the concept of class struggle for autonomy of politics turned ontology. In this sense, the opportunity (the *chance*) is inscribed as an *internal distance* in the *complex ensemble of the existent*—only to be experienced as a *familiar strangeness*: a liminal space, the immanent border that indicates an *irrepresentable* limit in the discursive materiality that systematically escapes and marks thought with real historical tensions, while it symptomatizes its incapacity to capture them immediately and to offer its concept. And, as it is already said, the—necessarily displaced—presentation of the irrepresentable is the point where, reading Machiavelli, Althusser discovers the suspended temporality of that *unsettling familiarity* that evokes the Freudian notion of *Unheimlichkeit* and allows us to outline the opening of the conjuncture to the opportunity for political action (Althusser 1995, 54).

SOME CONCLUDING REMARKS

With Pêcheux, Althusser's disperse and fragmentary developments about discourse could be brought together through the weak but suggestive thread that connects the critique of idealist and empiricist epistemology under the "religious myth of reading" of a manifest discourse; materialist critiques of classic theater, inspired by Brecht and Bertolazzi (Althusser 2005); critiques of the political anthropologies of the "State of Nature" that replicate the scheme of the *Edenic Myth* (Althusser 2014b); and the references to the *theoretical dispositive* in Machiavelli (Althusser 1995, 1997). It is a weak connection, where the discursive questions are invoked apropos other questions, regarding science, theology, politics, and so forth.

The Pêcheutian operation *produces* the discursive question that pushes the Althusserian theory of ideology forward. The emphasis on the *scenic* condition of interpellation brings forth the weight of fantasy, *jouissance* and desire as constitutive components of the materiality of power—the "psychic violence" of the *decree*—both in the ideological operation as well as in its discursive existence. It takes the interweaving of ideology and discourse to an extreme point that allows us to recover the epistemic sense of *conjunctural thinking*.

The materialist stake of a theory of discursive processes is rooted at the same time in the Freudian theoretical novelty, which, among other things, exposes the bond between fantasy and unconscious repression, and in the Marxist theoretical novelty, which, among other things, breaks away from the myth of the small producer by developing its theory of primitive accumulation. In both cases, a complex, plural, and non-contemporaneous conceptualization of temporality is set in motion. It is that complexity that remains ignored in the theories of discourse that ask the question about its mechanism, ignoring the problem of historical causality (or pretending to resolve it with an ontological jump toward an affirmation of pure contingency). The reading of the mythical fantasy as a dispositive of discursive production clarifies that it requires the repression of the material objectivity of the imaginary—in other words, the complex transindividual, overdetermined (hierarchical and unevenly articulated) *ensemble* of apparatuses and real discursive formations of a given conjuncture (educational, moral, legal, etc.) whose concrete existence as a *contradictory unity in dominance* is a product of the determined state of the class struggle, in the context of a given social formation. The class struggle does not respond to any kind of sociological position or to a *combat between ideologies* (neither "proletarian and bourgeois," nor "dominant and subordinate"), as Althusser (2018a, [MS 1978] 2018b) denounces as a reformist reading of the Gramscian theory of hegemony. The primacy of the class struggle may only be read in the concreteness of an order of *formations* that exists as a (metastable) equilibrium between contradicting relations of production and the transformation of the articulated complex in dominance. That means that it exists in a determinate conjuncture and never "in general": never in a structural comprehension of its formal mechanisms, which, imposed on the conjuncture (without a concrete analysis of the situation), reproduce the "point of view of the state."

Pêcheux understands better than Althusser his thesis about the clinical theory of temporality in the analytic of the "case": "It is only possible to give a content to the concept of historical time by defining historical time as the specific form of existence of the social totality under consideration, an existence in which different structural levels of temporality interfere" (Althusser and Balibar 1970, 109).

And he produces *avant la lettre* the critique of the process that operates today as the supposed "overcoming" of the concepts of class struggle and unconscious, not only in the images proper to common sense, but also in the abstractions and ontologizations that slip into the field of allegedly critical thought.

NOTES

1. This is not a new concerning, but the very pulse of his writings, since the early 1960s (cf. Althusser 2005).

2. For an approach to these formulas in the framework of the political discourse of the PCF, cf. "George Marchais: avancer sur la voie de XXII Congrès" *L'Humanite*, April 28, 1978, 7.

3. Not only the fledgling antidemocratic tendencies denounced in the countries from the old Soviet bloc, but also the dictatorships in Latin America, the place where the neoliberal reforms began.

4. These articles, due to the electoral defeat of March 1978, were summed up in the volume titled *Ce qui ne peut plus durer dans le parti communiste* (cf. 1978a).

5. Since *Lire le Capital*, Althusser notices this: "The historicism Gramsci affirms means a vigorous protest against this aristocratism of theory and of its 'thinkers,' . . . a direct appeal to 'practice,' to political action, to 'changing the world,' without which Marxism would be no more than the prey of bookworms and passive political functionaries" (Althusser and Balibar 1970, 129). But Gramsci's proposal fails in its effort to capture the concrete insofar as it proposes an immediate relationship between theory and its object, restoring among them an expressive causality that is more appropriate to the ideological link (a worldview) than to the theoretical one: "He tends to think the relationship between Marxist science and real history according to the model of the relationship between an 'organic' (historically dominant and active) ideology and real history; and ultimately to think this relationship between Marxist scientific theory and real history according to the model of a relationship of *direct expression*, which does give a fair account of the relationship between an organic ideology and its age." (Althusser and Balibar 1970, 131) As Morfino (2019a) has shown, Althusser's reading of Gramsci is very far from being simple or capable of being reduced to a mere critique or a rejection. It must be considered instead as an unavoidable step not only in Marxist theoretical and political tradition, but especially in the questions related to ideology, political thinking, and discourse.

6. "Wiping out the role of Althusser in this period is a typical aspect of a more general censorship, which has a very precise meaning: it means denying that Marxism in the post-war period (and especially in the 60s and 70s) was not a simple repetition of dogmas drawn from Marx, Engels, Lenin and Stalin (or even Mao), denying therefore that changes and events took place in its realm, bearing an objective relationship to the social and political issues of the period. It seems important now to deny that there was intellectual activity—therefore productivity—within Marxism, not only illusions. Marxist intellectuals, and especially communist intellectuals, must be portrayed as either passive victims or impostors, the mere instruments of a gigantic conspiracy. They should not have been able to think by themselves, just as Marxism and communism should not have had any real history, except the history of a catastrophic imposture." (Balibar 1993, 2)

7. "The whole of the Hegelian dialectics is here, that is, it is completely dependent on the radical presupposition of a simple original unity which develops within itself by virtue of its negativity, and throughout its development only ever restores the original simplicity and unity in an ever more 'concrete' totality" (Althusser 2005, 197).

8. "That every case (medical or otherwise) is singular, everyone will admit with no difficulty. But that a singular case is at the same time universal is what constitutes both a problem *and a* scandal! . . .

". . . [H]ow could it be said better than by Marx himself, who wrote that there is never production in general, labor in general, and so forth, and that every history is always a singular "case"—and likewise for [psycho]analysts: they never encounter "the same case" again, but always and uniquely singular and, therefore, different "cases." . . .

"Yet Spinoza ignores this objection, just as Marx and psychoanalysis so blithely take exception to Popper. . . . [I]t is only in the individual and social life of singularities (nominalism), really singular—but universal, for these singularities are as if traversed and haunted by repetitive or constant invariants, not by generalities but repetitive constants—that one can rediscover under their singular variations in other singularities of the same species and genus. . . . He rediscovers generic constants or invariants, as one wishes, which arise in the existence of singular 'cases' and which permit their *treatment*. . . , constants and not laws, which obviously do not constitute the object of a will to verification in an abstract renewable experimental dispositive . . . . It is obviously a question here of a test (*ipreuve*), which has nothing to do with experimental proof (*reuve*) in the physical sciences, but which possesses its rigor, whether it be in the knowledge and treatment of individual singularity (medicine, analysis) or social singularity (history of a people) and action over history (politics)." (Althusser 1997, 8–9)

9. The lack of a concept of class struggle and of the unconscious in Foucaultian theory marks limits to its capacity to produce a critique of the present beyond description because it fails to capture the material contradictions of the current regimes of domination. Hence the catastrophic tendency of many of his followers.

10. "It implied the two complementary postulates he defined in the Sixth Thesis on Feuerbach: (1) that there is a universal essence of man; (2) that this essence is the attribute of '*each single individual*' who is its real subject. These two postulates are complementary and indissociable. But their existence and their unity presuppose a whole empiricistidealist world outlook. If the essence of man is to be a universal attribute, it is essential that *concrete subjects* exist as absolute givens; this implies an *empiricism of the subject*. If these empirical individuals are to be men, it is essential that each carries in himself the whole human essence, if not in fact, at least in principle; this implies an *idealism of the essence*. So empiricism of the subject implies idealism of the essence and vice versa. This relation can be inverted into its 'opposite'—empiricism of the concept/idealism of the subject. But the inversion respects the basic structure

of the problematic, which remains fixed. In this type-structure it is possible to recognize not only the principle of theories of society (from Hobbes to Rousseau), of political economy (from Petty to Ricardo), of ethics (from Descartes to Kant), but also the very principle of the (pre-Marxist) idealist and materialist 'theory of knowledge' (from Locke to Feuerbach, via Kant)." (Althusser 2005, 227–28)

11. "Ideology is neither the cause (in any commonly accepted sense of the term) nor the effect of the apparatuses that constitutes its material form. We can now understand Althusser's comment . . . , 'to be a Spinozist or a Marxist...is to be exactly the same thing.' As is well known, Spinoza questioned the model of every conception of the original subject (or actor or agent of an action): God. [. . .] God can only be an immanent cause whose will and intentions exist solely in an actualized state: 'God could not have been prior to his decrees nor can he be without them." [fn. Spinoza E I, P33] . . . [T]he concept is there: ideology is immanent in its apparatuses and their practices, it has no existences apart from these apparatuses and is entirely coincident with them. Ideas have thus disappeared into their material manifestations, becoming like causes that 'exist' only in their effects (or, to add a Freudian reference that is entirely in keeping with both Spinoza and Althusser, ideas in this sense are causes that are ever only constituted *nachträglich*, retroactively, as the effect of their material effects)." (Montag 2013, 151–52)

12. "That the subject turns round or rushes toward the law suggests that the subject lives in passionate expectation of the law. Such love is not beyond interpellation; rather, it forms the passionate circle in which the subject becomes ensnared by its own state. . . .

. . . According to the logic of conscience, which fully constrains Althusser, the subject's existence cannot be linguistically guaranteed without passionate attachment to the law. This complicity at once conditions and limits the viability of a critical interrogation of the law. One cannot criticize too far the terms by which one's existence is secured." (Butler 1997, 129)

13. "Under what conditions does a law monopolize the terms of existence in so thorough a way? Or is this a theological fantasy of the law? Is there a possibility of being elsewhere or otherwise, without denying our complicity in the law that we oppose? Such possibility would require a different kind of turn, one that, enabled by the law, turns away from the law, resisting its lure of identity, an agency that outruns and counters the conditions of its emergence. Such a turn demands a willingness not to be—a critical desubjectivation—in order to expose the law as less powerful than it seems. What forms might linguistic survival take in this desubjectivized domain? How would one know one's existence? Through what terms would it be recognized and recognizable? Such questions cannot be answered here, but they indicate a direction for thinking that is perhaps prior to the question of conscience, namely, the question that preoccupied Spinoza, Nietzsche, and most recently, Giorgio Agamben: How are we to understand the desire to be as a constitutive desire?" (Butler 1997, 130).

14. As we will argue, this "development" pays some prices that should be considered before dropping the notion of ideology.

15. That force is productive is something Foucault rightly pointed out, but for Althusser, Machiavelli says more, because when saying that force is productive, he points toward the *product*: force produces *ideology* (Althusser [MS 1978] 2018b, 109).

16. "Althusser introduces the term 'individual' as a place-holder to satisfy provisionally this grammatical need, but what might ultimately fit the grammatical requirement will not be a static grammatical subject. The grammar of the subject emerges only as a consequence of the process we are trying to describe. Because we are, as it were, trapped within the grammatical time of the subject (e.g., 'we are trying to describe,' 'we are trapped'), it is almost impossible to ask after the genealogy of its construction without presupposing that construction in asking the question.

"What, prior to the subject, accounts for its formation? Althusser begins 'Ideology and Ideological State Apparatuses' by referring to the reproduction of social skills. He then distinguishes between skills reproduced in the firm and those reproduced in education. The subject is formed with respect to the latter. In a sense, this reproduction of relations is prior to the subject who is formed in its course. Yet the two cannot, strictly speaking, be thought without each other" (Butler 1997, 117). Among other circumstances, the reductionist reading is due to the extraction, that Althusser himself made, of the writing on *Ideology and Ideological State Apparatuses* from the general framework of the theory of social reproduction in which it took shape (cf. Althusser 2014b).

17. With different arguments, E. P. Thompson (1978), who finds it purely antihistorical; Rancière (1974), who finds it authoritarian; Foucault (1977), who finds it doesn't consider the productive condition of power; Dolar (1993), who finds it empiricist, among many others, read Althusserian theory of interpellation in a reductive way due to the misunderstanding of the complex temporality that underlies it. It is not that in Althusser writings, there aren't formulas, terms, or assertions that may lead to these conclusions, but each of them falls in the same sinecdochical reading because of choosing the portion of an ambitious philosophical process of thinking for the whole of it.

18. Carolina Ré (2011) has demonstrated that despite the differences there is a closeness between the criticisms raised by Butler and Žižek to the Althusserian concept of interpellation. . .

19. Some passages of Žižek intervention recall that of "Beyond Interpellation" by Mladen Dolar (1993), for whom Althusser could not fully consider the "remainder" of subjection process: for example "It is essential for psychoanalysis that the Althusserian alternative—materiality or subjectivity; exterior or interior—is not exhaustive." (Dolar 1993, 78) In other words, for Dolar, Althusserian interpellation places a clear-cut, living ideology for the "exterior" and psychic life for the "interior" space of subjectivity, disregarding "the point of exteriority in the very kernel of interiority . . . where materiality is the most intimate. . . . : extimacy" (1993, 78). Žižek was wont to follow this kind of Cartesian reading of Althusserian theory of ideology, but, to the extent that he rejects Althusser's material "exteriority," a kind of supposed dualism gets in through the window.

20. As emerges from the objections made by Balibar (2016) in his response to Althusser's essay, the distinction between elements that are significant for different discursive structures (ideological discourse, unconscious discourse) opens up a series of problems that are not at all resolved but are only indicated by Althusser in a fragmentary and erroneous way. Nevertheless, for the purposes of this chapter, the different structures of ideology and unconscious are sufficiently distinguished—a considerable difference between his way of conceiving the relationship between the ideological and the unconscious with respect to other searches, such as that faced by the Žižekian school.

21. The problem with this reduction is that it is situated in the bourgeois class struggle—that is, it does not see that, in political terms, the concept of class struggle involves an articulation of two struggles. Althusser puts forward this discussion in various writings. On the one hand, he insists on rejecting the concept of class struggle as a simple opposition between two forces (as if it were a playing field in which two already given teams meet) (cf. Althusser 1973). On the other hand, he states, particularly in *Que faire?* (2018), that the class struggle waged by the proletariat is not the same struggle waged by the bourgeoisie and that to confuse them is not only an error of strategy but also of theory.

22. The political immanence of theoretical discourse may support a dialogue between Althusser and Rancière, beyond the critiques of the latter (1974); and specially it may problematize the metapolitical consideration of Marxism (Rancière 1995).

23. It is in 1963 that the inflection in Freud's reading takes place, when it returns, with Lacan, the *libido* remaider in relation to desire and its cause as "the rock of the Freudian theory" (Consentino 1998, 101). Lacan introduces anguish, precisely in relation to the Freudian *Unheimlichkeit*, to indicate that irreducible pulsional point to the imaginary investment (Lacan 2004, 20).

24. "For you and for me, the category of the subject is a primary 'evident truth' (evident truths are always primary): it is clear that you and I are subjects (free, ethical, etc. . . .). Like all evident facts, including those that make a word 'name a thing' or 'have a meaning' (therefore including the evident fact of the 'transparency' of language), the 'evident fact' that you and I are subjects—and that that does not cause any problems—is an ideological effect, the elementary ideological effect." (Althusser 1971, 161; ellipsis in the original)

25. As Mara Glozman points out in her preliminary study to the Spanish edition of *Les vérités de La Palice*, "In many cases the use of notions (*discursive formation, pre-constructed, interdiscourse* to a lesser extent) or of expressions that carry their echoes (*discourse formation conditions, interdiscursivity*) directly omits the theoretical and militant framework from which they emerged. It eludes, in the materiality of the omission, not only the name but [also] a present and a way of inhabiting that present in which the positions and the theoretical interventions did not happen without getting involved and assuming the effects of that." (Glozman 2016, 7, my translation)

26. In the English edition of *For Marx*, Ben Brewster translates the French *décalage* as *readjustment* (e.g., Althusser and Balibar 1970, 78) and in his "Althusser Glossary 1969," Brewster suggests the term "dislocation." Those notions not always correspond to the use of *décalage* in Althusser's writings, while the concept of dislocation involves a certain temporal figure close to the notion of "event," the term "readjustment" is close to the idea of duplication but far from the idea of displacement or distortion. So, in the rest of this book the concept of *décalage* will be translated not only as *dislocation*, but also with different terms, such as *misadjustment* or *displacement*, depending on the context in the original text.

27. As Marilena Chaui has demonstrated, the Spinozian reading of Machiavelli entails the possibility of sustaining the knowledge of the political in the knowledge of nature, because it allows conceiving men as "parts of nature," as it is displayed in Parts II, III, and especially, IV of the *Ethics* (Chaui 2004, 87–208).

28. As Vittorio Morfino (2017, 445–65) has pointed out, in the first edition of *Lire Le Capital* in 1965, one can read a long meditation, eliminated from later editions, on the use of term *Darstellung* in Marx. This meditation connects the Althusserian question of causality with the figure of "theatre without an author"—on which Montag (2017) has worked—and the Spinozian thesis of the immanence of the structure in its effects, as the concept that Marx looked for to explain the peculiar kind of structure of the totality, according to a formula of causality that could escape as much to the Cartesian mechanicist tradition as to the Leibnizian idealistic thinking. But it allows the thinking of the presence of the whole, in the hierarchical and unequal relations of its elements, in a materialistic and historical way: "'Darstellung' means, among other things, in German theatrical representation . . . [,] 'presentation,' 'exhibition' and, at its deepest root, 'position of presence,' presence offered and visible. To express its specific nuance, it may be instructive to oppose 'Darstellung' to 'Vorstellung.' . . . In the Darstellung, on the contrary, there is nothing behind it: the very thing is here offered in the position of presence. The whole text of a theatrical piece is thus offered in the presence of the performance . . . . [I]t cannot be known, as presence itself of the whole, as latent structure of the whole, but in the whole; . . . it can be said that the 'Darstellung' is the concept of the presence of the structure in its effects—or, on the contrary, that the 'Darstellung' is the concept of the effectiveness of an absence. It is in this second sense that Rancière has used the decisive

concept, elaborated in depth by Miller last year, in the course of our seminar on Lacan, of 'metonymic causality.' I believe that, like the concept of the efficacy of an absent cause, this concept is considerably useful to designate the absence in a person of the structure in the effects considered in the perspective of its existence. But it is necessary to insist on another aspect of the phenomenon, which is that of the presence, of the immanence of the cause in its effects, said in another way of the existence of the structure in its effects" (Althusser 1996, 646, my translation).

29. In *L'archéologie du savoir*, Foucault unfolds a concept of history very close to the materialistic (Althusserian) concept of *process without subject*, which problematizes the type of structuralism of his previous works. For Lecourt, this would explain the absence of the category of episteme in this book (Lecourt 1970, 68–87).

30. Beyond the efforts of Butler to read in Foucault the *décalage* of the subject that allows the connecting of it with Freud (cf. Butler 1997) but also beyond Foucault's later works on the technologies of the self and *parrhesiastic* practices (cf. Foucault 2001), which are interesting elements for a rich genealogy of the encounters and disagreements with Althusserian materialism, Foucault himself accepts that he performs his task in the form of the *description* while "the time for theory has not yet come" (1972, 22). For Lecourt (1970), that "time for theory" was indeed inaugurated by Marx a long time ago, but it won't arrive for Foucault if he does not resolve to recognize the principles of this theory that are those of the science of history.

31. Terriles and Hernández (2014) take up a specific moment in Pêcheux's writing process, characterized as DA2 (Discourse Analysis 2) and which constitutes, in my opinion, the moment when the effort to articulate Marxism and psychoanalysis reaches its highest intensity. Toward the end of the 1970s and especially during the 1980s, Pêcheux's research will grow in complexity thanks to his reading of the Lacanian concept of the Real. In a context crossed by a weakening of the Marxist theoretical imprint in French philosophy, however, he will not succeed in sustaining with equal strength his project of articulating linguistics and psychoanalysis with the Marxist concept of class struggle.

32. The theoretical expression for this first current could be summarized in terms of the grammar of one part and the universal of another part, the whole resting on a philosophical conception according to which language is a timeless structure, guaranteed, in turn, by the structure of being and thought.

33. The philosophical conception underlying this second trend conjectures that languages form, differentiate, evolve, and die historically, as living species do. Philology—the research of affiliations, derivations, and disappearances—seems to constitute the classical form of this second trend.

34. It can be said, by the way, that this thesis is what Althusser develops in *Lire le Capital* (Althusser et al. 1965), as the theory of *symptomatical reading* (cf. 1965). A radically political reading, as Carolina Collazo has pointed out (cf. 2016).

35. From a strongly structuralist approach, Jean-Claude Milner (2002) recognizes it with the aporetic expression of an objectivity-thesei that allows the thinking of the possibility of a "political science" that pulsates in the long enterprise of Marx—his reading of Democrito, of Hegel, until his developments on political economy. For Milner, Althusser had touched Marx in the sense that the latter opened a crisis in thought related to the question of *necessity* and the way in which it affects the *physei/thesei* dichotomy that, for Milner, constituted one of the greater objects of Marx. He found, raised in terms of positive science, the question that only the Hegelian dialectic had seemed to articulate until then, in terms of speculative logic: the existence of a need freely created by men. It was no longer a question of convention but of history and politics. But these involved a paradox: if the whole of the *thesei* is understood as the whole of what depends on man, then it is also understood as the whole of what can be transformed by

man. Social relations are *thesei*, so they are not, therefore, immutable. *But they are modifiable by men because they are imposed on them.* Social relations are imposed with the force of inexorable laws to the isolated individual for the same reason that they are transformable by the conjunction of all men. For Milner (2002) it is, thus, *necessity* what opens a place for politics: social relations are imposed to each one in the exact measure in which they are transformable by the union of all. The "political" structuralism that Milner finds in the Althusserian reading of Marx dialogues with the reading of Marilena Chaui, who finds in Spinoza an ontology of the immanent relations between powers that, when rejecting all theological association between contingency, possibility, and will, allows ethics and politics to recover the foundations of a demonstrative speech that "from Aristotle had been denied to them." (Chaui 2004, 160, my translation)

36. "Ideology and the unconscious meet: in a forgetting deeper than any memory, because memory is nothing more than the forgetting of forgetting, the rendering absent of the absence that allows us to be stand-ins for ourselves, the disappearance of every gap into the density of a discourse without empty spaces, the writing without margins that covers the page, the uninterrupted murmur of incessant voices. . . . If ideology, in the concrete form of a specific ideological formation, rests on a 'primal or originary forgetting,' like Freud's *Urverdrängung*, it 'frees' the subject from the memory of the command that determines what he can and must say." (Montag 2015, §33)

37. This is meant in a sense that may open a dialogue with Butler's use of the notion of *iterability* rather that her readings on the figures of "bad subjects" (cf. 1997).

38. "In fact, every 'point of view' is the point of view of a subject; a science cannot therefore be a 'point of view' on the real, a vision or a construction which *represents* the real (a 'model' of the real): a science is the *real in the modality of its necessity-thought*, so the real with which the sciences are concerned is not anything different from the real producing the figurative-concrete that is imposed on the subject in the 'blind' necessity of ideology. . . . [The] true point of departure, as we know, is not man, the subject, human activity, etc., but, once again, the ideological condition of the reproduction/transformation of the relation of production." (Pêcheux 1982, 128–29)

39. "Yet to place oneself 'at the standpoint of reproduction' under the primacy of class struggle is necessarily to place oneself at the same time at the standpoint of what is opposed to this reproduction, at the standpoint of resistance to this reproduction, and of the revolutionary tendency leading to the transformation of the relations of production." (Pêcheux 2014, 3)

40. Althusser laid out this question in writings like "Sur la dialectique matérialiste" (in 1965), where he holds that the Marxist problematic inhabits simultaneously Marx's theoretical practices and the concrete thought of the Marxist political leaders obliged to mobilize the Marxist theory of history with regard to a singular case of the conjuncture they found themselves intervening in. Overdetermination names the *necessary combination* between two temporalities of thought: the thought of the "fait accompli" incarnated by the historian and the thought of the task—that is, the thought of the *fact to accomplish*, which is typically that of man of politics (Althusser 2005).

41. In the Appendix III "The French Political Winter" to the English edition of *Les vérités de La Palice* (1982), Pêcheux develops a rigorous critique of the Platonist deviation that could be developed from the idea of a kind of epistemological solution to bourgeois political practice (cf. also Pêcheux 1990): "Thus was evaded, with the utmost philosophical obstinacy, the fact that the nonsense of the unconscious, in which interpellation finds a pint of attachment, is never entirely covered or obscured by the evidentness of the subject-centre-meaning which is produced by it, because the moments of production and product are not sequential as in the Platonic myth, but inscribed in the simultaneity of an oscillation, of a 'pulsation' by which the

unconscious nonsense endlessly returns in the subject and in the meaning which is supposedly installed in it. There is no cause save for something jarring (Lacan). It is at this precise point that Platonism radically misses the unconscious, i.e., the cause that determines the subject at the point at which it is grasped by the interpellation effect; what is missed is that cause insofar as it is constantly 'manifested' in a thousand forms (the slip, the parapraxis) in the subject itself, for the unconscious traces of the Signifier are never 'erased' or 'forgotten' but work without intermission in the oscillation between sense and nonsense in the divided subject" (Pêcheux 1982, 216–17). A careful reading of this movement is still to be done in order to avoid considering it a mere rejecting of Marxism but a deepening of its encounter with psychoanalysis that reinforces the Pêcheutian development of analytic of discursive formations and the immanent reading of the ideological mechanism operating in them, which are also produced in the universal-singularity of the *case*. If Althusser arrives at the postulate of the mechanism of interpellation as a result of the critical analysis of *the concrete complex of formations in which that mechanism exists*, under the dominance of the formation of a *legal ideological formation*, then the theory of ideology is, in fact, immanent to the critical reading of this concrete ideological formation. When Pêcheux distinguishes between ideology in general, particular ideologies, and dominant ideology, he allows us to return to that crucial writing that is *Marxisme et humanisme* (Althusser 1965) and understand that the so-called "ideology in general" is the immanent structure of the dominant ideological formation of capitalism: *Humanism*. It is in this critique of humanism that psychoanalisis and Althusserian Marxism find their conjunction.

42. This is the *material* reason of the paradox of the indetermination of first names: they reject any determination (in spite of requiring it *by necessity*) because other terms, without being such, offer a placement from which they support their imaginary effect of singular designation: "Designation by a proper name correlatively implies the possibility of designating 'the same thing' by a periphrasis like 'he who discovered . . .' ." (Pêcheux 1982, 65; ellipsis in the original)

Chapter Two

Against Humanism and Denunciation of Alienation

> *Debout! L'heure est venue, à chaque travailleur*
> *Le pain (bis) qu'il a gagné, qu'importe sa couleur.*
> ....
> *Allons! malgré votre race,*
> *Hommes de couleur, unissez-vous;*
> *Car le soleil luit pour tous.*
> *Que chaque peuple heureux, prospère,*
> *Au fronton de l'humanité,*
> *Grave ces mots: en toi j'espère,*
> *Tu règneras, Égalité.*
>
> —Camille Naudain, "Marseillaise Noir," 1867

It is already well-known that the word *zombie* becomes from the Haitian Creole *zonbi*, which is a declination from the Kikongo, the Bantu language spoken in Congo and Angola and imported to Caribbean by former African slaves. Far from ethnographic or folklore studies approaches,[1] the Haitian genealogy of the mass-cultural figure of zombies could be useful to explore some dimensions of the ideological crisis in late capitalism in terms of a crisis of the long-fertile articulation of two ideological configurations: the myth of the "small producer" and the liberal myth of the "State of Nature."

On the one hand, it could be said that the figure of the zombie offers a metaphor for alienation in capitalist social formation. In this sense, it is an evocation of the alienation of the will, the capture of the sovereignty of the subject by thinking that is alien to him. The zombie could thus iconize the ideological capture of working-class subjectivity, in the very process of reproduction, in terms of "real subsumption" (Marcuse 1964; Foucault 2010; Baudrillard 2000; Han 2015; Guattari and Negri 1999). Undoubtedly, on the other hand, another very eloquent reading is the one that associates the postcolonial critic of universality with the Marxist reading of the "primitive accumulation" and offers accessible images to understand a critic of capitalism in its neoliberal form, in which, as diverse authors have raised, the processes of intensive dispossession permeate the expropriation of the collective wealth and offer new forms of servitude. This dialectical view has the virtue of placing a problem that is not exactly the one that can be formulated in "anthropological" terms as a problem of "otherness"—because the figure of the zombie is not the metaphor of a radical "other," entirely an outsider from civilization, a "nonhuman" in the sense of a distinction proper to former colonial relations. The zombie is, instead, of a type of nearer foreignness, a "familiar stranger"—to reclaim the Freudian expression that we registered in the previous chapter in relation to the figure of the interpellation—that indicates the strange as temporary *décalage* in the constitutive matrix of the Subject of Culture. This strangeness that connects the margins of the civilized world with its constitutive otherness has been taken up again by postcolonial studies, race, queer, and gender intersectional studies in their discussion with the figures of universality and deployed in approaches to neoliberalism in relation to the critique of the original accumulation, as a permanent and structural process of violent accumulation woven into the very surface of "capitalist normality" and its frequent cyclical crises of accumulation (Bishop 2010; Lauro 2015; Bohrer 2020; Coulthard 2014; Moore 2015; Getachew 2016).

Taking some of these tools, this chapter proposes a tour with a different nuance. In principle, it does not rely on the theory of alienation, since it does not aim to offer a cultural-critical analysis of "*zombie* culture" aimed at "unveiling" the mystery behind its forms. In fact, part of our effort will consist in stating that, in order to think about it from its "behind the scenes,"[2] critical analysis must cross the scene of the philosophical problem of consciousness and recognition.[3] Rather, the chapter aims to think of this figure as a *symptom of the process of de-dialectization* that takes place within the liberal-humanist ideological formation in late capitalism. This claims for a kind of symptomatical reading that, as Carolina Collazo has pointed out, involves a radically political conception of reading as "a way of understanding *otherness* as the siege that has always been imposed on consciousness in its attempt to determine itself as the Origin" (Collazo 2016, 15).

In this framework, the appeal to the critique of alienation is also part of the object of the critique, since it forms a unity with the humanist position, which is opposed only by its speculative investment. That theoretical reading is trapped in the circularity offered by the mechanism of the liberal myth itself. This "critique" of the humanism contained in the theory of alienation extends to the historicist gesture—which constitutes its *partenaire*—and consists of a "return to the origins" in the sense of a will to confront the cyclical capitalist "normality" with the violent truth of its *genesis* (cf. Romé 2020).

Based on this double caution, I will try to inscribe the figure of the *zombie* as a symptom in the complex assembly of relations and temporalities in which it takes shape. This complexity leads to a conception of historical time that, as we have already indicated following Althusser, acts in a practical way in the developments of Marx and Freud. This embrace will allow us to think about how the inherent politicization of the ideological processes of neoliberalization might recover the contradictory consistency of its figures. With this approach, I expect to contribute to the development of the links between Marxism and postcolonial, intersectional, and subjectivity studies, deploying the theory of social reproduction and the concept of historical time, while pointing out the risks of the ideological siege of liberal humanism.

To open up this idealistic circularity of humanism and historicism, psychoanalytic theory offers a noncontemporary conception of historical time that puts in check every genetic and historicist figure of temporality, and Marxist theory allows us to read a structural causality that demands our assuming the differential articulation of practices: the "relative" condition of their autonomy—that is, not their pure, disperse multiplicity or their indetermination, but their unequal and hierarchical articulation in an overdetermined and dominant totality. In this sense, the figure of the *zombie* brings into the attention the question of the link between *law* and *violence*, in the "origins" of humanism. But we will say that, far from doing so in terms of "unveiling" the violence that is hidden behind bourgeois juridical ideology (or "exposing" that behind the capitalist normality of wages, savings, and production lies the political truth of war and dispossession by force), it shows the contradictory consistency of the humanist-historicist ideology—that is, its condition of ideological formation as a divided unit. This exposes the misadjustment of dominant ideology as constitutive precariousness and, therefore, the politicization that is inherent to it—not as its repressed historical *genesis* but as the constitutive weakness of its structure and of the tendential laws that sustain its duration, a trace of the immanent exteriority of its historical determination.

In this sense, it is possible to think about that which by convention we can call "neoliberalism" as an agonizing process of mutual decomposition of the dominant humanist ideology in the complex assembly of relations of the regime of imperialist accumulation, under the condition of abandoning all teleology that summons the images of engendering and filiation, in order to capture the concrete conditions of the historical transformation.

It is a matter of accepting the bad news that the decomposition may last too long: "When Lenin says that imperialism is the last stage of capitalism, and that afterwards it's all over, we must realize: 1. that this last stage can last a long time; and 2. that afterwards we will find ourselves facing an alternative: afterwards is 'either socialism or barbarism'" (Althusser 2018a, 49).

This expression, taken up again by Rosa Luxemburg and Lenin from Karl Kautsky, offers in its disjunctive thesis a rudimentary concept of historical time, which Althusser underlines in his book on Imperialism (1973), published posthumously in the volume *Écrits su L'Histoire* (2018a), insofar as he assumes that history does not tend "naturally," nor only, toward socialism, because history does not lead to the achievement of an objective. On the contrary, from a political position of reading, attentive to the contradictory conditions, the disjunction means that, if the circumstances are favorable, if the proletarian class struggle is well conducted, it can be thought of as the end of capitalism; but "at the same time," its non-culmination can be thought of as *barbarism*. "What is barbarism?"—asks Althusser—. A regression in the same place, a decadence in the place, like the hundreds of examples offered by the history of humanity. Yes, our 'civilization' can perish right here, . . . accumulating all the sufferings of a birth that is not fulfilled and of an abortion that is not a liberation" (2018a, 50,).

In this sense, one could think that, although in many aspects it is fruitful to think of so-called "neoliberalism" as a "neo-colonialism," it is nevertheless risky to simply homologate them or to think of them in a sort of causal linearity because, among other things, that does not allow us to weigh the historical specificity of the regime of imperialist accumulation, in the process of its decomposition—but also because the juxtaposition of times in figures like the one evoked by the notion of "accumulation by dispossession" (Harvey 2005) or the idea of a structural and permanent "original accumulation" has the effect of homologating the tendential logic of expanded reproduction of Capital with the problem of *transition*, or worse, of confusing it with the figure of the Absolut Power that is a mythical figure of the Origin. This may result in an immediate politicization of Capital that does not allow us to think about the nonsubjective, contradictory dynamics of its expansion, and correlatively, it could consecrate an omnipotent figure of the global Power that has as its effect a diagnosis of current conjuncture, blind to the real contradictions (cf. Romé and Collazo 2017).

TEMPORAL COMPLEXITY AND THE MYTH OF THE ORIGIN

With respect to the worth of the category of primitive or original accumulation with which the economic role played by the Latin-American former slavery system in the birth of Capitalism and Modernity may be conceived, one of the most delicate and interesting points is the notion of "accumulation by dispossession" (Harvey 2005; Federici 2004) to the extent that it offers a complex approach to the concept of time while inscribing the mechanism of violent expropriation as a *(non)contemporary temporal* form of "original" accumulation, which pushes the modernity myth itself into a liminal experience. Especially in Federici's works, "noncontemporary" temporality could mean that the "origin" should be read as a precariousness that coexists within "structural" duration. In this sense, the notion of politics of the commons recalls a wide tradition in Latin American Marxism focused on discussing forms of noncapitalist social organization and struggle entangled with monopolistic capital forms. There, where eurocentrist or teleological ideas (be they of Marx or others) tend to accept the ideological operation of primitivization of peripheral capitalist zones operated from colonialism to imperialism, many heterodox Marxist thinkers introduce ideas of plural temporalities, dislocations, and temporal paradox within forms of property, social production, reproduction, and so forth, and produce original readings of Marx's writings, Kobalevsky's notebook, Vera Zasílich's correspondence with Marx, and so on (cf. Mariátegui 1928; Aricó 1982; dos Santos 1970, Marini 1973; Furtado 1964 Echeverría 1994; Dussel 1990, García Linera 1989).

Within this tradition, Eduardo Grüner (2010) has considered the historical experience of the Haitian Slaves Revolution of 1791, *more French than the French Revolution*—not only because it had pursued an wider universality of values, such as freedom or equality, but also because it has searched the most paradoxical universality of a *Black Citizenship*, even more a *Black Jacobinism* (James 1989).[4] As long as it could be seen both as a "chapter" and as an *excess* of Jacobinism, it could *objectively* expose the historical *limits* of French Revolution universalism (Grüner 2010, 320).

I will follow this idea of the "noncontemporary time" of this contradictory *ensemble*—the excess of the *more French than French* Haitian Revolution—in order to address the ideological function from which current zombies tales seem to arise. In this respect, the concept of *noncontemporary temporality* performed by Althusser in his reading of Marx can be recalled to develop the heuristic power of the non-teleological conception of history. In addition to this materialist position conceiving of theoretical effect as the result of a critical operation, the concept of time must emerge from the permanent exercises of critique of the various figures of historicism (and humanism, which is its specular-*partenaire*) that constantly return to our theoretical developments. In this sense, ideological notions of time must be the object of analysis because they already are the operations of ideology that must be considered in order to develop the type of connection that "brings back" the experience of the first slaves revolution of the capitalist world-system, in the core of imperialist popular culture, with its singular complexity of contradictions and paradoxes (between archaic—almost mythical—traces and very modern conditions, including some bourgeois-ideological topics). Researchers have taken into account, in this sense, not only the aporia (modern/not modern) of a violent appropriation of labor force productive capacity by the slavery (but quite *rationally* organized) system in Caribbean plantations,[5] but also the decisive role that Creole religion played in the process of this sort of *modern* revolutionary organization:[6]

> Religion played a main role that could be considered a signal of some restorative or traditional tendency; but the fact that it was *that* religion, which is a result of syncretism, and very complex transculturation, is in its own way a "modern" phenomenon—if we accept including it—as we are convinced it should be—in this "modernity," not only the "official" or hegemonic one, represented by Europe, but also that *other* "modernity," much more intricate and contradictory, composed by the (socioeconomic, cultural and even philosophical) *unequal* and *combined* effects of the expansion of the world-system to the extra-European confines (an expansion that, we pointed out, is in *itself* the very condition of the advent of this world-system as it is). (Grüner 2010, 319, my translation)

Grüner gives an interesting characterization of the Haitian Revolution as a *meta-revolution*, as far as it "objectively" called into question the universal pretentions of the so-called modern revolutions, "beginning with that one which was supposed to have 'inspired' it and has posed itself . . . as the paradigm of modern revolutions: the (so-called) French Revolution." He argues recalling a Trotsky's concept, which Haitian can be called a *meta-modern* (meta)revolution that has "*anachronically* challenged in its own *unequal and combined* temporality the ethnic question together with the class question and even the gender question . . . . But, precisely: we consider that Haitian Revolution was that one which showed another modernity: a modernity . . . *divided against itself* (Grüner 2010, 269, my translation).

Doubtless, the problem posed here in terms of a divided-unity is the one of the *Myth of the Revolution as an origin*. There, where the narrative points toward a meta-level of History (which might have meant that the Haitian Revolution is a kind of "veiled" Truth of Revolution), Grüner decides to conceive of it as the symptom of a constitutive, *immanent division* of the image of Modern Revolution. This idea arises from the critique of the genetical narrative history (the very identification of *das Geschehen* and *das Geschichte-erzahlung*) that is tacit but practically involved in historical approaches that conceive of research concerning a social formation as a question about *filiation*. As it has been pointed out by Althusser (2018a; 1995; 1965), this historicist topic connects every figure of historical, "evolutive" temporality with the philosophico-theological Myth of the *genesis*, and this idealist solidarity reappears as the humanist conception of ideology within the *theory of alienation*. They converge in the empiricist background that assumes a relationship of immediacy in which knowledge is already contained in the object (which is itself nothing but the objectification of the "Essence of the Subject"). The historicist form of this thesis is that which immediately identifies the concept of history with the historical object, with the consequence of an epistemological relativism (cf. 2018a).

The rupture that materialism exercises with the figures of the genesis leads to a critique of the theological commitment of the modern myth of the "State of Nature," by means of which it has built up the illusion of immediacy that ties together the assumption of linguistic transparency—that supports empiricist-idealist epistemological tradition—and the image of "superabundance" that makes work dispensable (or *insignificant*). Therefore, Eden becomes here the name of a double imaginary immediacy of "Nature": that one of a human being with the necessity of work neither to survive nor to acquire knowledge (Althusser [MS 1969] 2014a, 150).

The image of a God that leads human beings toward their own good matches the idea of humans following their *right reasoning* and the *movement of nature* (Althusser [MS 1969] 2014a, 152). Althusser exposes that "transparency" and "immediacy" are supported by a paradox: almighty God is himself subjected to a kind of absolute law—the prohibition to eat the fruit from the Tree of Knowledge of Good and Evil. God himself is *subjected* to the omnipotence of some abstractions that place "immediacy" in a regression *ad infinitum*. *God himself cannot make abstraction of the universal law of abstraction* (Althusser [MS 1969] 2014a, 154). The myth, we may say, is constitutively divided by it "inner" contradiction that is the symptom of the "exteriority" that determines the closure of it "inner" space of experience. The "original immediacy" is always already *divided* because it is the result of a prohibition or a "forgetting" (cf. Pêcheux 1982). Consequently, the original plenitude should be considered always-already an effect.

Materialism can be thus considered as a reading position of this constitutive opacity, which assumes the unavoidable secondary order of philosophy considered as a *discourse*. This fact rejects the very idea of a *Prima Philosophia*.

The assumption of the condition of "second order" of every discourse constitutes a criterion of demarcation between the materialist and idealist positions: where philosophy intends to be a discourse on *Origin* or *genesis*, it again takes up the place abandoned by religion. Philosophy that denies it second place in relation to the transformations of existence is a philosophy that has become an ideology, a mythical discourse, a "philosophy of resignation" (Althusser [MS 1969] 2014a). Although this development is usually associated with his theses on aleatory materialism where, against the association of genesis and origin, he recalls the figure of the *clinamen* under the axiom of the primacy of the encounter over form, [7] nevertheless, the struggle with the diverse figures of Origin, and especially of the historicist narratives of filiation or engendering that put the recourse to genetic temporality into play in an explicit or overlapping way, is permanent throughout his writing. But in addition, and as can be deduced from the 2018a publication of an unpublished work from 1966, the critique of *genesis* is at the foundation of his theory of historical time and of the developments on structural causality in which Marxist and psychoanalytical theories converge.

> Thus, to return to the example of the logic of the constitution of the capitalist mode of production in *Capital*: 1. The elements defined by Marx "combine." I prefer to say (in order to translate the term *Verbindung*) that they "conjoin" by "taking hold" in a new structure. This structure cannot be thought, in its irruption, as the effect of a filiation; it must be thought as the effect of a *conjunction*. This new Logic has nothing to do with the linear causality of filiation or with Hegelian "dialectical" causality, which merely says out loud what is implicit in the logic of linear causality. 2. Yet *each* of the elements that come together and combine in the conjunction of the new structure (in the case to hand, accumulated money-capital; "free" labour-power, that is, labour-power divested of its work tools; and technological inventions) is itself, as such, a *product*, an *effect*. What is important in Marx's demonstration is that the three elements are not contemporaneous products of one and the same situation. . . . Each of these elements has its own "history" or genealogy . . . [that] excludes any possibility of the resurrection of the myth of the *genesis*. (Althusser [MS 1978] 2018b, 33)

"This excludes all possibility of a resurgence of the myth of genesis: the feudal mode of production is not the 'father' of the capitalist mode of production in the sense that the latter is contained 'as a seed' in the first," concludes Althusser ([MS 1978] 2018b, 34). Although linear causality can participate in certain, specific historical processes, it is always subordinated to structural causality, says Althusser (Althusser 2018a, 34).

The search for this "singular dialectic" has been present in Althusser since the early 1960s and runs through his readings of psychoanalysis, as it emerges from his correspondence with René Diatkine (cf. Althusser 1993). But this search also appears in *Lire le Capital*, as a theory of reading, in the form of a radical critique of what he calls the "religious myth of reading" a manifest discourse, which brings together, in the various modes of the illusion of immediacy of meaning, the empiricist and idealist traditions. This is the key to the materialist apodicticity that Althusser reads in a "practical state" in Marx's mature writings and the way the former understands the theoretical work, which connects with Spinoza's influence in his materialism.[8] No matter if the original purity is recognized in the Book of Nature or in the Holy Scriptures—if it is bitterly grey or richly green—it always alludes to the process of imaginary simplification of the practical-material *thirdness of production* implied in the very existence of language.[9]

This perspective offers a way of reading Marx's gesture in his chapter 24 on the "so-called primitive accumulation," which begins with an ironic evocation of "Adam Smith previous accumulation" in terms of the *Edenic myth-*

of the small saver—"the diligent, intelligent and above all frugal elite" (Marx 1906, 784).[10] The main mythical function does not lean so much on the denial of a "portion" of history that would consist of its *genesis*. If this were so, it would be enough to "see" that portion of history denied by the modern narrative of the individual who "makes himself," in order to deactivate, by inversion, its ideological force. But if, on the contrary, that force continues acting, it is due to the fact that the material efficacy myths work structurally, denying the relational matrix that causes them. It is the relational condition of the real, the "primacy of the relations of production" on the productive forces, the mechanism on which rests the ideological efficacy of the myth of the "small producer" and what ties it in a singular way to humanist *iusnaturalism*. A historical complexity is irreducible to a single simple "relation", not even to a single contradiction" (cf. Althusser 2005); it involves the overdetermined opacity of a complex of displaced and condensed relations, summoned by a *thirdness*, in the sense of a "relation of relations" causality.

> Observing the opposition between the class that owns the means of production and the class that is deprived of them—in other words, the exploiting and exploited classes—we may be tempted to say that this relation of production is a "human" relation, since it involves *only human beings*, distinguished by the fact that some are rich and others poor. This would be, in some sense, a *two-term* relation: the rich exploit the poor. To say so, however, would be to neglect the crucial fact that wealth and poverty are determined by a *third term*, the means of production . . . . This brings out the specific structure of the abstraction of the relation of production: it is not a two-term, but a three-term relation, in which the relation between classes is determined by the distribution of the means of production between classes.
>
> With that, we glimpse the possibility of a form of abstraction that is utterly disconcerting for idealist philosophy, whether empiricist or formalist. For empiricist or formalist abstraction is always conceived on the model of a "two-term" or an *x*-term abstraction, where *the objects in question are all on the same level*—horizontal, let us say. (Althusser 2017, 88–89)

The idealist depuration—that produces simplicity—thus becomes thinkable by restoring the structure of the real complexity of whose denial is effect. The "myth" is not criticized by the "unveiling" of that which it represses and which would be a "more natural" or authentic truth of history, but by making thinkable the contradictory condition of its material effectiveness, as "part of history," in the Spinozian sense (cf. Romé 2020).[11] The theory of that material complexity takes shape with the discovery of the continent of history to thought, from the Marxist theoretical revolution. But its deployment demands a perpetual fight in the philosophical field against the siege of idealistic tendencies, in whose battle the class struggle in theory is waged.

The theological (or philosophical) conception of a world involved in both images of Paradise and the State of Nature includes—as in a displaced mirror—the *recognition* of the material reality of existence conditions in their structural causality: the overdetermined condition of (sexual) reproduction, material-practical production, and human knowledge. Material transformation pulses in a contradictory way inside idealist myths that aren't there just by chance, but for a very deep historical necessity.[12]

This idea has the merit of connecting Marx's historical references to the violence of capitalist primitive accumulation (where Caribbean slavery have a place) with the critique of the idealist modern theory of social totality as a "spiritual totality" inherent to a homogeneous-contemporary conception of time, from Modern *iusnaturalism*—the Theory of Natural Right—to Hegel. But it introduces them as a counter-mythical exercise and therefore not as an empirical series of facts, but subordinated to the principle of historical contradiction and class struggle.

The question is then whether to read the myth of "so-called primitive accumulation," just like that, as a *myth*. Althusser does this in his unpublished work on imperialism, of 1973, published in *Ecrtis sur l'historire* (2018a), in order to introduce a demarcation with respect to the figures that are *staged* there. This demarcation advances some interpretations that Marx himself offers and on which are based many of the readings of chapter 24, which rediscover in the *genesis* of capitalism, the authenticity of the "small independent producers." For Althusser, these "small producers" can't be but the mythical figures that work on a dis-adjustment, a jump of meaning between three conceptual terms that are those that Marx actually writes: that of the *peasant-proprietors*, "whatever was the feudal title under which their right of propriety is hidden" (1906, 788), which is to say, a *form under feudalist historical relations*; the *wage-workers* (1906, 789), those who are already capitalist dispossessed-workers; and the *immediate-producers* (1906, 787), which is the *theoretical* name of a nonexistent (an x), an conjectural negative entity that only becomes real *as a result of the expropriation process*. The *immediate-producer* is the *prior*-to-existence name of the "wage-workers" (1906, 786).

What is in discussion here is the conception of historical time within the problem of *transition*. It is the temporality of an absolute, previous question: "the pre-historic *stage* of Capital and of the mode of production corresponding to it" (Marx 1906, 786, my emphasis), a temporal gap that can't be "solved" with a biographical or sociological narrative of individual transformation or sociologist transformation of individual attributes. Historical-materialism, in contrast. conceives of the historical principle of individuation within a determined mode of production. Hence, according to Althusser, the circumscription of the figure of the "small independent producer" constitutes an idealistic capture of the problem of historical transition—

> the idea that the independent petty producer is in some sense a "natural" reality. Marx thereby endorses willy-nilly an essential category of bourgeois ideology; the category of "Nature," which is quite simply intended to found existing fact in its origin in Right [*origine de droit*]. (Nature is which possesses Right [*droit*], and this is why all natural law [*droit naturel*] jurists talk precisely about "natural law": nature is what is rightful [*de droit*] . . . . Similarly, the monogamous family (woman and children) seems "natural" as a unit of production and consumption. Similarly it seems natural that the independent petty producer . . . if he is meritorious enough to have accumulated the wherewithal to employ wage-workers, becomes a capitalist. He is the *homo* [*individuum*] *oeconomicus* in originary form. (Althusser 2018a, 91, French included in the original)

What particularly concerns Althusser is that Marx seems to "discover," in real history, the actual existence of small independent producers, who correspond to this ideological figure (Althusser 2018a, 91). As if this figure were a *germ, embryo,* or the *kernel* (in the sense of an *essential form*) of the capitalist mode of production. In effective historical processes we can find the *peasant-producer* as an organic form of the feudal mode of production (that could survive in some areas as a structural "reminiscence" of that mode of production unequally articulated under the dominant capitalist mode of production), not as a *pure form.* As a "figure," there is nothing "natural" about it; it forms an ideological-unity with the myth of original accumulation. It cannot be "unveiled" as a form of nature *denied* or *inverted* in the "mercantile" alienation because its mythical existence as "natural" indicates the articulation of the "so-called primitive accumulation" with the myth of the origins that *iusnaturalism* offers to the dominant ideological consecration, within the capitalist social formation.

A *counter-mythical* reading, which is affirmed in an sort of material "exteriority" that is not properly "outside" of the ideological space, does not demand an *inversion* of the myth and the consequent restoration of the *denied authenticity*, but the assumption of the inherent conflict of its *unity-interiority*, which points, as we have seen in the previous chapter, to the double principle of "the reproduction point of view"—the primacy of the social relations of production over the productive forces and of the unconscious, in terms of a *décalage* or temporal gap over the form of conscience of an individual unitary figure (Pêcheux 2014).

Liberal theories of the Myth of the State of Nature appeared within the process of unification of the ascendant bourgeoisie cementing its own unity, while grouping around itself the popular masses; the very existence of these masses with their material conditions and practices is contradictorily inscribed in the discursive materiality of the myth as a trace of counter-resistance *avant la lettre*. In this contradictory unity of philosophical idealist discourse lays the historical experience of material struggle, and every idea, every image or abstraction is, therefore, a land divided in itself by this *polemos*.

A deconstructive process of this kind works from "inside" the *deafening silence* of the Haitian revolutionary experience,[13] in the image of Revolution that rules the "history of revolutions." The concrete and overdetermined process that no philosophical category could successfully discipline involves not only the dialectical movement that ties the French revolution to this Afro-American slave revolution—which lead to a scandalous *Republique Noir*—but also the complexity of historical contradictions and temporal paradoxes that the latter had condensed.[14] As Grüner pointed out, from the very beginning of the sixteenth century, modernity was menaced by the struggle between Spain, England, and France to reach the control of non-European land where the economical materiality of colonization was displaced by the semiology of the *Imperium*. Although from the sixteenth century the Ciceronian etymology shifted it into the concept of *sovereignty*, most of these classical meanings (such as a conquest land, or the territorial extension covered by the *auctoritas* of People, or the Aristotelian idea of *"perfecta communitas"*)[15] persisted up to eighteenth century, when a new ideological connotation overdetermined the others: the identification of *Imperium* with Civilization as such. This sealed the material basis of a capitalist world-system with the philosophical category of *Imperium Universalis*, "and therefore, in our case, slavery" (Grüner 2010, 342–43, my translation): in other words, the consolidation of the *world-system* is correlative to the subjection-theatrical-*dispositif* within which the stranger—or the slave—is the gap-in-the-Sovereign Subject.

WHAT DO ZOMBIES STAND FOR TODAY?

The statement of this idea will allow me, on the one hand, to discuss the *ideological* worth of this peculiar *figure* of the *non-talking* undead, which takes place in our singular neoliberal conjuncture, in order to deal with the traumatic experience of liminal terror that arises with the de-democratization tendencies proper to imperialist capitalism's, barbarian and agonic-declination. In this sense, this figure symptomatizes the "internal" contradictions of liberal ideology: the dominant ideological formation that, under the (juridical-moral and theological) form of humanism and historicism, constitutes the very matrix of subjective experience as we know it, in terms of an *interpellation* that organizes the reasons of the subject as an effect of a subjection. The figure of the *zombie* is staged in a "scene" of battle for survival in apocalyptic contexts; this allows us to read the crisis of humanism and its effort to persevere as a formation, in a framework of weakness-in-dominance, in the complex of ideological formations contradictorily articulated with it. In this sense, it also shows the weakness of the working-class and the struggle of the popular masses in an ideological field. Reading this crisis in articulation with the neoliberal transformation of the regime of imperialist accumulation—that is, in the framework of a concrete situation—allows us, on the other hand, to avoid relapsing into analyses that restore an idealism of history of the kind that is subordinated to very eloquent and descriptive expressions of the "Crisis of Modernity" or the "fall of the Symbolic Order" or "*thanato-politics*", as if they were ineffable phenomena disconnected from *contradictory* historical causality.

If the figure of the *zombie* symptomizes the uneasiness of a phantasmic hesitation of the *scene of the sovereign subject*, which with Pêcheux we have named in terms of the "little theoretical theatre of consciousness" (Pêcheux 1982, 107–8), this is part of a historical process that, according to Althusser's reading, we can call "barbarism," in the sense of a historical "transition in place." And this demands long-term research of which we could hardly pose the main ideas. In principle, ours is an ideological conjuncture characterized by the simultaneous crisis and vacillation of the correlative figures—Subjective and State—of the *imperium*.

For this, we may start from some works of Susana Murillo, who states that neoliberalism is the weakening of the denial of the constitutive violence of state power that liberalism makes work through the dominant juridical-moral ideology (Murillo 2012). This implies, in our opinion, that forms of anguish and malaise characteristic of the contemporary neoliberal scene can be seen as indicial signs, not of the growth of a new form of power, but of the *weakening* of the modern dispositive of political handling of social violence; deeply woven into the contradictory ideological fabric of modern formations where sociability and subjectivity take form. It is within this *dispositif*, tightened between the *Hobbesian pact of obedience to the Sovereign* and Rousseau's notion of a Social Contract founded upon *piety*, where the vacillation of our *vivid world* occurs. And in this sense, neoliberalism could be thought of as the extreme tension of a contradiction inherent in the liberal ideological formation and its subject-effect.

As Murillo underlines, neoliberal tendencies seem to increase the primacy of the Hobbesian extreme of this dialectics, where "the subjection pact that leads to the transit from the multitude to the People, supposes the subordination to a Sovereign that is placed simultaneously over the law while he institutes it . . . . [T]his modality of the pact has *security* as its ultimate cause" (Murillo 2008, 48, my translation). Correlatively, Epstein remarks, Derrida has argued that the relation between *sovereignty* and *security* commits the most singular experience of the subject:

> Hobbes' sovereign is the Absolute Terror who is the amalgamation of all men's fear of vulnerability in the State of Nature. In the other hand, with respect to *foreignness*, the *sovereign is the amalgamation of all men's existential fear that they are mere beasts who are foreign to themselves qua* ostensibly self-identical men. The existential fear is that self-identity is always already lost. The Absolute Sovereign alone, in his approximation of the divine . . . is an artificial Monster, a Leviathan, summoned and forged by men to guide them towards their teleological destiny of self-identicality and *ipseity* by protecting them against the *monstrous foreignness* of ineliminable difference and heterogeneity that deforms mankind as such. (Epstein 2016, 102, additional emphasis is mine)

If the "death of God" announced by Nietzsche is about to be translated, in neoliberal terms, as the death of *Leviathan* and with it, the very category of *sovereignty* that has given consistency both to modern State and modern Subject, then, as in Nietzsche, this should not be interpreted as any kind of "liberation"—a plain disappearing of God is a paradox with no solution—but as the reinforcement of its *doubles*. This idea, which will help me to analyze the ideological procedure that zombies embody, must not be understood as a *requiem* for politics itself. In this sense, some readings based in the Foucaultian tradition (Murillo's reading, also) build a figure of this process in a non-dialectical way—as a pure and successful, omnipotent, Absolute Power (cf. Agamben 1998; Mbembe 2019). This pendulum extreme must be rectified in the sense of what Étienne Balibar has suggested in a reading of Wendy Brown's "Neo-Liberalism and the End of Liberal Democracy" (2003). As Balibar (2012) says, the "crisis of representation" that could be read in the neoliberal scene should not be intended as the *end* of political struggle (what would directly imply a kind of acceptance of the end of History itself) but as a process of *de-democratization* of politics *within democracy*. Neoliberalism is not the very dissolution of traditional structures of domination resistance and struggle, but the invention of another—probably, not so new—historical solution to the problem of the adaptation of subjects to capital. It must not be thought of in terms of the *genesis* of the new, nor as the *negation of negation*; it is, instead, a historical crisis of the figure of Social Citizenship—which is both the result of a historical revenge of the capitalist class after welfare state and the development of the Social Citizenship inner contradictions—that matches with tendencies of weakening-within-mundialization of the universalizable rights, those which had involved a dialectical productiveness of an "equal-liberty"—*egaliberté* (Balibar 2013). As Carolina Ré (2020) points out, in neoliberalism an ideological formation about time is configured, a particular homogenization of time, which blocks the emergence of emancipatory political practices under the logic of a continuous transformation, a mandate to permanent revolution, to enjoyment as an imperative and to the vindication of systematic crisis as a norm. Perhaps because the violence with which the process of production/reproduction of capital develops reaches atrocious dimensions, it is such that a common construction is erected over its own obscene reverse: the homogeneous common (cf. Ré 2020).

In this respect, it is also necessary to carefully distinguish between the imaginary experiences of the "declination of the Order," or the manifestation of "anomic forms," and the historical process in which these ideological experiences are overdetermined. In political terms, this process should be read neither as a decline, nor as a reinforcement of a unique power, but as a weakening of the internal dialects of dominant forms of capital power, between force and fantasy. It is not just a pure widening of the Hobbesian form of the pact—historically linked to the experience of the absolute state—but as a retroversion of the Rousseauean type of pact that is contradictorilyy articulated with it: the union pact that opposes the Hobbesian sociability based on the *desire to cause damage* with another sociability based on the *desire of no damaging* (Althusser [1972] 2012).[16] This retroversion may be considered as what has paradoxically promoted the increase of what can be expressed as a kind of "desire of a Leviathan." The very dangerous conservative drives that arise in current neoliberal sociability can thus be interpreted in the sense of a violent fear of social/subjective disaggregation—the reinforced experience of the "existential fear" of the "monstrous foreignness" (Epstein 2016)—connected to the historical transformations operated within of disciplinary society's ideological formations—or, what is the same, the experience of the Social Citizenship contradictions, in times of a regime of accumulation where the concept of collective and subjective Sovereignty itself is suffering violent transformations, connected with very fast geopolitical and economical reorganization toward processes of tendential, homogeneous mundialization. This terrifying experience, which can be considered as the effect of the weakening of liberal democracy's institutions, images, and practices, is nevertheless manifested as extreme hatred of democracy.

Neoliberal violence could be considered the vacillation of the ideological complex of discoursive formations that had supported the material reproduction of bourgeois class dictatorship. Rousseau's Social Contract, Kantian categorical imperative, and Beccaria's concept of the mathematical relationship between crime and penalty had constituted the theoretical basis for the fictions of a symbolic order that had organized social relationships during industrial capitalism (Murillo 2008, 52). Desperate experiences of "preventive" terror (cf. Žižek 2008, Davies 2016; Miller 2010) in the form of segregation, neofascism, racism, gender violence, Islamophobia, homophobia, and transphobia may not be a result of an "excess of power" but of an impoverishment of this kind of power. This impoverishment coincides with a sort of literal poorness of metaphors—linked to a political incapacity to represent social conflict—that, as Balibar has said, alludes to the very crisis of representation principle itself. Because it is not the mere elimination of conflict—in the form of an absolute total power of capital—what neoliberalism performs, but it is the conduction to certain delimited zones of social life (a subjective life) that can be "sacrificed" to the extent that they aren't directly exploitable and remain as "inner" fragments of "monstrous foreignness." Conflict is, in this movement, applied onto sacrificial zones for disposable human beings, while it is at the same time *particularized* and devoid of its *constituent* force (Balibar 2012).

NEOLIBERAL HUMANIST FANTASY: ANTAGONISM WITHOUT CLASS STRUGGLE

If we accept that the figure of *zombies* symptomatizes this experience of declination of the forms of *sovereignty* linked to the de-democratization of Social Citizenship figure (both in a political and a subjective way), we should distrust the first impression that could lead us to interpret the "scene" of the struggle in which many *zombies'* stories are organized (the dead versus the alive; the nonconscious versus the conscious, the masses versus the individual, etc.) as a direct "expression" of struggle. It is not only in order to reject mechanical determination, but also because, theoretically, the kind of image that subordinates the struggle to the *prior* existence of "classes" (that being the name of any social "part" or identity) is connected to humanist commitment, which is unable to think the historical contradiction as inscribed in historical *objectivity*, in the very *materialities of the real* (cf. Althusser 1995, 169–244).[17]

History, considered as a "process without Subject": "an immense natural-human system in movement," whose motor is *class struggle*, discards the bourgeois idealism of the Subject recalled in the leftist-humanist thesis (embodied in the name of John Lewis, with whom Althusser established a discussion published in the British PC organ, *Marxism Today*, in October-November of 1972) that considers Man (or Class) as the artisan (or the Creator) of History (Althusser 1972, 29). Rejecting the theological-heritage that lays in the identification between Human Being and Creator, the Althusserian materialist position rejects the idealist epistemology based in the category of consciousness that supports a theory of ideology as *alienation* with which materialism must break through. Althusser recognizes the themes of humanism (a "fetishism of man") in the recovery of a philosophical idea of *praxis* as "creation" of history and of *freedom* as man's capacity to "transcend history." He finds these theses in the interpretations of fetishism as a *reification* and consequent exaltation of the *person* (rewriting of the *person/thing* pair of bourgeois philosophy). This mechanism is repeated whenever a social relationship is conceived as a natural quality or attribute of a *substance* or a *subject* (cf. Althusser 1995, 169–244).

In a similar way, Roberto Esposito (2015) analyzes this *dispositif* of the *person*, as the logical structure of "unity and separation" (person/thing) that organizes the functioning of a genealogy of discourses that go from religion to law and philosophy. In this framework, he recalls that the Catholic philosopher Jacques Maritain, one of the drafters of the *1948 Declaration*, defines the person as *an absolute master of himself* (1942). But according to Esposito, it is in Hobbes where the relationship between subjectivity and subjection implicit in the juridical and philosophical decline of the person becomes clearer—in its transposition to the political terrain, oriented to the absolute foundation of *sovereignty*. This process of acquisition and confiscation of *political personality* finds its center in the paradigm of *authorization* through which each subject authorizes the *Sovereign Person*—defined in its ancient theatrical root as an "actor"—to *represent* him. This gesture makes each subject the "author" of his condition (Esposito 2015).

While among those who offer approaches to personality that challenge this dialectical unity of personalization-depersonalization, Esposito recognizes Freud. In his *Zur Psychopathologie des Alltagslebens* (1901), Freud extracts the individuation of an impersonal background that calls for an exchange between identity and otherness. As we have pointed out with Pêcheux (2014) in the previous chapter, the divided unity of an ideological formation connects the concept of *class struggle* with that of the *unconscious*, as Althusser suggests. But this demands the understanding that when the latter raises the irreconcilable condition between the figures of humanism and the concept of *class struggle* (cf. Althusser 1973), it conciliates a singular sense for this concept. As Balibar has pointed out in a footnote to *Écrits pour Althusser* (1991), the concept of "class" (always subordinated to that of relation-struggle) must be taken in Althusser in two simultaneous ways: as a *historical concept* and as a representative of the *philosophical name* for identity (the *idem est ac*, or the *tauton gar esti* of philosophers), which allows us to say that *identity is always division*. This thesis is also stated by saying that class struggle and the existence of classes are one and the same thing. This is supported, we recall with Balibar, by the cornerstone of the Althusserian theory of the "point of view of reproduction" that implies a shift within the very idea of historical (over)determination: instead of founding historical variations on an invariance, it means that all (relative) invariance presupposes a relation of forces; all structural continuity is the necessary effect of an irreducible contingency (Balibar 1991). This means that contingency, *chance* or fortune, have their opportunity *in* the structure.

The recovery of the concept of contradiction in the structured order of reproduction (in a sense of an immanent tension of *conjoncture/conjonction*) allows the putting in question of some derivations of the Marxist thesis of the "*real subsumption.*" According to Balibar in *Cittadinanza* (2012), these readings shift to think of late capitalism as a system of *immediate* technological (re)production of the labor force as a *commodity* that conditions the qualitative aspects of individual life—and the plain principle of individuation—to its logic. This series, which brings together Marcuse, Foucault, Baudrillard, and Agamben and which finds in Hardt and Negri a less apocalyptic formulation, has as an effect a non-dialectical reading of the processes of de-democratization in the sense of a totalizing logic of power in the terms of a new cultural "rationality."

The concept of class struggle within the framework of a theory of social reproduction allows us to think of superstructural formations as constitutionally divided-units; this requires us to rigorously assume the thesis of the *primacy of contradiction over opposites*, so as not to restore humanist reformulations of the concept of class struggle. Neither is it a question of finding class struggle "everywhere."

In this sense, I propose that the scene of a battle for surveying, in which *zombies* figures are staged, should be read as the ideological "scene" into which we "wake up" from the traumatic experience of our "inner" *monstrous foreignness*, reinforced in (over)determined *conjunctural* conditions—those that offer specific discursive materialities for fantasies of Absolute Power. As Penha and Gonzalves point out, following the analysis of Mladen Dolar (2018), *ten* years before the Haitian genealogy of the *zombie* figure "returned" as a monstrous form in American popular culture, Freud (1919) had already worked with that disturbing position in which a subject is confronted with the ambiguous figures of *foreignness-intimacy*, at once proximate and unrecognizable. Looking for the etymology of the German word *unheimlich* and the conceptual ambivalence it draws with its "opposite" *heimlich*, it designates the ominous as a kind of "family strangeness" (Penha and Gonsalves 2018, 12). As M. Dolar warns, this figure of the strange as monstrous is developed by Lacan in the concept of *extimacy*, to account for the unconscious *topique* that rejects interior/exterior spacialization, associated with the notion of *jouissance*. In this sense, it is interesting to take up again the reading that Jacques Alain Miller (2010) offers of the relationship between the concept of *extimacy* and the logic of *racism*, as hatred of castration, which finds particular conjuncture conditions within the expansion (and totalization) of humanist discursive formations in the globalizing tendencies of its alleged universality. In relation to this, Balibar (1997) links the processes of neoliberal "globalization"—not as a repetition of colonialism, but with new forms of "differential racism" that replace even the biological racism of the nineteenth and twentieth centuries. What is at stake here, he says, is the vacillation of the *representation of the frontier* and the consolidation of an imaginary relationship with the otherness, based on the experience of proximity-alienness that results in radicalized affections of "insecurity." This process, which unfolds at the level of nation-states in the form of repressive increase, retraction of civil rights, and criminalization of minorities, exposes the mechanism of *preventive counter-violence* required by the precarious duration of state power, whose sovereignty is tied up in the current conditions: between punitive social drives and pressure from supra-state financial powers.

Within this framework, the *lack of self-sovereignty* of the undead, their disconnection between "body" and "soul," points toward the question of the *imperium* (the liberal image of man as *an imperium in an imperium*). It does not indicate the *un-representable* condition of fear, nor does it "unveil" a historical violence that has been turned invisible. It symptomizes the historical (*conjunctural*) current experience of the very frontiers of representation/subjection dispositive itself (the correlative "evidence" of Subject and Meaning) in the singular forms of its discursive and ideological formations (Pêcheux 1982).

It is in this sense that the current figure of the *zombie* evokes, in a displaced way, the scandalous figure of the Haitian slave who demanded to self-govern and exposed the founding contradiction of humanism, the most effective ideological formation in the history of capitalism, in whose transformations the traces of the crises of accumulation and the survival of this mode of production are read;—from imperialism, with its eugenic theories and its racist positivism, to neoliberalism with its multicultural and, at the same time, hyper-racialized and patriarchalized segregations. The figure of the *zombie* connects the neoliberal ideological formation with the contradictions of liberalism, in an *amalgamation of times*. So, it is not the isolated figure of the *zombie* as a representation of alienated beings, but the whole theatrical representation where it is staged that embodies the nostalgic *drama* of our ideological configurations.

This requires another kind of critical procedure, because it is not the relation between the characters (the "actors") in the scene that must be focused, but the whole theatrical dispositive that organizes the relation of the "spectator" to the scene (the frontier of the scene itself), where a struggle-to-death is performed (the dead versus the alive, the conscious versus the non-conscious; the masses versus the individuals) that has to be the object of concrete critical interrogation. This kind of procedure recalls the materialist position that assumes the reading of every conjuncture in which objective and subjective forces are overdetermined in the terms of the structural causality (which, among other metaphors, Althusser has called a "theatre without author"[18]). As a reader of Brecht, he has shown that it is not the scene "inside" (the theatrical representation of life, with its actors, and script that actualizes the concentric scheme of modern consciousness) that could give space for an ideological critique. On the contrary, the whole theatrical-machinery (including public) is the field for an actual *ideological struggle*.[19] Where, "one can say that, in the majority of cases, the function of philosophy and of the theater consists in smothering the voice of politics" (Althusser 2002, 140).

In this regard, it can be suggested that the ideological performance of current *zombies*, staged in an apocalyptic time and playing a struggle-to-death scene, should be assumed to be in terms of the phantasmic "scene" that lets us forget that our existence is placed in a conjuncture where the productive relations are organized (or, paradoxically, structurally disorganized) in a regime of accumulation that feeds on crisis and incertitude, while revolutions itself permanently, producing the vacillation of the ideological principle of political or semiotic representation, supported by the modern universal categories of *imperium* and *sovereignty*.

If this is correct, we might consider that the almost classic battle between the dead and the alive—and with it, every simplified specular-dialectical image of political antagonism—may be the fabric of the ideology into which we "wake," just to stop dreaming that we are always-already the *zombies* that we already are. Images of war between parts of society (which are also battles between the inner space and the outer space of the theatrical scene) may not be the representations of class struggle anymore, but their imaginary denegation. Rather than the ideological staging of political struggle, *zombies* tales should be understood in connection with the performance of the desperate and unutterable wish of an Absolute Power in the process of a vacillation of the dialectical dispositive of sovereignty that leads to tendencies of de-democratization of so-called democracies. We might be aware of, against the simplified images of very polarized struggles, that which will to actualized, political representations of class antagonism. They could be the "dream" where we aren't always-already *zombies* that dream they still live in the self-*imperium* and among the alive. We must be aware of those fantasies into which we wake up to avoid facing our own desire of Leviathan.

NOTES

A partial version of this chapter has been published in Portuguese in Diego Penha and Rodrigo Gonsalves, comps., 2018, *Ensaios sobre mortos-vivos. "The Walking Dead" e outras metáforas*, trans. Rodrigo Gonsalves. (São Paulo: Aller Editora).

1. This anthropological tradition dates back to the beginning of the twentieth century and could be thought of in relation to the consolidation of the ideological forms of imperialism in the inscription of the figure with Haitian roots in the American popular culture. (Cf. Seabrook 1929)

2. In this sense, for example, the whole discussion that involves different Hegelian positions, such as those posed by Lauro (2015) with Bishop (2010), must be abandoned.

3. I thank my colleague Elena Mancinelli, of the Universidad de Buenos Aires, whose reading of the draft of this chapter allowed me to be confident in some remarks included here.

4. The Imperial Constitution of Haití, 1805, states in its article 14, "All acception (sic) of colour among the children of one and the same family of whom the chief magistrate is the father, being necessarily to cease, the Haytians shall hence forward be known only by the generic appellation of Blacks." The 1805 Constitution of Haiti, 1805, http://faculty.webster.edu/corbetre/haiti/history/earlyhaiti/1805-const.htm

5. As Mintz pointed out, the Caribbean plantation system was a capitalist form of economic development, even though this fact was partially covered by it's dependency from slavery and the agricultural production, it was highly industrially organized (Cf. Mintz 1971).

6. And as James describes it, "Voodoo was the medium of the conspiracy. In spite of all prohibitions, the slaves travelled miles to sing and dance and practise the rites and talk; and now, since the revolution, to hear the political news and make their plans. Boukman, a Papaloi or High Priest, a gigantic Negro, was the leader. He was headman of a plantation and followed the political situation both among the whites and among the Mulattoes. By the end of July 1791 the blacks in and around Le Cap were ready and waiting" (1989, 86).

7. "Once they have thus 'taken hold' or 'collided-interlocked,' the atoms enter the realm of Being that they inaugurate: they constitute beings, assignable, distinct, localizable beings endowed with such-and-such a property (depending on the time and place); in short, there emerges in them a structure of Being or of the world that assigns each of its elements its place, meaning and role, or, better, establishes them as 'elements of . . . (the atoms as elements of bodies, of beings, of the world) in such a way that the atoms, far from being the origin of the world, are merely the secondary consequence of its assignment and advent [*assignement* et *avenement*] . . . . [This is a] situation that puts discourse on the world forever in second place, and also puts in second place (not first, as Aristotle claimed) the philosophy of Being—thus making forever intelligible, as impossible (and therefore explicable: see the appendix to Book I of the *Ethics*, which repeats nearly verbatim the critique of all religion found in Epicurus and Lucretius) any discourse of first philosophy, even if it is materialist." (Althusser 2006a, 192).

8. "The first man ever to have posed the problem of reading . . . was Spinoza, and he was also the first man in the world to have proposed both theory of history and philosophy of the opacity of the immediate." (Althusser and Balibar 1970, 16)

9. The theoretical consequences of abandoning a question for historical causality, from a materialistic and dialectical approach, can be clearly registered in the lectures given by Stuart Hall in 1983, at the University of Illinois (especially in lectures 5, 6, and 7), where the effort to overcome the "structuralist" burden of the concept of ideology results in the simultaneous abandonment of the concepts of *unconscious* and *class struggle*, causing a relapse of Culture Studies in the idealist field of Consciousness. (Cf. Hall 2016)

10. "This primitive accumulation plays in Political Economy about the same part as original sin in teology" (Marx 1906, 784).

11. The critical operation is not solved in a simple rejection of the idealism of "Theory," but in a work of dispute that demands the identification of a double front: not only that of the omnipotence of the concept, but also that which results from its speculative pair, that of the affirmation of the authenticity of Life (or of pure praxis or abstract activity) to demonstrate the profound connection between them.

12. Étienne Balibar has posed this necessity in terms of a contradictory or *conflictive necessity*. As he says, against rationalism and positivism, Althusser let us think that the "conceptual division" (the one that divides itself in two) and the division of controversial interpretations (the struggle of tendencies) belong intrinsically to the singular apodicticity of science of history. As the object is always intrinsically conflictive, the theory is always conflictive too, and only moves forward by dividing itself. This Althusserian idea leads Balibar to conclude that a sort of epistemological singularity exists for both Marxism and Psychoanalysis: they are to be considered as *"schism-sciences,"* which means, determined in their very constitution—for the mode in which they are placed in the conflict, which they are simultaneously intended to *represent* in knowledge. These sciences aren't just "spectators" of an object, nor are they expressions of conflictive "facts" or related to political "objectives," but *parts* playing a role in a conflictive process (Balibar 1991, 60–61, my translation).

13. The Haitian revolutionary experience is even absent from the most interesting revolutionary history, such as Hobsbawm's work, such as *The Age of Revolution 1789–1848* (1996).

14. Saint-Domingue (Haiti) was such a condensation of contradictions that it could have fit the Leninist concept of the weakest shackle of the chain (weaker from the whole capitalist world-system in its moment of faster accumulation) for it was the richest and most productive Caribbean colony while the most committed by the juncture of very contradictory political, religious, ideological forces (cf. James 1989; Grüner 2010).

15. "If all communities aim at some good, the State or political community, which is the highest of all, and which embraces all the rest, aims at good in greater degree than any other, and at the highest good (Aristotles *Politics*, Pt. 1, Ch. 1).

16. For Rousseau, says Althusser in his course on Rousseau on March 17, 1972, piety is not a positive social relationship; it does not have the effect of bringing men together but only prevents the desire for harm. Althusser relates this figure of piety in Rousseau to his reading of Hobbes and the examination of his hypothesis of a sociability based on the desire to cause harm, rather than as an active foundation of the pact (cf. Althusser [1972] 2012).

17. "You have to go beyond the football match idea, the idea of two antagonistic groups of classes, to examine the basis of the existence not only of classes but also of the antagonism between classes: that is, the class struggle." (Althusser 1973a, 28–29)

18. "When we enter Althusser's little theater of philosophy (*'notre petit théâtre théorique'*): a contradiction or, more precisely, a contradiction that opens onto a series of contradictions inseparable from Althusser's dramaturgy, his staging of the fact that philosophy is by its nature compelled to perform (that is, act or act out) its theses in the field of visibility (that is, the theater) proper to it. His dramaturgy might be summarized as the work of staging philosophy's staging of itself, like a play about the way plays are 'made,' a play within a play, a meta-

commentary or meta-theater that nevertheless cannot step outside that which it dramatizes or that on which it comments. And nothing that Althusser has written more dramatically illustrates the aporia that makes his work what it is than the notion of the authorless theater (*un théâtre sans auteur*) that makes a brief appearance near the end of his introduction to *Reading Capital*." (Montag 2017, 440 for the Spanish version; version in English from the author)

19. "'Playing' should be understood in its double sense. First in the traditional sense of theatrical playing (the theater is playing: the [*actors*] play, the theater is a fictive representation of reality. Playing is not life, it is not reality. . . . It is represented, hence is not present). But 'playing' should be understood in the second sense: theater allows this 'playing' (in the sense that there is some 'play' in a door, a hinge, a mechanism). This means that it belongs to the nature of the theater, to contain *some room*." (Althusser 2002, 138)

Chapter Three

Against Neo-Anarchism

Toward a Radicalization of Social Reproduction Theory, within Plural Temporality and Overdetermination

Starting with the first inquiries into unpaid reproductive labor and black feminism (Dalla Costa and James 1975; Hartmann 1979; Barret 1980; Davis 1983; Brenner and Ramas 1984; Vogel 1983; Hayden 1985; among others), up until the most recent Marxists feminist, queer, and intersectional theoretical developments, *Social Reproduction Theory* has grown in such a powerful manner that it constitutes today one of the most promising ways of counteracting the lethargy of leftist thinking in this era that presents itself as post-critical. Set within the wider frame of a question regarding political imagination and the possibilities of agency, it opens itself to a conjunction of other traditions of Latin-American Marxism, anti-imperialist theories, and postcolonial studies that share a decentered reading of history. In this sense, it takes shape in the concatenation of problems and developments, the problematization of the concept of historical time, dear to Marxist theory and critical tradition in general.

But the singularity that marks feminist theories' especially interesting spot in the current conjuncture stems from the mode in which its theoretical pursuits are stirred up in the heat of a massive political practice in process. Thus, it is a mass of thought woven from diverse inputs that flow together in one and the same field of debates and that also flesh out controversial tendencies between which the dilemmas that could offer a strategic horizon for emancipatory imagination are settled and dispute the future.

As philosophical as it may sound, the problem of temporality does not constitute a minor topic today. Instead, it is the precise spot where critical thought faces the regime of temporality that in *Left-Wing Melancholia: Marxism, History, and Memory* (2017), Enzo Traverso calls "presentism," described as a regime of temporality that threatens to dissolve, in its cyclic and expansive experience, past and future, provoking a sort of "historical dead end."

That regime marks the limits of critical theory and forces contemporary leftist thought to face its own impotence; on the other side, the exercises of political thinking, linked to concrete experiences, appear but in spontaneous irruptions without dialectically impacting the regime of theoretical thought. Not to diminish the relevance and weight of the political onslaught that looms above, one may also point out that the impoverishment of the global left imagination finds reasons in its own weakness too. Many political practices do not elicit wide intelligence of the situation, nor do they manage to produce a theoretical sediment of their own experiences and defeats; neither do they propel theoretical thought to assume an open and hospitable condition to that which is foreign to itself. In many of the cases the commitment does not exceed a philosophical romanticization of social movements; it would be much better if they saved themselves from being contaminated with power. Theory gloats on politicist tendencies, which either only render the struggles and their actors folklore, or revel in a narcissist practice of philosophy, to which the world of real suffering is barely a source of inspiration.

It is precisely on that spot of actual fragility where feminist intelligence meets its opportunity—not only as a *foreigner* in the field of philosophical combat, but as a real political collective force and as the historical process of reparation of the damages symptomatized in the global homogenization of thought, in different forms of philosophical affectation or technocratic positivism.

The dimension of the task of repairing the faintest threads that bind life in common is immense, but harkens back to an effort that is not in itself political, but merely is its formless and available matter. It turns out to be indispensable for a comprehension of the conjuncture to include the capacity of connecting the subjective affections and imagination, the quotidian experience, the memories of the popular sufferings to the processes of collective *experimentation*, as a precise reading of the conjuncture. Accordingly, feminist theory is today one of the richest developing lines of *historical materialism*, in this strictly sense.

> Historical materialism can be called quite literally the experimental science of history, using the distinction between *Erfahrung* and *Experiment* . . . . Indeed, it can be said that, compared with the empirical and spontaneous political practice which forms under the domination of bourgeois ideology as political *Erfahrung*, the Marxist-Leninist practice of politics constitutes a true "historical experimentation" (Balibar 1974, 86); *Experiment*, simultaneously knowledge and transformation, knowledge in order to transform, in the specific conditions of the process "history." (Pêcheux 1982, 148)[1]

Theoretical feminism is not in this sense a "perspective" or a discipline, but what can be rigorously called a *position* in the theoretical field; a *partisan* practice of theory that requires tracing demarcations in order to politically affect the knowledge production.[2] Beyond the content of its theoretical discourses, feminism is inscribed in a way of exercising thought that has been, if not inaugurated by Marx, then consolidated by his materialistic contribution: the conception of theory as a practice of *positioning* theses and tracing demarcations between existing theses (cf. Althusser 1997).

But feminism, in order to produce effects in ordinary life also develops its struggle within a concrete ideological field, which must be conceived, as Pêcheux has posed it, as a hierarchical, contradictory complex of formations unequally articulated with a *dominant*. The theoretical dimensions, linked to the capacity of producing rigorous readings of the conjuncture are, therefore, stressed by two logics—one that involves the theoretical space in itself, which could be considered the development immanent to theoretical practices (the conceptual permanent adjustment of its categories and the refinement of its heuristic capacity to give account of concrete processes, etc.); another, that requires indispensable attention to the permanent siege of dominant ideological formations (by means of spontaneous philosophy's notions, categories that function as "evidences" of meaning, or empiricist abstractions)—that mark theoretical discourses with the force relations of their conjuncture.

We need to see clearer within the field of feminist theories, understanding that it is unescapably knotted in the material imaginary complex of discursive and ideological formations. In this sense, current feminism is the most powerful *rarefaction* of neoliberal thought, the opportunity of a politization of its very contradictions, a chance for real historical counter-tendencies. As political thinking, feminism can be considered, within the current neoliberal ideological conjuncture, as its *immanent exteriority*; but it must be said that, as such, it is dangerously traversed by the same threats that have impoverished the left's intellectual and political capacity since the second half of the twentieth century. The arms against these dangers are feminist politics and feminist theory if, and only if, they manage to work in a material dialectical articulation.

TECHNOCRATISM AND HUMANISM: TWO DEVIATIONS OF THE SAME THREAT IN THE CONJUNCTURE OF THE NEOLIBERALIZATION OF THOUGHT

Feminism can be in this sense as one of the most powerful weapons to fight against the forms of neoliberalization of the leftist intellectual field. As Nancy Fraser (2009; 2020) has warned, in order to do so, feminism mustn't be considered a homogeneous entity, plainly exterior to historical contradictions, but a material field where struggles also occur. Postcolonial feminism, black feminism, and queer studies have developed a great critique of phallocentric-teleological Universal History, and this must be applied also to the feminist theories history that can't therefore be considered a homogeneous evolutive unity. Far from this, the long-term history of feminist movements and positions is in itself a permanent part of feminist research, critical analysis, and debates.

This historical multiplicity is not just a history of a disperse plurality; it is a history of concrete contradictions and force relations within which feminism is placed and overdetermined, while articulated with different processes of struggle, conjunctural conditions, and long-term tendencies. If we agree with Fraser (2017) in recognizing neoliberalism as a *historical block*,[3] and notice with Harvey (2005), among others, that it have arisen from the contradictory conjuncture of post–New Deal world, we must notice that, at the same time, it was contradictorily furnished within the heritage of new left and civil and social rights struggles, May 1968's legacy, and third world movements, as a sort of process of political retroversion of social state (cf. Balibar 2012) and left positions within the theoretical field—as, for example, Badiou (2008) has underlined for the French philosophical scene, hegemonized by the so-called "new philosophers." Therefore, we must pose the question about the partnership of intended left thinking in this historical defeat.

Accordingly, on the one hand, the historicization of the links between Marxism and feminism proposed by Cinzia Arruzza (2015) allows us to identify a particularly contradictory moment, between the 1960s and 1970s, in which the accumulated dissatisfaction resulting from the retroversion of pro-feminist positions since the *Third International*; the traditional sexism of party and trade union structures; and the new forms of abuse within the new left took the form of a modality of critical attitude that led to problematic consequences in the theoretical sphere that matched the depotentiation in the political sphere. From the consolidation of *separatism* as a political practice, beyond the fact that in many cases the theories invoked offered brilliant and extremely fruitful developments for critical reflection,[4] a *practical* shift can be observed in the diagnosis of social and historical inequalities: from the question of social totality, toward the interior of leftist organizations (student, worker, pacifist, or black activist), which had disintegrating effects even on the feminist and gay organizations themselves. And, on the other hand, the resurgence of essentialist and individualist forms of understanding psychic, affective, and sexual life, whose diagnoses of inequalities and injustices slide toward essentialist naturalisms or philosophical abstractions, around categories such as "self-consciousness," "clitoral woman," "work," "life," "*ethos*," not only leads to an indistinction and subsumption of the political in the ethical, but does so under a significant humanist emphasis that makes the very idea of feminism problematic, beyond a simple inversion of sexism.

In this sense, some passages of the *Manifesto* of *Rivolta Femminile*, from 1970 (Lonzi 2017), or the documents about "The Meanings of the Self-Consciousness of Feminist Groups" of the same group, or Carla Lonzi's famous writings "Let's Spit on Hegel," from 1971 (Lonzi 2017), and "Clitoral Woman and Vaginal Woman," from 1971 (Lonzi 2017), offer a condensation of elements that situate the emancipatory effort in problematic terms. In particular, to the extent that the critical operation is thought of as a pure *inversion* of those theories or positions that are recognized as patriarchal, the efforts are restricted in their potency by the counter-identifying scheme in which they are organized and that is none other than the space of *Meaning* of the phenomenological circle—that which governs, for example, the dialectic of the master and the slave (that is supposed to be questioned). In this sense, it is especially illustrative the gesture of claiming the clitoral woman as a way of criticizing the Freudian affirmation of the vaginal woman as a feature of sexual maturity. In this example, it is clear that the effort of impugnation is nullified by adopting the same terms that are intended to be questioned because of their dichotomous formulas, their nineteenth-century biologicism, and so forth. The impugnation of the relational condition of the feminine—its reduction to an abstract essence that is self-sufficient and asserts itself as natural, to "express the *meaning* of its own existence" (cf. *Rivolta Femminile* 1970, in Lonzi 2017)—is nothing but the phallocentric structure of liberal Humanism, which has (white) man as the form and measure of all things.[5] What is under discussion here is not only the strategic question—although it is also about this—but also a profound theoretical question about how to understand the critical operation—if, to "spit on Hegel" is to "turn him upside down,"[6] it does not seem to be in itself a very novel operation, nor is it understood why it would be especially "feminist."[7] In a different sense, Cristine Delphi's developments are also tendentially reductive of the critical operation by producing an abstract reading of the category of labor and by offering an inverse homologation between class and gender, inverting the workerist reductionism of gender to class with the "naturalistic" effects of reducing the historicity of gender relation to a link between genderized individuals (1999).[8]

In the diversity of their objectives and causes, both in strategic and theoretical terms, these strongly contradictory processes are not dissociated from the vicissitudes of the global defeat of the emancipatory and contentious forces. The consolidation of this process of retroversion toward the 1990s would be supported by what Fraser calls the "neoliberal left," which had no need but to once again put *back on its feet* what had been *inverted* or "turned upside down."[9]

> It fell, accordingly, to the "New Democrats" to contribute the essential ingredient: a progressive politics of recognition. Drawing on progressive forces from civil society, they diffused a recognition ethos that was superficially egalitarian and emancipatory. At the core of this ethos were ideals of "diversity," women "empowerment" LGBTQ+ rights, post-racialism, multiculturalism, environmentalism. These ideals were interpreted in a specific limited way that was fully compatible with the Goldman Sachsification of US economy. (Fraser 2017, 12)

Fraser focuses on the specific transformation within the process of neoliberalization itself, which has been mapped out by W. Davies (2016) as the transit of a *combative* neoliberalism—especially dedicated to make of the crisis of Marxism its defeat and definitive elimination—toward a *normative* form that wanted to affirm itself in projective speeches and in a capture of utopian thought with discourses on "globalization." This was supported by a renewed technophilia, thanks to the technological leap of the so-called "third industrial revolution," and to political transformations aimed at the thickening of the so-called "third sector," under the anti-statist dictum of the citizen comptroller—"transparency" based on management and the figures of "empowerment" of an atomized and fragmented society in identitarian microcommunities. That process had as its main target of attack, as Fraser (2017) emphasizes it, the consolidated forms of trade-union and worker organizations, by means of a mechanism that could be considered "pincers" (*pincer*) between the persecution of its bases and the transformist absorption of its leaders. But it also had as its result, historical conditions under which all the social and communitarian forms of critical thought and desires of emancipation were decimated as real possibilities of consecration.[10]

In this sense, in addition to working on diverse political, ideological, and cultural fronts, it is indispensable to open up a series of questions regarding the conditions and possibilities of the production of current critical feminist theory. Without that task we would not only be facing, unarmed, a historical torsion of a large magnitude in the history of capitalism, which within so-called "neoliberalism" is experiencing a strong authoritarian shift since the financial crisis of 2008, whose autophagic exhaustion threatens to unleash an unprecedented civilizational crisis, whose victims are specially poor, racialized women and LGBTQ+ communities; we would also run the risk of seeing the greater part of the thought that one assumes to be emancipatory, assisting in a naive and collaborationist manner to this process.[11]

Because the forms antagonistic to feminist and popular emancipation always work inside our "critical" languages, it is in this sense that theoretical demarcations and collective intelligence take on special importance in order to elaborate *conceptual* categories to name our time and its conditions.

Within this frame, feminist thought offers an especially vibrating territory, both in its potency as well as in the strength of its controversies and contradictions. On one side, in its most explicit or belligerent forms of inheriting the crisis of Marxism and opening it up to a new productive impulse, it offers a series of political and theoretical debates that revitalize the diverse traditions of critical thought. On the other, its socially and culturally current manifestations are drawn in the tension of an *immanent exteriority* to the neoliberal Present and, therefore, find themselves in an ambivalent and liminal relationship to the dominant forms that stalk its critical condition. Against what could be misinterpreted, in its capacity to participate in the composition of a counter-power of significant weight at the global level ,this constitutes a strength, not a weakness, of the feminist struggle in the ideological field. To understand this, it is worth recalling the warnings regarding how the concept of dominant ideology relates to ideological struggle:

> Ideology is not reproduced in the general form of a *Zeitgeist* (spirit of the age, "mentality" of an epoch, "habits of thought," etc.) which would be imposed in an even and homogeneous way on society understood as a space prior to class struggle . . . , which means that it is impossible to attribute to each class its own ideology, as if each existed "before the class struggle" in its own camp, with its own conditions of existence, its institutions, its specific "habits" and "mentalities," which amounts to conceiving of ideological class struggle as the encounter of two distinct pre-existing worlds—an encounter followed by the victory of "the stronger" class, which would then impose its ideology on the other. In the end, this would be to multiply the conception of ideology as *Zeitgeist* by two. (Pêcheux 2014, 4)

If the feminist tendencies of the current conjuncture show a force that is able to move across and connect a diversity of sufferings and injustices and influence the composition of a counter-power, this is to the extent that, inscribed in counter-tendential forces, current feminism could not be but contradictory intertwined—in a subordinate mode—within the dominant formations: and therefore it could be read as the "weakest link in the chain," in a Leninist sense.[12] That is the coincidence of feminism's political potency, its theoretical task, and its ideological struggle. A critical diagnosis requires a concept of social totality and complex temporality such as those offered by Marxist theory, at least for those feminisms concerned with historical transformation in a profound sense and especially for those who share the idea that, in order to understand the way in which inequalities, battles, and resistances *exist as* and, at the same time, *modulate* the subjective and linking aspects.

The menace of the retroversion within the left intellectual field under the specific form of a liberal "solution" to the *crisis of Marxism*, constitutes the backdrop against which Louis Althusser deploys his critical interventions during the early 1960s and his insistence on a *recommencement* of the reading of Marx. That is why tracking those tendencies, which in their time formed a unity with the consolidation of the crisis of Marxism in its regressive forms, turns out to be especially fruitful today. To present the question very schematically, one could say that the preoccupation with deploying the theoretical *anti-humanist* and *anti-historicist* imprint in his philosophical reading of Marx constitutes the specifically theoretical and philosophical intervention of a much broader struggle—against two wide, ideological tendencies that outline and shape the dominant ideological conjuncture that permeates diverse registers of thought, since the early 1960s up to today: *technocratism* and *humanism*.[13]

In this sense one could read in a 1963 manuscript kept at the Institut Mémoires de l' édition contemporaine (IMEC), properly titled with the above-mentioned conjunction, some preliminary developments of his theory of ideology. And, first of all, the idea of the primacy of the struggle over the ideological unity, which leads to a characterization of what he calls there "proletarian ideology," a constitutive contradictory process that "gains terrain in the heart of dominant ideology itself" (Althusser 1963).

In this writing, what Althusser understands as "Marxist science" keeps close to the definition, borrowed from Pierre Macherey for *Lire le Capital*, which suggests conceiving Marxist theory in terms of a "science of ideology" (Althusser 2005, 31).[14] It is inflected in three features: (1) the theory of ideology, (2) the theory of ideological struggle, and (3) the specific knowledge of the conditions of the ideological conjuncture.

Regarding this last one, a large part of the manuscript strives to characterize the political and intellectual conjuncture during the early 1960s as gravitating toward *technocratism*, conceived as a process of articulation between monopolistic capital and some ideological formations that associate humanitarianism and technocracy.[15] In general terms, it is a constellation of discursive formations that connect theoretical ideologies, such as empiricism, formalism, and pragmatism, to "new topics and forms"—in sum, "everything that, from up close or afar touches, not reality, but the myth of computers, cybernetics and electronics" (Althusser 1963, 23, my translation). This renewed tendency of technocratic economicism meets its "soul supplement," says Althusser, in the diverse forms with which *humanism* is reissued. On one side are the "humanitarian" forms that psychosociological technologies of adaptation tend to flow into, which aim to deploy "pacifying" strategies in the capital-labor relations and management techniques in the bond of political representation. In this sense, Pablo Rodríguez (2018) has developed the concept of "informational *episteme*" as the result of analyzing a wide scope of discursive transformations in the field of very distant theoretical disciplines—such as cybernetics, general theory of systems, molecular biology, ideas on the "Society of Information," neurosciences, systemic psychology, sociology systems theory, post-humanist philosophies, data management, the ideas on bio-capital—to conclude their convergence (cf. 2018).

Correlatively, Sergio Caletti (2006) has analyzed what can be called the *opinion dispositive,* as the process of the introduction of management *intelligence* (in the sense of technologies and in the sense of forms of collective perception and representation of the social totality) that performs a huge political, non-democratic transformation within the *informational* discursive formation (Caletti 2001).

Similarly, for Althusser, as the necessary counterpart of the technocratic tendencies, the theoretical ideologies of a "scientific" sociology of culture, which tend to replace the concept of *classes* for a particular notion of "masses"—not conceived as a political category, but as an anthropological notion immediately associated to the idea of *audience*, in the aesthetical key of the cultural industry—also come into play.[16] These latter tendencies are joined, says Althusser, by subaltern and petit bourgeois forms of dominant ideology in which diverse forms of anarchist individualism stand out, which associate with popular or erudite forms of existentialism and phenomenology, popular refluxes of the moral and judicial consciousness. These forms are Leftisms and neo-anarchisms, modern forms of aestheticism and of the "religion of art and the artist" that extol the condition of the "creator" and are grounded on "a spontaneous ideology of liberty and revolt," with which leftist intellectuals "console their own impotence by 'participating' in the victories and defeats of all the revolts in the world," while living out its conditions within the ideology of a people "that is not them or is no longer them, taking the place of a myth capable of calming down their impatience regarding a revolution that lasts too long" (Althusser 1963, 24, my translation). These "subaltern position" tendencies function under the domination of entrepreneurial *humanitarianism*, which combines with *technocratism*.[17]

This controversy sketched out by Althusser in 1963, will receive a renewed impulse after the episodes of May 1968, at the height of which he wrote the posthumous published *Sur la reproduction* (2011) in which *technocratism* and *anarchism* would constitute the two tendencies that embody the pincer-like device into which materialist thought falls as Marxism's theoretical and political crisis worsens (cf. Althusser 2014b). In a broad sense we could understand these two tendencies as "tones" in the way to read the articulation between the instances of the Marxist *topique* and its overdetermined causality; accents that are, in a way, not pure but as emphasis or slips tend to simplify the complex social totality from hypertrophizing some of its aspects, blurring the economic determination in the end. In this sense, what is identified here as "technocratism" supposes the reduction of the *social relations of production* to their *technical-economic* dimension, either under the form of a substantialization of means of production or of the subsumption of the concept of social reproduction into a reproduction of skills and technical competences. And what is called "politicism" (or neo-anarchism) consists of the reduction of the *social relations of reproduction* to a juridical-political dimension in the concept of "property" or to a philosophical-political one: the subsumption of economic *exploitation* in the notion of "domination." Briefly, what *Sur la reproduction* (2011) exposes is that, since late 1960s, the problem of reproduction constitutes the territory in which the ideological threat prowls the Marxist field, and it is therefore the reason for Althusser's understanding of the strategic value of theoretical work. It does not seem to be incidental that this same question that strikes one of the most interesting fibers of feminist thought, strikes those which develop among different theoretical tendencies within the Marxist field of the problem of social reproduction. Addressing it continues to be particularly strategic.

TOWARD A RADICALIZATION OF SOCIAL REPRODUCTION THEORY

Since the 1980s, the development of a feminist position within the Marxist question of *reproduction* is undoubtedly one of the richest efforts to face these impoverishing tendencies and the menaces of weakening critical thought and emancipatory politics (Hartman 1979; Vogel 1983; Barret 1980). In this sense, the so-called Social Reproduction Theory, especially those studies dedicated to pursuit a *unitary theory* (Vogel 1983; Brenner and Ramas 1984; Laslet and Brenner 1989; Young 2004; Arruzza 2015; Bhattacharya 2017; Merteuil 2017; among others), have taken into their scope many of the theoretical questions with which Marxist theory fell into an impasse.

Among various issues, the way in which Social Reproduction Theory is shaping the problem of materialist causality in terms of the articulation between the theoretical, quite abstract concepts (to take into account macro-structural logic and long-term processual tendencies) with concrete conjectural dimensions of reproduction and transformation (not only of political transformation, but also technical transformation) is particularly interesting. In this regard, in the foreword of the book compiled by Tithi Bhattacharya,

Social Reproduction Theory Remapping Class, Recentering Oppression (2017), Lise Vogel proposes the direction of the theoretical program that will make it possible to articulate the contributions of Social Reproduction Theory itself to studies on *intersectionality* and other concrete analyses in the field of feminist studies in terms of the problem of what we could call *historical causality*—that is, in terms of the principle of differential and hierarchical articulation of the complex of differences, which allows the accounting of not only its connections, but also of its various indices of efficacy in the articulated whole.

> I think we must jettison two dearly-held [sic] assumptions. First, the assumption that the various dimensions of difference—for example, race, class, and gender—are comparable. Second, the implication that the various categories are equal in causal weight. . . . With these assumptions gone, we can break out of the tight little circle of supposedly similar categories. Our theoretical task would then be to focus on the specificities of each dimension and to develop an understanding of how it all fits—or does not fit—together. Out of this process could come a lens, or perhaps several lenses, with which to analyze empirical data. (Vogel 2017, xi)

In this sense, in the introduction to the same volume, Bhattacharya adds, with respect to the way of defining the field of work of Social Reproduction Theory, first, that it can be considered as a "*methodology* to explore *labor* and labor power under capitalism and is best suited to offer a rich and variegated map of capital as a social relation." And second, she underlines that it is a methodology that privileges *process*, based on the idea that "developing tendencies of history constitute a higher reality than the empirical 'facts'" (2017, 4, my emphasis).

As we can see, the project consists of conceptualizing the type of process-articulation that allows us to think about the whole dynamic of capitalist social formation. And this opens up a position with respect to the non-empiricist way of understanding material and historical concrete processes and events. In other contributions, the question of causality appears to be raised in relation to a question of temporality and historical time. In this sense, for example, as an effort to think theoretically about the articulations between the subjective and the historical, starting from the identification of unequally articulated temporalities, Cinzia Arruzza (2015) has posed a possible dialogue between Marxist studies on the problem of plural temporality (Tombazos 1994; Bensaïd 1995; Tomba 2012) and Marxist studies on the subjective temporality of *queer* theory (e.g., McCallum and Tuhkanen 2011), paying special attention to the works of Butler (2006; 2011) on temporality and performativity.

Together with materialistic causality, the question of temporal complexity constitutes one of the cores that allow structuring the encounter of diverse contributions to the problem of social reproduction in a way that gives account of the articulation of the inequalities. If, on the one hand, as we read in Vogel, the development of a finer conceptualization of historical causality would allow us to understand the way in which differences coalesce in their unequal efficacies, the postulation of the problem of temporality would allow us to think about the processual condition of that articulation in the long term of historical transformation and to place it in the singular forms of individuation and subjectivation that constitute the concrete fleshing out of its relations and tendencies. In this sense, Arruzza's proposal is not to recover the false dichotomy between structuralism and historicism in order to opt for the latter against the former, but to place the specific form of the abstract structural temporality of subjection, which Butler identifies, within the frameworks of a historical conjuncture that makes it possible. Accordingly, Arruza proposes that Butler's formal and abstract temporality of gender performativity must be placed in its conjuncture, as a distinctive feature of the construction of gender and sexual identities in advanced capitalist countries, to the extent that the empty time that takes place in forced repetition must be, in her reading, conceived as mediated by the generalization of abstract time given by the diffusion of the commodity form (2015, 51). By introducing the temporal complexity of historical time, Arruzza is able to restore to Butler's concept of gender processes its condition of historical subjective *formations*—which is to say, the rejection of considering them as philosophical *a priori forms*.

This latter question also animates the work of Silvia Federici and her effort to articulate feminism and Marxism, making room for historical singularity, especially in relation to the concrete historical processes that must be read in the gaps of Marxist theory and that demand a critical development of historical materialism in a feminist and anticolonial perspective.

In Federici's work, the intention is to expand on Marx's theory of productive labor to include reproductive labor in its manifold dimensions, with the aim of "understanding the class struggle and the means through which capitalism reproduces itself, through the creation of different work regimes and different modes of unequal development and underdevelopment" (2018, 87, my translation).

The operation that the point of view of reproduction opens up to thought, interrupts the teleological and contemporaneous temporality that allows for a critique of the neoliberal *presentist* temporality regime. In *Caliban and the Witch* (2004), the problem of historical temporality involves the feminist revision of the critique of *primitive accumulation*. Federici expands and complexifies the Marxist critique of capitalism's imaginary temporality, based on the bourgeois myth of the State of Nature, introducing genealogies that place the material processes of generization, and the social division of labor articulated with them, among the conditions for the emergence of the capitalist social relation of separation of the immediate workers to the means of production. In that sense, the operation opens up and enables to think the expanded mode in which the cyclical temporality of expanded reproduction of capital establishes a necessary relation with the repression of a complexity of times, which are expulsed to a sort of "prehistorical" time of capitalism but pulsate in the groundwaters of the abstract temporal *presentist regime of temporality* of capitalism's mode of production.

The multiple and complex conception of historical time that presents itself in Federici's writing may also be read in the temporal scheme of reproduction, which marks the history of capitalism within the links between social division, international division, technical division, and sexual and gender-based division of labor. As Arruza's, the work of Federici points toward the double historical and structural operation that constitutes the constitutive-double-consistency of the problem of historical time: the problem of the *mechanism* of a mode of production and the problem of a social formation as a *result* or an *emergence*. This double question regarding temporal complexity can be posed in terms of a search for a conception of time at once plural and structured. And it can be at the same time the main scheme of the research program that Vogel (2017) suggested to address for the development of a feminist Social Reproduction Theory, capable of taking into account the articulation of diverse inequalities; each inequality involves a specific temporality but must be considered in the historical causality in which they all fit (not without contradictions and hierarchical relations).

It may be meaningful here to remember the sense of the introduction of the concept of *overdetermination* to think about the specificity of the principle of contradiction in the materialist dialectic, in the Althusserian *reading* of Marx:

> The "contradiction" is inseparable from the total structure of the social body in which it is found, inseparable from its formal conditions of existence, and even from the instances it governs; it is radically affected by them; determining, but also determined in one and the same movement, and determined by the various levels and instances of the social formation it animates; it might be called *overdetermined* in its principle. (Althusser 2005, 101)[18]

As we have developed in other chapters of this volume, the concern for the elucidation and development of a rigorously materialistic conception of historical time is found in the heart of the Althusserian reading of Marx, in *Lire le Capital* (Althusser et al. 1965). Against what readings such as those of E. P. Thompson (1978) have interpreted, the singular Althusserian "structuralism" (cf. Balibar 2003, de Ípola 2007, Romé 2015) understands that the project of giving an account of the principle of Marxist structure summons three theses derived from Marx's metaphors and expressions. By means of recalling the uses of *Verbindung* and *Gliederung* (in the sense of a *combinatory* of elements) and *Darstellung* (as the effectiveness aspect of an absence), V. Morfino (2017) notices that it is possible, "to make emerge clearly the novelty of the Althusserian concept . . . focusing on the point of intersection of three theses: the thesis of the constitutive character of the relations or of the primacy of the relation over the elements; the thesis of the contingency of the relations; [and] finally, the thesis of the plural temporality" (Morfino 2017, 455, my translation).

The research destined to give an account of the noncontemporary and nonhomogeneous temporality radically distinguishes the concept of Marxist historical time from the Hegelian teleology—in the terms of a plural *but unequally articulated* historical temporality. A materialist concept of time is not just a pluralist concept; it also aims to make thinkable the differentially structured unity of times in each conjuncture:

> We can argue from the specific structure of the Marxist whole that it is no longer possible to think the process of the development of the different levels of the whole in the same historical time. . . .
> . . . The fact that each of these times and each of these histories is relatively autonomous does not make them so many domains which are independent of the whole: the specificity of each of these times and of each of these histories—in other words, their relative autonomy and independence—is based on a certain type of articulation in the whole, and therefore on a certain type of dependence with respect to the whole. . . . [T]he mode and degree of independence of each time and history is therefore necessarily determined by the mode

and degree of dependence of each level within the set of articulations of the whole. (Althusser and Balibar 1970, 100)

The relative and differential condition of the concept of plural time requires a concept of its historical contradictory unity. These theses can be useful to understand that the approximation to a plural conception of time, incarnated within feminist thought in Federici's proposal, turns out to still be *descriptive*—in the same sense of "description" that Vogel (2017) attributes to *intersectionality*. The problem is that if we do not pursue the concept of its *unity*, an important concept for historical materialism is lost on the way; this concept is precisely the "economic determination in the last instance."[19]

> It is not enough, therefore, to say, as modern historians do, . . . that each time has its own rhythms, some short, some long; we must also think these differences in rhythm and punctuation in their foundation, in the type of articulation, displacement and torsion which harmonizes these different times with one another. To go even further, I should say that we cannot restrict ourselves to reflecting the existence of visible and measurable times in this way; we must, of absolute necessity, pose the question of the mode of existence of *invisible times*, of the invisible rhythms and punctuations concealed beneath the surface of each visible time . . . . Marx was highly sensitive to this requirement. . . . [T]he time of economic production is a specific time (differing according to the mode of production), but also . . . , as a specific time, it is a complex and non-linear time, *a time of times*, a complex time that cannot be read in the continuity of the time of life or clocks, but has to be constructed out of the peculiar structures of production. The time of the capitalist economic production that Marx analysed must be constructed in its *concept*. (Althusser and Balibar 1970, 101)

Without a *concept* of temporal contradictory and unequal unity, which is to say without a concept of the hierarchical and conflictive articulation of *differences*, the plurality of "observable" genealogies is caught up in Hegelian contemporary time: as the *inverted* form of the counter-mythical operation that reduces critical reading to an unveiling of "hidden" histories (by means of an *inversion* of the myth of small producer that involves *salary* and *property*, to find the truth of *slavery* and *community*). In this sense, the special way in which historical research is placed in Federici's *Caliban and the Witch* (2004) puts into trouble the richness of the plural historical temporalities that her great research discovers.

To claim that "unity" is not and cannot be the unity of a simple, original, and universal *essence* is not "to sacrifice unity on the altar of 'pluralism,' it is to claim something quite different: that the unity discussed by Marxism is the unity of the complexity itself that the mode of organization and articulation of the complexity is precisely what constitutes its unity. It is to claim that the complex whole has the *unity of a structure articulated in dominance*" (Althusser 2005, 202).[20]

The historiographic work can, at this point, be kept at a descriptive level while waiting for a concept of the differential unit of historical time. The point is that this concept, if the principle of historical materialism is followed, cannot be for capitalism but a principle of economic determination—not as a mechanical or expressive cause, but as *time of times*, "invisible time," an index of the efficiency of the hierarchical articulation of the plurality of temporalities. Here a gap opens up in Federici's analysis, which dialogues with a certain displacement of many postcolonial studies that subsume imperialist determinations into colonial ones. As Didier Contadini (2018) has shown, this gap is symptomatic of the identification of violent dispossession in the capitalist mode of production with the singular dispossession mythologized in the figure of "so-called primitive accumulation." The projection of primitive accumulation on the forms of violent capitalist accumulation has, as an effect, the subsumption of the notion of expanded *reproduction* of capital and the omission of that of *transition*. The absence of this distinction and, consequently, the elision of the historical singularity of capitalist social formation in which, unlike feudal social formation, economic *determination* (relative to the *hierarchical law* of relation between *instances*) and *dominance* (relative to the *fact* of subordination or domination between contradictions in a determined situation) tend to coincide in the invisible time of capital, produce the politicization of historical causality and the subordination of the problem of economic exploitation to that of state domination. We find ourselves within the Hegelian principle of the state as a concrete universal

> because natural or historical conditions of existence are never more than *contingency* for Hegel, because in no respect do they determine the *spiritual totality* of society; for Hegel, the absence of conditions (in the non-empirical, non-contingent sense) is a necessary counterpart to the absence of any real structure in the whole, and to the absence of a structure *in dominance*, the absence of any *basic determination* and the absence of that *reflection of the*

conditions in the contradiction which its "overdetermination" represents (Althusser 2005, 208–9, my emphasis).

The plurality of times becomes then irrelevant, if, in the concrete condition of its determinations, it does not offer more than the possibility of finding behind the modern myth of the bourgeois state the "truth" of the Absolute Power. To subsume a necessary theory of temporal complexity under an *inversion* of the temporality of capital (undistinguished from that of state), which would thus make room for the emergence of a hidden multiplicity, places Federici's work in a specular opposition to the "Hegelian principle of explanation by consciousness of self (ideology), but also with the Hegelian theme of *phenomenon essence-truth-of*" (Althusser 2005, 111); which is to say: *Humanism*.

It is not incidental that the result of this analysis leaves feminist political thought entangled in a specular relation, either with the bourgeois myth of the small producer or with the economicist myth of the English proletariat. Humanism, which is inseparable from colonial and patriarchal genealogies, continues to lurk within feminist thought, even in the best feminist theories. In this sense, the debate on the causes of the transformation that, toward the end of the nineteenth century and the beginning of the twentieth century, consecrated a new advance of the sexual and gender-based division of labor in Great Britain, is particularly illustrative. Following the studies of Wally Seccombe, Federici argues in the chapter "La construcción del ama de casa a tiempo completo y del trabajo doméstico en Inglaterra de los siglos XIX y XX" (2018)[21] about the existence of a confluence of interests among liberal governments, capitalists, and male proletarians represented in the unions, from 1840 onward, in promoting legal reforms and policies that would expel women from factories. Since the enactment of the *Mine Act* (1842) and the *Ten Hours Act* (1847), among other social reforms, the relative increase of 30 percent in the worker's wage toward the end of the nineteenth century would have consolidated the figure of the "family wage," under which the subsumption of non-remunerated reproductive work under the "wage form" took place. This is not a minor circumstance; it is the moment in which, in the core of the imperialist world-system and as part of the process of international division of labor, the wage-form is configured.[22]

In this framework, the emphasis of the analysis is not focused on the global imperialist scheme of capital forces that determines the form of labor in the center of capitalism (cf. Althusser 2018a), but on the set of legal and political reforms that tended to consolidate the sexual and gender-based division of labor as a process of confluence between the objectives of the bourgeoisie to discipline the labor force with the objectives of the unions to discipline women by confining them to reproductive work. If, as Federici suggests, the consolidation of the "full-time housekeeping" form is, in part, the product of a transformation in the exploitation of labor, from the extraction of absolute surplus value to the extraction of relative surplus value, this suggests that the ideological "sexism" of the trade union referents would explain the connivance of the proletariat in the intensification of its own exploitation, in the form of state power.

Notably, in this singular issue, Federici's analysis coincides with that of other Marxist feminists, supporters of the "dual-system" approach, such as Hartmann (1979) and Barret (1980), which has already been discussed within unitarian perspectives of the Social Reproduction Theory. Against the former, in "Rethinking Women's Oppression" (1984), Johanna Brenner and Maria Ramas have demonstrated the questionable character of the thesis that supports the consolidation of the *imperialist* form of the sexual and gender-based division of labor in the confluence of interests between capitalists and male trade unionists, for two different types of reasons. The first concerns inaccuracies and simplifications in the historiographic analysis. In this sense, for example, questions related to the gendered distribution in different industrial branches show that, on the one hand, while women were indeed expelled from some industries with union support, on the other hand they were encouraged to create unions in other branches. The thesis also disregards different moments in that struggle and ignores the tactical questions related to the reading of the use of women's employment as a kind of reserve army of labor by the capitalists in order to consolidate the decline of wages, among other questions.

Mainly, however, what Brenner and Ramas (1984) demonstrated is the insufficiency of the juridical-political and ideological hypothesis to account for the material causality of the transformation in the modes of capitalization. In short, what the authors criticize is the politicist (and ideologist) deviation that identifies *exploitation* with *domination*. It is not a question of details but of the type of analytical operation that is put into play. The *method* is not a secondary issue—as Bhattacharya has pointed out (2017) for Social Reproduction Theory—in historical analysis, as in fact it is not in any science, because it compromises its theoretical and philosophical foundations. The question here is not to reject ideological or political effectivity in historical processes. The question is, in the case of Federici, whether "laws" and political pacts can fully determine the wage-form in the transition to absolute surplus-value. The politicist subsumption of complex historical overdetermination seems to be connected here with the subsumption of the specific imperialist form in the more general, and therefore abstract, category of dispossession that uses *primitive accumulation* as its model.

Finally, as it is deduced from the development of his article, in addition to theoretical consequences that hinder the growth of the Theory of Social Reproduction by maintaining the principle of causality abstract, this kind of subsumptions has strategic consequences, because the identification between exploitation and domination (and therefore between the class force of capital and the power of the state) leads to abstractly anti-statist (and neo-anarchist) positions that see in the state the historical continuity that consecrates the juxtaposition between inequality of class, gender, and race.

In this sense, in their reading of Althusser's theory of ideology, Brenner and Ramas (1984) are right to point out the ambivalence of Barret's dualism. We could add that this reading, supported by the extract "Ideology and Ideological State Apparatuses,"[23] is fragmentary and dualistic, since it is divorced from the complete volume *Sur la reproduction* (Althusser 2011) which remained unpublished until after Althusser's death and where he places the problem of ideology in the framework of a materialistic theory of *social reproduction*, based on the materialistic principles of *overdetermination* and the *non-contemporaneity* of historical time.

It is possible to establish distinctions inside Federici's writings and emphasize some articulations with other feminist theorists who are committed to introducing the question regarding multiple temporality into the very core of the critique of capitalism. These would help to avoid reducing every conjuncture to the abstract scheme of *inversion* or demystifying operations, aimed at unveiling the "mystery" of the political violence of radical dispossession hidden in the cyclical temporality of state power. This kind of analysis, purely based on an idealist reading of the critique of the "*so-called primitive accumulation*," allows the restoration of a Philosophy of History that meets, in each one of its phenomenic manifestations, the "essence" of the original violence of its *genesis*. The immediate association between counter-mythical readings and empirical descriptions is, rigorously, a pure *inversion*, which is not only theoretically insufficient for lacking a just intelligence of historic causality, beyond the descriptive plane, but also runs the great risk of nourishing political programs that may only strengthen the liberalism and humanism that constitute the philosophical tools of the mode of life proper to the imperialist social formation and whose historical processes of configuration connect racism and sexism with exploitation.

In this direction, Tithi Bhattacharya (2015) introduces an interesting nuance with regard to the consideration of the link between production and reproduction in Marx's writings. With a great interest in developing a unitarian perspective, she proposes a global comprehension of the problem of reproduction—not in the strict sense of the reproduction of the labor force, but in the broader sense of the *reproduction of the complex totality of capitalist relations,* from which the capital/labor relation is but the most abstract theoretical form.

> In her terms this may be stated as the fundamental insight of Social Reproduction Theory.
>
> The fundamental insight of SRT is, simply put, that human labor is at the heart of creating or reproducing society as a whole. The notion of labor is conceived here in the original sense in which Karl Marx meant it, as "the first premise of all human history"—one that, ironically, he himself failed to develop fully. Capitalism, however, acknowledges productive labor for the market as the sole form of legitimate "work," while the tremendous amount of familial as well as communitarian work that goes on to sustain and reproduce the worker, or more specifically her labor power, is naturalized into nonexistence. Against this, social reproduction theorists perceive the relation between labor dispensed to produce commodities and labor dispensed to produce people as part of the systemic totality of capitalism. (Bhattacharya 2017, 2)

It can be pointed out that the difference between Bhattacharya's and Federici's approaches stems from the way of considering the problem of reproduction. In Bhattacharya's approach, we can discover a materialistic conception of reproduction under the thesis of *the primacy of the relations of production over the productive forces,* which distances it from a more idealistic critical conception closer to the humanist theory of *reification-alienation.*[24] In a similar direction to that of Arruza's, Bhattacharya advances the recognition of a contradictory and complex temporality, the materialist fiber of Marx's thought, which is distorted in economicist readings and therefore restricts their concept of the working class to the canon of the apparent forms of capitalist economy.

In this sense, an internal principle of the theoretical developments of Social Reproduction Theory functions as a demarcation operator preventing what could be the other extreme of the theoretical pendulum in the heritage of the Marxist tradition: the *technocratic* deviation that is embodied in a purely technical conception of reproduction, under a purely technical conception of work, which could be derived from the very definition that Bhattacharya offers of "human labor as the heart of social reproduction" (2017, 2). The principle that avoids the technical (then, idealistic) reduction of this centrality of work is the development of the question about the complexity of the social totality as determinant (an *overdetermination*, I may say). This avoids the reduction of the concept of social reproduction to the reproduction of the productive forces independently and restores the historical materialist principle of the *primacy of the relations of production over the productive forces*. In this way, the conceptual register of social reproduction is extended by involving in the concrete existence of these relations the superstructural configurations in which *economic causality exists as an abstract cause or as a presence (by absence) of the structure in its effects*.[25]

Accordingly, Bhattacharya reads in Marx that, from the point of view of a "connected whole," the processes of production are, at the same time, processes of reproduction,[26] in which not only the labor force is reproduced, but the relation of *capital* itself.[27] This allows us, on the one side, to recover the thread of economic exploitation in the complexity of *concrete* reproductive relations (within culture, ideological formations, education, subjective dispositions, etc.) and, at the same time, to point out that exploitation does not exist as such in an immediate or pure way, but in particular historical forms of apparition on which capital sustains itself—which allows us to think that class struggle has its opportunity in the complex world of capitalist social life and in the variety of cultural, ideological, political (and so forth) forms in which the working class endeavors to attend to its own needs and the complex variety of the struggles through which popular sectors dispute "a share of civilization" (Bhattacharya 2015).

From Bhattacharya's developments, we can differentially deduce that the primacy of the labor force contained in Federici's program leads to a restricted reading of reproduction—one that emphasizes the reproduction of the labor force over the reproduction of the overdetermined *relation* of capital/labor. This tends to divorce domination from economic exploitation and undoubtedly has consequences, not only related to the theoretical assumptions set in motion, but also in terms of political strategies. When the different temporalities of *transition* and *reproduction* are mixed up, the result is the restoration of the historicist conception of time in terms of a *genesis*, which is, as I have already stated in other chapters, the theological commitment of liberal philosophy. Accordingly, a myth of nature is invoked when politization of capital subsumes, with no rest, imperialist forms into colonialist forms.[28]

ANARCHISM AND TECHNOCRATISM: NEOLIBERAL MENACES TO THEORETICAL MATERIALISM AND EMANCIPATORY POLITICS

In the 1980s, Michel Pêcheux—one of the best readers of the problem of reproduction in Althusser—forewarned about the Stalinist operation as a *regression* of Marxist thought to a pre-Leninist status such as that of the *Second International*. In a manuscript allegedly written in 1983, currently kept at the IMEC and titled "Anarchisme/Reformisme" (1983), Pêcheux defines Stalinism as the practical outcome of the decomposition of the contradiction between anarchism and reformism, on which Leninism works (1983). He then found a paradoxical affirmation of Stalinism in the forms of its alleged critique (which, by then, already assumed the accents of technological fetishism and neo-anarchist politicism), in the unnoticed recuperation of the *primacy of the productive forces over the relations of production*.

The crucial point for a theory of social reproduction, in terms of the primacy of the relations of production over the productive forces, had been underscored by Althusser in 1975 as the strategic question necessary to understand *imperialism*:

> knowing what productive forces and relations of production are, not only for a given mode of production, but [also] for a social formation, in which several modes of production exist under the domination of one of them; that of knowing what becomes of this unity in a capitalist social formation in the Imperialist stage, which adds supplementary determinations that are not secondary but essential to the question of this "unity." (Althusser 2014b, 216)

Some of these risks in which politicism and technocratism dramatically coincide were seen in relation to the 2019 Bolivian coup, when feminist voices rose to distinguish the authenticity of certain Aymara sectors from the spurious condition of Evo Morales as a "trade unionist more than an Aymara."[29] As previously developed, this is not about an individual reading of a singular conjuncture and not only the result of a political position that can be discussed in tactical or strategic levels; it is about theoretical, subtle displacements and deviations that expose the *cyphers* of the neoliberal conjuncture in its discursive divided-unity.[30] We may say, thus, that for developing the Social Reproduction Theory as an effective *critical* theory, it would be not only interesting but also necessary to analyze and rectify these theoretical dilemmas—among others, the question of the different temporalities of *reproduction* and *transition* and the materialist development toward an *imperialist* determination of neo-colonialist relations—in order to understand the hierarchic differences among current neoliberal contradictions under the reproduction of social relations of production, conceived in an overdetermined way.

The emphasis that may be read in the works of Bhattacharya and other theorists who are interested in producing a unified theory of the links between patriarchal and capitalist relations, regarding the *primacy of the relations of production over the productive forces*, allows us to conclude that, in their perspective, it is the overdetermined "invisible time of capital" that accommodates a temporal conjunction of existing social relations in their historical, technical, institutional, cultural dimensions that perpetuate the amplified reproduction of the diversified capital/labor relation.

> Understanding the complex but unified way in which the production of commodities and reproduction of labor power takes place, helps us understand how the concrete allocation of the total labor of society is socially organized in gendered and racialized ways through lessons learnt by capital from previous historical epochs and through its struggle against the working class. The process of accumulation, thus, in actuality cannot be indifferent to social categories of race, sexuality or gender, but seeks to organize and shape those categories that in turn act upon the determinate form of surplus labor extraction. The wage labor relation suffuses the spaces of non-waged everyday life. (Bhattacharya 2015)

This is a necessary revitalization of materialist and dialectical thought, to the extent that the complexity of the concretely historical does not dissolve the determination "in the last instance" through the capitalist relation of production. It assumes, at the same time, that it is itself *abstract with regard to the complex of relations in which it exists as an absent cause*—in other words, always displaced, de-centered in its effects. It is a similar approach to the one recognized by Althusser in the Marx's materialist conception of historical time, which takes shape as an immanent critique of the contemporary and homogenous temporality of Hegelian historicism, which survives in the same body of thought. According to Althusser, the materialist temporality inscribes the complexity in the bosom of the capitalist contradiction itself; which turns the abstract time of production, a "time of times," at once determinant and invisible.

Within this framework and on the supposition of a temporal multiplicy, a unified theory offers the theoretical basis to reconcile zones of feminist thought that seem to erect walls between undoubtedly connected, but relatively autonomous in their specific logics, problems—such as aspects related to the feminization and racialization of poverty, the sexual and gender-based division of labor or the imperialist financial exploitation based on "gender" and "race," problems related to genderized identities and the election of a sexual object, and so forth.

This is the way in which, for example, Cinzia Arruzza critiques the reduction of historical to performative time in Butler, avoiding an economicist misrecognition of the affective and identitary problem, but placing it within the framework of a program of reconciliation of the subjective, affective, or psychical and the historical, determined by the class struggle and its transindividual forms (Arruzza 2015). In a radically anti-economicist way, the economic exploitation thus becomes the *absent cause* (which is to say, *present in it effects*) of a multiplicity of concrete configurations of the capitalist social relation, which allows us to reencounter, both in critical theory as well as in political thought, the threads that reinscribe the local processes within a global logic of the complex and overdetermined social totality.

It would not be excessive to remember, at this point, that it is the downfall of this question about the totality that brands the political weakening and the theoretical impoverishment of the left, trapped in an age of an extremely globalized capitalism. This impoverishment, in some of its political drifts, adopts the shape of identitarian struggles, while, in its philosophical courses, under diverse inflections (pandiscursivism, politicism, pluralism, autonomism, technocratism), suffers a process of simplification of the concept of historical time, in the shape of the hypertrophy of a temporal mode over others or in the affirmation of the equality of differences—both of which involve the incapacity to think about their articulation with a totality of heterogeneous times.

Therefore, it is not about comprehending feminism as such; there is no feminism "in general." The real challenge—the one that requires a greater intellectual audacity—is to acquire the instruments to see more clearly into the field of feminist thought, aiming to identify the opportunity that it offers for the singular conjunction between theoretical and political practices. This is in order to propel the processes of the feminization of politics and the composition of a popular feminism capable of revitalizing an anti-authoritarian front. In our particular conjuncture, many reactionary and neo-conservative tendencies that expose the crisis of imperialist regime of accumulation remind us of the ones that marked the history of dependency. If the so-called neoliberalism is, in one of its dimensions, the "long conjuncture" of the decomposition of *imperialism*, it can be read about in the global topography of neocolonial relations in geographic peripheries that display, with total brutality, the marks of a condensation of "times"; but this complexity may not be understood if we abandon the thesis of the determination in the last instance, which presupposes the ontological primacy of the class struggle *based on the supposition of the primacy of the relations of production over the productive forces.*

It is within this framework that the role that feminist theory is developing becomes vital in its effort to reconstruct the complex plot that connects diverse subjective sufferings to the capitalist structure of economic exploitation. What is at stake is not only the future of the feminist movement, in its capacity to expand and articulate on a global level, but also the possibility for emancipatory thought to repair the horizon of the future for all forms of life.

This might be achieved, however, as long as feminist thought does not confuse theory with strategy—as long as it does not turn its own words of order into an immediate and impoverished reading of the complexity of the conjuncture, as long as it does not become an immediate inversion of the technocratic reduction of time to the administration of the same. A renewed materialist feminist position has a lot to offer for that task.

NOTES

1. "On the one hand, . . . the idealist repetition of the subject-form characterized by the coincidence of the subject with himself (I/see/here/now) in the 'seen-ness' of a scene, in the evidentness of the *experience* of a situation, in the sense of the German *Erfahrung*, i.e., of an experience which can be transferred by identification-generalization to every subject; a coincidence, then, which guarantees continuity in the evidentness of meaning between empirical lived experience and speculative abstraction, continuity between the concrete subject and the universal subject, supposed to be the subject of science (notional-ideological operation)" (Pêcheux 1982, 139). And "On the other hand, . . . the materialist process of knowledge, a process without a subject, in which *experimentation* (in the sense of the German *Experiment*) realizes the body of concepts in devices which contain the objectivity of the science considered, without any foreign admixture (conceptualscientific operation)" (141).

2. We have developed this concept of materialistic apodicticity in other chapters of this volume.

3. Despite the fact that we would rather prefer to speak of *dominant ideology*, for the reasons already settled in the chapter 1 of this volume, Fraser's analysis appears to be a fair reading of the neoliberal conjuncture—to the extent that it assumes the dilemma of her own left thinking, and in such terms she reads the concept of *hegemony* in a quite close meaning to that of *dominant ideology*.

4. Simone de Beauvoir's writings, frequently invoked, although rarely read fairly, offers such a theory.

5. The developments of Firestone (1970) and Fouque (1995), among others, could also be reviewed in this sense.

6. It was Marx, who first posed it in his foreword to the second German edition of *Das Kapital* (1873): "The mystification which dialectic suffers in Hegel's hands, by no means prevents him from being the first to present its general form of working in a comprehensive and conscious manner. With him it is standing on its head. It must be turned right side up again, if you would discover the rational kernel within the mystical shell."

7. In the text "Prologo.#Estamos para nosotras," incorporated as a preface to the latest Spanish re-edition of the writings of Lonzi and some of the documents *Rivolta Feminile*, Veronica Gago and Raquel Gutiérrez Aguilar suggest a reading of those writings that inscribes Lonzi's contribution in a feminist genealogy of the "communitarian question," in which Selma James and Mariarrosa Dalla Costa and Silvia Federici's contributions participate and which moves it toward richer and more complex formulations, in which not by chance, the Marxist theoretical bet returns. However, as the authors themselves state, Lonzi's operation consists of finding feminism, by means of *reversing* Hegel. (cf. Gago and Gutiérrez Aguilar, in Lonzi 2017, 6)

8. Developments in lesbian thought and queer studies, especially those that approach the category of gender with contributions from linguistics, psychoanalysis, and structuralist perspectives—such as those of Julia Kristeva, Judith Butler, and Peter Druker—have opened a path against essentialisms of this type. For an introductory mapping of these debates, see Arruzza (2015).

9. "I think that, in its approximation, this metaphorical expression—the 'inversion' of the dialectic—does not pose the problem of the *nature of the objects* to which a *single method* should be applied (the world of the Idea for Hegel—the real world for Marx), but rather the problem of the *nature of the dialectic* considered itself, that is, the problem of *its specific structures*; not the problem of the inversion of the 'sense' of the dialectic, but that of the *transformation of its structures*. . . .

". . . [I]f the Marxist dialectic is 'in principle' the opposite of the Hegelian dialectic, if it is rational and not mystical-mystified-mystificatory, this radical distinction must be manifest in its essence, that is, in its *characteristic determinations and structures*. . . . [T]hese *structural differences* can be demonstrated, described, determined and thought. And if this is possible, it is therefore *necessary*, I would go so far as to say *vital*, for Marxism. We cannot go on reiterating indefinitely approximations such as the difference between system and method, the inversion of philosophy or dialectic, the extraction of the 'rational kernel,' and so on, without letting these formulae think for us, that is, stop thinking ourselves and trust ourselves to the magic of a number of completely devalued words for our completion of Marx's work. I say *vital*, for I am convinced that *the philosophical development of Marxism currently depends on this task*." (Althusser 2005, 92–93)

10. In this sense, it is especially suggestive, the implementation of the dictatorial experiences of the 1970s in South America where the forms of a democratic-socialist, popular government (in Chile) and the strong structures of an organized labor movement articulated to a radicalized middle class (in Argentina) made these countries the "laboratories" of the neoliberal

experiences implemented later with the Reagan-Tatcher alliance, in the 1980s. The bases for the pillage of natural resources, the privatization of public services, the subordination of the incipient industrializations to the voracity of financial capital, the *reprimarization* of the economies and the consolidation of a series of structural reforms that substantially modified the sociability and subjectivity of their citizens found in those processes a main enemy: the workers' and peasants' movement. In the case of Argentina, this can be seen very clearly in the numbers of victims murdered and disappeared by the systematic plan of state terrorism that greatly exceeded the persecution of armed organizations and left-wing partisans, in order to attack all kinds of workers' delegates and trade union leaders, agrarian and neighborhood militants, even though they did not profess any revolutionary ideology whatsoever (cf. Unzué 2012; Abós 1984; Pozzi 1988).

11. During November of 2019, when this book was being written, public declarations regarding the coup in Bolivia from a series of great intellectuals and feminist militants (such as María Galindo; Silvia Rivera Cusicanqui, Rita Segato, etc.) circulated through different media. Beyond the understandable fine aspects of a living politics, which, at certain junctures, can provoke tactical or strategic divergences among those who, in global terms, seem to have to articulate their struggles if they want to effectively produce a historical transformation, the sayings of the feminist intellectuals were particularly inopportune due to the international transcendence of their voices at a time when the dramatic political circumstances in Bolivia were attracting attention because of the ferocity with which the functionaries and political leaders representing a majority popular force were violently uprooted from their homes, their families kidnapped, by a coalition of a manifestly pro-imperialist right in alliance with the military forces. The most striking thing about the episode was that they were anti-colonialist feminists who have dedicated their lives to political militancy, with great commitment to Latin-American feminist thought, because beyond the exquisiteness of their readings and intentions, their interventions could not but provoke, in light of the real power relations of the situation, a further weakening of the outgoing government and with it, consecrate a tactical victory to the representatives of a profoundly colonialist and reactionary right. In general terms, the sayings poured into journalistic columns, radio interviews, and public pronouncements aimed to correlate the violence of a manifestly dictatorial process and the imperialist technocracy and financial capital interference for the plundering of natural resources to forms of male chauvinism and "*caudillismo*" within the popular movement lead by Juan Evo Morales Ayma, as if it was a battle of two devils .

12. "The unevenness of capitalist development led, via the 1914 War, to the Russian Revolution because in the revolutionary situation facing the whole of humanity Russia was the weakest link in the chain imperialist states. It had accumulated the largest sum of historical contradictions then possible; for it was at the same time the most backward and the most advanced nation, a gigantic contradiction which its divided ruling classes could neither avoid nor solve. In other words Russia was overdue with its bourgeois revolution on the eve of its proletarian revolution; pregnant with two revolutions, it could not withhold the second even by delaying the first. This exceptional situation was 'insoluble' (for the ruling classes) and Lenin was correct to see in it the objective conditions of a Russian revolution, and to forge its subjective conditions, the means of a decisive assault on this weak link in the imperialist chain." (Althusser 2005, 97–98)

13. From different approaches, many studies have developed the critical analysis of these tendencies, despite conceptual and terminology options (cf. Rodriguez 2018; García Linera 2011; Lordon 2013; Fisher 2016; Sadin 2013, among many other).

14. Althusser refers here to Macherey 1965, 139.

15. For the case of France, Pêcheux also links technocratism to the what he calls the ideology of the Gaullist state.

16. Special attention should be taken to not fall into the mistake of understanding that Althusser confronted the very concepts of masses to classes as if they were in the same conceptual level and for every purpose, or as he rejected the idea of popular masses being the vital force for political struggle in the second half of the twentieth century—articulated, in this sense, in his *Résponse à John Lewis* (1973b).

17. In this sense, see also Balibar 1997; Žižek 2008; Rancière 2009.

18. Following the theoretical conclusion from Lenin's concrete analyses of the situation in revolutionary Russia, Althusser concludes, "If, as in this situation, a vast accumulation of 'contradiction' comes into play in the same court, some of which are radically heterogeneous—of different origins, different sense, different levels and points of application—but which nevertheless 'merge' into a ruptural unity, we can no longer talk of the sole, unique power of the general 'contradiction.' Of course, the basic contradiction dominating the period (when the revolution is 'the task of the day') is active in all these 'contradictions' and even in their 'fusion.' But, strictly speaking, it cannot be claimed that these contradictions and their fusion are merely the pure phenomena of the general contradiction. The 'circumstances' and 'currents' which achieve it are more than its phenomena pure and simple. They derive from the relations of production, which are, of course, one of the terms of the contradiction, but at the same time its conditions of existence; from the superstructures instances which derive from it, but have their own consistency and effectivity, from the international conjuncture itself, which intervenes as a determination with a specific role to play. This means that if the 'differences' that constitute each of the instances in play (manifested in the 'accumulation' discussed by Lenin) 'merge' into a real unity, they are not 'dissipated' as pure phenomena in the internal unity of a simple contradiction. The unity they constitute in this 'fusion' into a revolutionary rupture, is constituted by their own essence and effectivity, by what they are and according to the specific modalities of their action." (Althusser 2005, 100)

19. "Marx has at least given us the 'two ends of the chain,' and has told us to find out what goes on between them: on the one hand, determination in the last instance by the (economic) mode of production; on the other, the relative autonomy of superstructures and their specific effectivity. This clearly breaks with the Hegelian principle of explanation by consciousness of self (ideology), but also with the Hegelian theme of phenomenon essence-truth-of."(Althusser 2005, 111).

20. The notion of dominance concerns "the law of uneven development. For, as Mao puts it in a phrase as clear as the dawn, 'Nothing in this world develops absolutely evenly.'

"To understand the meaning of this law and its scope—and, contrary to what is sometimes thought, it does not concern Imperialism alone, but absolutely 'everything in this world'—we must return to the essential differences of Marxist contradiction which distinguish a principal contradiction in any complex process, and a principal aspect in any contradiction. So far I have only insisted on this 'difference' as an index of the complexity of the whole, arguing that it is absolutely necessary that the whole be complex if one contradiction in it is to dominate the others. Now we must consider this domination, no longer as an index, but in itself, and draw out its implications.

That one contradiction dominates the others presupposes that the complexity in which it features is a structured unity, and that this structure implies the indicated domination-subordination relations between the contradictions. For the domination of one contradiction over the others cannot, in Marxism, be the result of a contingent distribution of different contradictions in a collection that is regarded as an object." (Althusser 2005, 201)

21. From "Feminism and the Struggle Over Sexual Labor: Origin and History in 19th and 20th Century Europe and US." Published for the first time in Spanish, translated by Maria Aránzazu Catalán Antuna. Cf. Federici 2018, 65–76.

22. As we have pointed out in chapter 2, the absence of the historical concept of imperialism synthesizes the tendency to blur the conjunctural (imperialist) determination in capitalist temporality, in benefit of a "colonial" continuity, which contributes the crystallizing of a relatively abstract scheme in the historical critic and blurs the temporal complexity and the singular condition of the concrete conjunctures. This analytical tendency that can be recognized in some developments in postcolonial studies and even in postcolonial feminism (cf. Rivera Cusicanqui 2018) appears in some of Federici's works—especially in *Caliban and the Witch* (2004)—but it is tensioned and problematized by other studies closer to the theory of social reproduction. Examples of these studies include those inscribed in the compilation we discuss here and in which the consolidation of imperialism is thought of in terms of a transformation in the form of accumulation from light industry to heavy industry that demanded a more rigorous disciplining of labor (cf. Federici 2020).

23. The well-known article "Ideologie et appareils idéologiques d'etat. (Notes pour une recherche)," originally published by Althusser in *La Pensée* no. 151 (June 1970), was extracted by its author from a volume that was kept unpublished until 2011, under the title of *Sur la reproduction*.

24. For an approach to a materialistic critique to the theory of alienation, see chapter 2 of this volume.

25. In previous chapters, I have presented the Althusserian structural causality in these Spinozian terms. For an overview of the variations on this topic, compare Morfino 2017.

26. "It is important in this regard to clarify that what we designated above as two separate spaces—(a) spaces of production of value (point of production) (b) spaces for reproduction of labor power—may be separate in a strictly spatial sense but they are actually united in both the theoretical and operational senses." (Bhattachayra 2015).

27. This is a conception that reads a transindividual ontology in the passage from concrete to abstract labor and that suggests that every reading that tends to keep the focus on the individual scene of production (as a process of labor) or on reproduction (a woman, a family, etc.) remains on the abstract temporality of purely economic logic. With this idea, Bhattacharya says, "Beyond the two-dimensional image of individual direct producer locked in wage labor, we begin to see emerge myriad capillaries of social relations extending between workplace, home, schools, hospitals—a wider social whole, sustained and co-produced by human labor in contradictory yet constitutive ways." (2015)

28. Against this subsumption, a huge debate took shape within Latin-American Marxism. In diverse forms, Latin-American Marxists took into account the danger by proposing different discussions and concepts—from the essays of Mariátegui (1928), who underlined the historical role of the "*indio*" in terms of a material force within monopolistic capital relations and who criticized, since the early decades of the twentieth-century, exoticization and "authentical" ideologies of the "Indian" form; to conceptual developments of *Dependence Theory* and the discussions that took place in Mexico during 1970s and 1980s between diverse Latin-American Marxists about "development" and against the pure identification, between noncapitalist forms, of local production and property with "feudal" or "pre-capitalist" relations. In this sense, a huge bibliography can be recalled, in which Marx's later writings are rediscovered (Dussel 1990; Aricó 1982; García Linera 1989).

29. The characterization was made by the well-known Argentinian feminist, Rita Segato, in her dialogue with the Bolivian feminist María Galindo, leader of *Mujeres Creando*, for *Radio Deseo*. The Spanish transcription of Segato's words can be read in "Rita Segato sobre Bolivia:

'Es el momento oportuno para pensar a Bolivia críticamente,'" Lavaca, November 20, 2019, https://www.lavaca.org/notas/rita-segato-sobre-bolivia-es-el-momento-oportuno-para-pensar-a-bolivia-criticamente/.

30. For an approach to the type of unity of discursive formations, see chapter 2 in this volume.

Part II

For Theory

Chapter Four

No Theoretical Thinking without Political Thought; No Political Thinking without Theory

In 1967, in the context of the growing popularity achieved through the publication of those works that doubtlessly would turn out to be his most celebrated ones, Louis Althusser undertook a process of severe self-criticism and correction of some of the thesis he had presented.

> If I did lay stress on the vital necessity of *theory* for revolutionary practice, and therefore denounced all forms of empiricism, I did not discuss the problem of the "union of theory and practice" which has played such a major role in the Marxist-Leninist tradition. No doubt I did speak of the union of theory and practice within "theoretical practice," but I did not enter into the question of the union of theory and practice within *political practice*. Let us be precise; I did not examine the general form of historical existence of this union: the "fusion" of Marxist theory and the *workers' movement*. . . .
>
> . . . I did not show what it is, as distinct from science that constitutes *philosophy proper*: the organic relation between every philosophy, as a *theoretical* discipline and even within its *theoretical* forms of existence and exigencies, and *politics*. I did not point out the nature of this relation, which, in Marxist philosophy, has nothing to do with a *pragmatic* relation. So I did not show clearly enough what in this respect distinguishes Marxist philosophy from earlier philosophies. (Althusser 2005, 14–15)

The self-inflicted accusation had a philosophical sense that few of his readers managed to notice and, far from an intentional effect, it worked as a functional argument, which, in his posterity, fed both the incomprehension of his detractors as well as that of many of his disciples and followers[1] —in most cases, promoting allegedly critical readings of his thesis that remained captive by the dominant interpretative tendencies, which, in the name of politicizing theory, would broaden the channel of a general displacement toward forms of theoreticism, empiricism, and, in its worst manifestations, plainly relativist positions (not only in their conception of knowledge but also in their political analysis). The last decades of the twentieth century would sanction their paradoxical posterity.

Time has gone by and the captivating power of the accusation of theoreticism has lost some of its efficacy. It is fair to admit that it is not due to the innocent passage of time, but because many of the passions that fueled the controversies that vied for the exegetical key to Marxist theory in the 1960s and 1970s have weakened to the extreme. Moreover, it is necessary to point out that the release of a significant amount of Althusser's unpublished writings, the circulation of lesser known articles,[2] and the revitalization of a field of readings through the work of several thinkers who, in some sense, could be considered Althusserian or post-Althusserian,[3] opened up an opportunity to return to certain areas of his work with more resources and fewer prejudices.

Within this framework, I propose to revisit some of the classical developments of what could be considered the matrix of Althusserian theoreticism, intending to reconstruct its coherence, in order to demonstrate that it says much more than what has been attempted to read in them. I will develop two interrelated conjectures: (1) That the problem of the articulation of political practice and theoretical practice is already inscribed—and enacted—within the early development of the category of *overdetermination*, with which Althusser pursues the materialist figure of Marxist dialectics, even in its most "theoreticist" formula: the definition of philosophy as the *Theory of Theoretical Practice.* (2) That, beyond the cartography Althusser himself traced of his writings, critical access to the epistemological field, in order to give theoretical shape to Marxist philosophy in relation to the question of science, is required by the proper political determinations of his intervention. Althusser's critique of classical epistemology is directed toward the conceptualization of political practice as a specific practice and political thought as a singular kind of thinking. This question is already posed (in a practical state) in the category of *overdetermination*, which requires the theoretical distinction between different practices in order to enable the conceptualization of its concrete articulation in a conjuncture.

In short, the revision of the so-called "theoreticism" I propose aims to emphasize the magnitude of the Althusserian contribution to the development of a critical conception of science and knowledge, remarkable in itself, but also crucial as an opportunity for *political thinking* in its full right. I will not focus on his posthumously published correspondence, nor on his unpublished manuscripts or posthumous publications, which would offer a kind of shortcut to read the canonical writings in hindsight, once the problem of the junction of theory and practice has been posed explicitly.[4] I will focus, instead, on the classical texts, in order to read what was already there.

OVERDETERMINATION: *TOPIQUE* AND PROCESS

The notion of *overdetermination* is recovered by Althusser from Freud, who develops it within his study on the interpretation of dreams, in order to describe the type of operation proper to unconscious thought: "Each of the elements of the dream's content turns out to have been 'overdetermined,' to have been represented in the dream-thoughts many times over" (Freud 2010, 301).

From the Freudian approach of this notion, I am interested in highlighting some features that, as I understand them, survive in the Althusserian employment of the term and, in different ways, will compromise vast regions of his problematic. First, unconscious thinking is a decentered process that produces *formations*. Second, its structure is characterized by a certain disproportion or *misadjustment* (*décalage*).[5] Third, the figure of misadjustment that the notion of overdetermination supposes is drawn in opposition to the notion of direct transparent representation and presupposes an omission; but omission and misadjustment do not operate on a lack, but due to an *excess*.[6]

The Freudian notion of *overdetermination* takes the shape of a concept in Althusserian thinking in relation to the search for a kind of apodicticity adequate to the materialist position (which acts in the Marxist theory of history) and consequently responds to the problem of the conditions of intelligibility of a social formation. Althusser says that it is necessary to question about *"what is the content, the* raison d'etre *of the overdetermination* of Marxist contradiction, and how can the Marxist conception of *society be reflected in this overdetermination*. This is a crucial question" (Althusser 2005, 107).

In this deep rationality that inhabits psychoanalytic theory, Althusser pursues a solution to the problem of the relationship between structural legality and singularity (which is vital to the materialist theory of history),[7] understanding that the theoretical development of Marxism requires an accurate conceptualization of the singular legality that responds to this *processual topique*.[8] His texts are seeded with invocations to those aspects of the psychoanalytic problematic that correlatively call for a decentered *topique* and a complex temporality, neither homogeneous nor contemporary. Thus, it is convenient to clearly establish, in principle, that the appeal to the Freudian notion does not operate as a kind of culturalist (or paralinguistic) reformulation of Marxism, but assumes the extremely complex philosophical problem of *reading*, which is another way to pose the "problem of knowledge" within the framework of a theory of history.[9] Against this problem of the "religious myth of reading" of the manifest discourse of the "Great Book of the World" (Althusser and Balibar 1970, 16), Althusser proposes another conception of reading that, honoring the psychoanalytic genealogy, he calls *symptomal*, but has precedents in the history of philosophy far beyond Freud. In that sense, Althusser highlights:

> The first man ever to have posed the problem of *reading*, and in consequence, of *writing*, was Spinoza, and he was also the first man in the world to have proposed both a theory of history and a philosophy of the opacity of the immediate. With him, for the first time ever, a man linked together in this way the essence of reading and the essence of history in a theory of the difference between the imaginary and the true. This explains to us why Marx could not possibly have become Marx except by founding a theory of history and a philosophy of the historical distinction between ideology and science, and why in the last analysis this foundation was consummated in the dissipation of the religious myth of *reading*. (Althusser and Balibar 1970, 16)

This reading is not the reading of a manifest discourse, the pursuit of a *voice*, but a *reading of readings*, the pursuit of symptoms and misadjustments: it is the reading of a *topique*,[10] because starting with Marxist theory, the text of history is not a text where a voice speaks (the *Logos*); it is instead the "inaudible and illegible notation of the effects of a structure of structures" (Althusser and Balibar 1970, 17). What the Marxist theory of history mobilizes is an internal differentiation of the concept of history, an increase of the complexity that turns useless the dyads that organize classic epistemological thought (subject-object, theory-praxis). And it does this to the extent that it forces the posing of the problem of the historicity of theory itself, in order to turn thinkable that of its object and, therefore, requires the effort of reconsidering the concept of *time*.

As a result, it is clear that, if the problem that the category of overdetermination means to conceive is posed by Althusser in the language of the Marxist problem of determination, it is, however, not referred to a mere question of the (direct or indirect) relations or interdependence between regions of social life, but to the historical and philosophical problem of *forms* as *formations*.

> It is sufficient to retain from him what should be called the *accumulation of effective determinations* (deriving from the superstructures and from special national and international circumstances) *on the determination in the last instance by the economic*. It seems to me that this clarifies the expression *overdetermined contradiction*, which I have put forward . . . . This *overdetermination* is inevitable and thinkable as soon as the real existence of the forms of the superstructure and of the national and international conjuncture has been recognized—an existence largely specific and autonomous, and therefore irreducible to a pure *phenomenon*. (Althusser 2005, 113)

The main question, as this fragment raises, is the dialectic. And the formula Althusser pursues is that of an *impure dialectic*—or, broadly, the question about the problematic articulation between conceptuality and history, related to the question about the complex structure of temporality. Overdetermination, considered as a concept, deals with a dilemma I will attempt to develop. This *dilemma* is that of a concept that, as a concept, is not the unification of multiplicity but the indication of its impossibility. Overdetermination is proposed by Althusser as a name for the impossible task of conceptualizing the limits of the concept—that is, *the relationships between itself and what is not itself*. In order to understand the complex kind of articulation established between philosophy and science, this is a capital question.

Althusser arrived to this Freudian notion in the search for a formula of the Marxist dialectic capable of expressing the rationality that inhabits Marxist theoretical practices, those that enable the premises of *Capital*. This dialectic is not only conceived by Althusser in a completely different light than that of Hegel,[11] but it is also defined by its difference. This search leads to conceiving the materialist condition of the Marxist contradiction in the terms of *overdetermination*.[12] However, to the extent that the consistency of this concept rests on the Leninist (and later Maoist) reading of a given historical formation and its structural relationships in the key of *conjuncture* (that is to say, as a question about the concrete conditions of *political practice*), it already opens the philosophical space for problems that overrun the question of knowledge and that advance toward other zones of thought.[13]

It is important to underline that Althusser searches for the materialist definition of dialectics in a *double* movement: in Marx's theoretical work and in the experience of concrete revolutionary struggle (as recovered from the thought of Lenin, Mao, etc.). It is the very articulation of these heterogeneous practices what sets the complex space for materialist thinking.

So, we are lead to consider that it is the conjunction with Marxists' *political* thinking that furnishes the materialist nature of Marxist theoretical apodicticity.

We can find, here, the clues to a singular articulation between *philosophy and history* that lays down the thick—but not always visible—threads of what I understand as the Althusserian problematic. *Overdetermination* aims to a question about the *theoretical thinking* that is answered—since 1962, the date the first version of "Contradiction and Overdetermination" (cf. Althusser 2005) was published—in a detour through *political thinking*. It involves a philosophical position that requires an *open structure* for theory because it attributes to history the constitutive and permanent condition of an *exception to the law*. The category of *overdetermination* displays its particular condition of being an axis, around which the most classical Althusserian developments on science are organized, and a point of ambiguity that allows it to overflow its space, opening up its depths to new questions. On one side, this ambiguity stems from the formulas to which Althusser arrives in his search for the materialist formulation of the *theoretical necessity*, but on the other, it is itself an answer that places the problem of *the political* in the same field as the question of knowledge, producing a continuous misadjustment.

WHICH THEORETICISM? PHILOSOPHY AS THE *THEORY OF THEORETICAL PRACTICE*

The notion of overdetermination, coming from another tradition, constitutes Althusser's first attempt to positively theorize about the specific materialism that furnishes the *philosophical* position of Marxist theory. The field for the Althusserian problematic is the field of philosophy (and not social theory, nor historiography, nor cultural analysis).

> It is the existence of Marxist philosophy "in the practical state" in *Capital* that authorizes us to "derive" the Marxist conception of philosophy from *Capital*. . . . This work is a real theoretical work: not merely a work of simple extraction, abstraction in the empiricist sense, but a work of elaboration, transformation and production, which requires considerable effort. (Althusser 1990, 59)

The *philosophical* reading of Marx is organized by Althusser, in his first systematic attempt, as the question about *philosophy conceived as Theory of theoretical practice* and, even if this already exhibits an *aporia* (theory-practice) and a torsion (Theory of theory), it supposes some limitations that Althusser would point out sooner rather than later.[14] However, it is the growth of the premises that take shape in this field, which is assumed as the challenge of thinking of materialist philosophy in its relationship with history. This produces a permanent widening of the problematic field driven by the encounter and the tension between theory and politics.

Resorting to overdetermination to conceive the specificity of materialist dialectics constructs, in the same inaugural gesture, the direction of the philosophical process. From then on, the materialist position in philosophy always involves, from the Althusserian perspective, reflecting about its relationship to history—or better yet, its own place in history. From the start, the concept of overdetermination itself is committed to a singular conception not only of history, but also of *historicity* and of *time*[15] —not only of them, but also of the reach and the conditions of their *intelligibility*. And, in this sense, it unveils that the problem of historical complexity is itself the problem of the relationship between theory and non-theory that is subtended from the beginning in the materialist question of theory, opening up its space toward a point of irreducible excess to itself: the political practice. Something has emerged in Badiou's 2005 writings, when translating the problem of overdetermination in its (internal) tension with economic determination in the terms of the relationship between objectivity and politics: "Overdetermination puts the possible on the agenda, whereas the economic place (objectivity) is that of well-ordered stability . . . . Overdetermination is in truth the political space" (Badiou 2005, 65).[16]

Beyond how debatable this schematization can be, which offers the rather confusing idea that the objective and the political could be separated a priori, to be articulated later, Badiou notices that overdetermination points toward a sort of ambivalence of *articulation and difference* between objectivity and the political, signaled by the red thread of what could be called the "Althusserian problematic." If Badiou does not succeed in thinking through the Althusserian problematic fully, it may be due to his own subjective theory of politics, while in Althusser the concept of overdetermination is intended to name the radically dialectic condition of a political objectivity [17] Nevertheless, his remark enables us to encompass the relationship (twisted by the torsion) that is established between two concepts that involved two problematic dimensions that have been read separately: *theoretical practices* and *political practices*. Even more so, if a specifically Althusserian problematic can be spoken of (rather than a more generally Marxist or structuralist one), it is due to this perseverance in thinking jointly about that which, by definition, may not be joined. Overdetermination is, in this sense, the cypher of a process of thought that features a *contradictory effort of unification-differentiation*.[18]

Only by assuming the problematic magnitude of this thought can the series of theoretical developments that present a first approach to philosophy be considered, starting with the question of theoretical practice, formulated within the framework of a program that may give shape to a theory of science immanent to the Marxist theory of history. This is a zone of the Althusserian production that coincides with the formulation of some problems related to the concept of *conjuncture*. As I have said, the philosophical question of *theory* finds there its inconsistent consistency and, therefore, its concept and that of its torsion. In this sense, I understand that it is possible to contour the place of this axis in the general space of the Althusserian problematic, in the terms of the pair *theoretical practice-conjuncture*, in order to pursue this *deconstructive operation* (cf. Collazo 2016) that makes the problem of the political to appear "from within" the problem of theory, *as its excess*. As Balibar points out, the movement of that process results in the effect of a *non-null trace* that may only be noticed in the framework of a philosophical reading. This allows us, as Balibar has stated, to grant Althusser's texts something more than is usually searched within them: the *non-null effect* of a path that annuls his own thesis (Balibar 1991). In my opinion, the thickest stroke in this void strike that produces a *non-void effect* is noticed in the movement through which, at the core of this philosophical question of the theoretical, *a distance is placed* where the problem of the political appears. This absent-presence of the political is the mark of historicity on theory; and from then on it is possible to assume that the politicity of philosophy is the place for its commitment *to the real*, as Althusser would develop in the following years.

> All that can be truly philosophical in this operation of a null drawing is its displacement, but that is relative to the history of the scientific practices and of the sciences....
>
> ... Hence there is a history in philosophy rather than a history of philosophy: a history of the displacement of the indefinite repetition of a *null trace* whose effects are *real*. (Althusser 1971, 38)

The analytical deployment of the notion of overdetermination and of its theoretical consequences enables us to approach the problem of *conjuncture*—or of structure *as* conjuncture—that is organized around the question of theory in the key of the intelligibility of history. The theoretical zone that grants consistency to the interrogation of the materialist philosophical problematic is the key of its *scientificity*. Althusser's so-called "theoreticist deviation," far from constructing a pantheoreticism or a hypertrophied formalism, allows the pointing out of the *limits* of theory and, consequently, opens up the road to the possibility of thinking of a materialist philosophy in its full right—that means, one that attempts to make history thinkable without subsuming it into its own logic. We place the nerve of this movement in the concept of overdetermination that, by being proposed as a key to the intellection of a conjuncture, lays down the limits to the *intelligible* in the *conjunctural*.

History leaves its mark on theory in the shape of a rupture that is, at the same time, a historical event and a movement within the theoretical: a folding of theory upon itself. The *rupture* that Althusser identifies in Marxist theory with regard to its own Hegelian genealogy is not only historical or only theoretical. It is, rather, the *distance*, the twisted space that opens up between the historical and the theoretical, where the paradox of a *unity in disjunction* is at work.[19] Only this way can the notion of rupture be kept—only vaguely because of the Bachelardian encumberment that Althusser would later berate himself for and that Balibar rigorously defines (1978)—if any degree of precision needs to be established.

Marx's rupture with Hegel does not simply consist of a "cut," in the sense of a *demarcation* of theoretical formations with regard to its nontheoretical (ideological) predecessors; but rather, it is that and also the index of an *endless process* that turns the Althusserian position into a *(re)commencement* of the Marxist position: its reading, its transformation, and its struggle for existence. Its life and its crisis.

The Althusserian enterprise to produce a materialist philosophy by searching for it in Marx's theoretical production describes the form of a displacement that results in an *aporia*: the immanent philosophy of Marxist theoretical practices is, as such, its *interior criterion*. But it is not immanent only to Marx's theory; it is immanent also to the political practices of the workers' movement, as it stands out in a barely superficial reading of the classical texts: "So we shall start by considering practices in which the Marxist dialectic as such is in action: Marxist theoretical practice and Marxist political practice" (Althusser 2005, 173). The *aporia* is, then, that philosophy can only be thought of in its internal condition to a determinate science, if it is assumed also as the reading of that which results exterior to itself, because it is immanent to nonscientific practices. We have then that *philosophy is internal to science and overflows it at the same time*. This is the materialist philosophical position that will be built—not as a discourse but as an acting philosophy—in the process of theoretical work that encompasses almost three decades of writing.

If, as I said above, the Althusserian problematic consists of dealing with the *disjointed union* of the theoretical and the political, Althusser turns this aporetic solution into the materialist formula for the problem that Marx's "discovery" puts in tension: the impossible encounter of philosophy and history is reinscribed as a contradictory *union* between theory and politics.[20]

This underscores the need for a critique of the philosophical tradition that identifies knowledge with political action and of the emphasis on the rupture of the Marxist operation with humanist tendencies, which Althusser defines as the Philosophies of Conscience in a clear nod toward psychoanalysis and its counter-epistemological potency.

On this line, Althusser will hold that the Marxist problematic takes shape as an operation of rupture within the very field of that hegemonic cypher (the Subject) that identifies knowledge with history. This operates as a matrix not only of philosophical thought, but also of common sense. "All of modern Western philosophy [is] dominated by the 'problem of knowledge,'" says Althusser, and then clarifies: dominated by the ideological solution, imposed and anticipated to the formulation of the right question; imposed by "practical, religious, ethical and political 'interests' foreign to the reality of the knowledge" (Althusser and Balibar 1970, 53). The formulation of the materialist philosophy that takes consistency in this Marxist operation of rupture is only possible on the basis of producing a non-humanist conception of the process of knowledge—that is to say, one that does not require the figure of the knowing Subject as a mirrored construction—at once *form* and *norm*—of the empirical knowing subjects. This critique of epistemology itself coincides with the practice of the new problematic of overdetermination as the formula for the comprehension of a *processual topique*:

> I will note in passing that the concept of *process without a subject* upholds the work of Freud. But speaking of a process without a subject implies that the notion of subject is ideologic. If this double thesis is taken seriously: 1. the concept of process is scientific; 2. the notion of subject is ideologic; two distinct consequences follow; 1. the revolution of the sciences, the science of history becomes formally possible; 2. a revolution in philosophy: since all of classical philosophy rests on the categories of subject + object (object = mirrored reflection of the subject). But this positive inheritance is still formal. The question posed is then: Which are the conditions of the process of history? Marx owes nothing to Hegel there: he contributes on the decisive point something unprecedented: there is process only under relationships. (Althusser, in D'Hondt 1973, 119, my translation)

This means that, if science has itself a history, we need to accept that even if the "human individuals are its agents," knowledge may not be understood as the faculty of a subject, neither transcendental, nor empirical, nor psychological. Rather, thought develops as *a process under relationships*—this means, inscribed in the concrete framework of a historical complexity. The *processual* condition of knowledge is its *historical* condition. The ontological strength of this phrase may not be tamed in a few paragraphs. In order to comprehend it, a long *detour* I may not traverse is required here; but I may, nonetheless, extract some of its consequences. The first one is that the historical is part of the definition of the theoretical itself. Now, this strange "consequence" we extract from Althusser's intervention in the seminar dictated by Jean Hyppolite at the beginning of the 1970s, and that can therefore be conceived of as part of an operation of "rectification," was already drafted in *Lire le Capital* (*Reading Capital*), where Althusser does not refrain from insisting on the necessity of conceiving knowledge as a

> historically constituted system of an apparatus of thought, founded on and articulated to natural and social reality. It is defined by the system of real conditions which make it, if I dare use the phrase, a determinate mode of production of knowledges. (Althusser and Balibar 1970, 42)

This system of theoretical production is articulated in a conjuncture: its practices are articulated with concrete economical, political, and ideological practices; that is their *determined existence*. This is what defines and assigns functions to the thought of singular individuals "who can only 'think' the 'problems' already actually or potentially posed; hence it is also what sets to work their 'thought power.'" This way, it stops being conceived of within the scheme of a dichotomy that opposes a conscience to the material world without a remainder (and which therefore reflects it mirrorlike). And, in exchange, it results in a "peculiar real system, established on and articulated to the real world of a given historical society"; a specific system of articulated practices, defined by the conditions of its existence, with a structure of its own (Althusser and Balibar 1970, 42).

The specific feature of knowledge rests on its capacity to indicate its own place among the many other social practices,[21] and it is therefore capable of indicating its own historical conditions, because it can also indicate the place and the historical conditions of the ideology it transforms and relegates to its own prehistory. Thus, the perspective of a *process of production* of knowledge as a material production process can be conceived recalling Marx's *Einleitung zur Kritik der politischen Ökonomie* (Marx 1964, 632) the conception of a "labour of transformation (*Verarbeitung*) of intuition (*Anschauung*) and the representation (*Vorstellung*) in concepts (*in Begriffe*)" (Althusser and Balibar 1970, 42). In this conception, the "raw material" of the *intuitions* and *representations* is not thought of in the sense of a sensitive intuition or a pure representation, but consists *always-already* of complex articulations, which combine, in turn, "sensuous, technical and ideological elements" (Althusser and Balibar 1970, 43). There never is a pure object, identical to the real object, as the starting point in the process of knowledge. There is *ideological* raw material that is transformed in the process of knowledge that produces, as a result, knowledges.

Thus considered, knowledge

> does not fall from the sky or from the "*human spirit*"; it is the product of a process of theoretical labor, it is subject to a material history, and includes among its determinant conditions and elements non-theoretical practices (economic, political and ideological) and their results. But, once produced and constituted, the formal-theoretical objects can and must serve as the object of a theoretical labor in the strong sense, must be analyzed, thought in their necessity, their internal relations, and developed in order to draw from them all the consequences—that is, all their wealth. (Althusser 1990, 51)

It is the concept of (overdetermined) *process* that indicates the historicity of the production of knowledge and also, therefore, its *articulation with nontheoretical practices.* If in the course of his self-criticism Althusser berates himself for not having fully contemplated the political dimension of the notion of rupture,[22] and derives from there a certain "deviation" that could result in a reading of the science/ideology demarcation in the idealistic key of error/falsehood, it is necessary to underline that its very definition as a theoretical *practice*, developed in "On Materialist Dialectics" already contains the crucial elements to avoid such confusion:

> Theory is a specific practice which acts on its own object and ends in its own product: a knowledge. . . . The knowledge of the process of this theoretical practice in its generality, that is, as the specified form or real difference of the practice, itself a specified form of the general process of transformation, of the "development of things," constitutes a first theoretical elaboration of Theory, that is, of the materialist dialectic. (Althusser 2005, 173)

I hold that the concept of *theoretical practice*, which acts at the center of his conception of knowledge, forces us to consider the relationship (and demarcation) between *science* and *ideology*—in the framework of a philosophy of the *historical* distinction between scientific and ideological practices, correlative to a materialist theory of historical formations. This means, within the *overdetermined causality*. This is understood as the name of the condition at once specific to and differentiated from the general and theoretical practice or inscribed in the general process of transformation. What this enigmatic reference deploys is nothing but the emphasis on the strict, practical condition of theoretical production and therefore points out the place where its specificity should be considered—that place is the thinking of an articulated complexity or, rather, of an overdetermined causality. This in turn allows us to think of the difference and the articulation of theoretical practice with those that are not identical to itself: the ideological practices; but this way, it opens up the possibility (and the necessity) of thinking of its difference and its articulation with other practices, economic, political.

It is, therefore, to the same extent that the inscription of the problem of knowledge is produced in the decentered *topique* of overdetermination (and this occurs at the same instant that *theory is thought of as praxis*) that the science/ideology difference *occupies* the site of the idealist truth/falsehood dyad and places, in its stead, a criterion that introduces the historical condition of *the concrete* and singular to the terrain of Epistemology. Against what Althusser may suggest in his self-criticism, this critical movement is less indebted to the Bachelardian notion of "epistemological rupture" than to the concept of *theoretical practice*, and to the materialist problematic as a thought of the differential articulation of practices.

It is the notion of overdetermination that produces the entry of history into philosophy, with regard to the "problem of knowledge." And it does so, additionally, with the virtue of not leading to any kind of relativism, to the extent that it is solidary with the premise according to which scientificity is conformed as an *immanent system* of effective theoretical practices; this means, following a criterion of *radical interiority* of scientific practices, because the definition of theoretical practices in their specificity rests on the possibility of conceptualizing their *relative difference* with regard to other kinds of practices.

If Althusser berates himself for not having given an adequate theoretical form to this idea, this does not authorize us to suppose that it is not already practically in action in his classical texts. This way, reflecting on ideology, a new materialist philosophy is produced as a *displacement*, taking the stead of the "problem of knowledge," historically occupied (constituted) by modern philosophy,

> since in this work of investigation and conceptualization we have to learn not to make use of this distinction in a way that restores the ideology of the philosophy of the Enlightenment, but on the contrary, to treat the ideology which constitutes the prehistory of a science, for example, as a real history with its own laws and as the real prehistory whose real confrontation with other technical practices and other ideological or scientific acquisitions was capable, in a specific theoretical conjuncture, of producing the arrival of a science, not as its goal, but as its surprise. (Althusser and Balibar 1970, 45)

And so much so that Althusser recalls Macherey's expression to hold that every science, in their relationship with ideology, can only be conceived as a "science of ideology"; assuming at the same time that "the object of knowledge, which can only exist in the form of ideology at the moment of constitution of the science" (Althusser and Balibar 1970, 46).

This issue is developed by Badiou under the idea that the pair science/ideology exists before each of its terms separately and this presupposes accepting that it is not a *distributive opposition* that could allow allocating the different practices and discourses, let alone valuing them abstractly. Their difference may not be apprehended as a *simple contradiction* but as a *process*: science is a process of *transformation-differentiation* and ideology is a process of *repetition-unification*. Saying that science is "science of ideology" implies that science produces the knowledge of an object of which a determinate region of ideology indicates the existence. But, additionally, science is the science of ideology because, reciprocally, ideology is always ideology for a science: The only discourses that are known as ideological are such in the retrospection of a science (cf. Badiou 1967).

We return, in this way, to the idea of "rupture" and somehow begin to glimpse, in the form of its relationship to ideology, the topological character of the weave that makes up the Althusserian problem of knowledge (in its processual and complex condition). The topological figures announce the relationship between the "problem of knowledge" and the notions of *conjuncture* and *overdetermination*.

> It is not exaggerated to say that DM [dialectical materialism] is at its highest point in this problem: How to think the articulation of science onto that which it is not, all the while preserving the *impure radicality of the difference*? How to think the non-relation of that which is doubly related? From this point of view, we can define DM as the formal theory of breaks. Our problem thus takes place in a much vaster conceptual context, which concerns all forms of articulation and rupture between and among instances of a social formation. (Badiou 1967, 20, my emphasis)

It is not about thinking the process of knowledge under the philosophical guise of a theater conceived as the *closed* and *mirrored* relationship of the protagonists of the epistemic bond, but about thinking it in the topological key of a problematic understood as a *combination* or *articulation* of elements resulting from a (theoretical and nontheoretical) *conjuncture*.

The ideological weave of classic philosophy, says Althusser, may be identified in the figure of the circle of *guarantee*, because it is the question about the guarantee of knowledge that places us in the ideological terrain of the philosophy that goes from the "Cartesian circle" up to the circle of Hegelian or Husserlian teleology (Althusser and Balibar 1970, 53). This circle explodes (and its explosion turns "visible") in the materialist premise that distinguishes, in order to never join again, the real object and the object of knowledge, such as Spinoza had noticed it earlier.[23] Althusser finds in Marx that *other* relationship of knowledge, understood now as a relationship of *appropriation*. That is where science turns out to be a specific (different) form from the several social forms of appropriating the world, politics, morals, aesthetics, and religion itself (Althusser 1998, 55).

Understanding the cognoscitive relationship as a form of *appropriation*, philosophy (as a "theory of practice") takes care of it, *but not only* of it; because in order to think about it, philosophy must be able to think about its difference—that is to say, its differential relationships to the other forms of appropriation that distinguish different practices. Every practice, as an activity of appropriation, presupposes two conditions: one is its *processual* and therefore *incomplete*, misconstrued character; the other, the always *improper* condition both of its object and of its result.

The "primacy of being over thought" may, in this framework, be translated in the sense of a *primacy of practices* (activity of conformation) with regard to the discourse of philosophy (having already become a form)—a primacy that, therefore, is in no way a "foundation." In this framework, philosophy becomes

> a discipline of this world, as a discipline that has this world as an object in the effective forms of its apprehension (of "its appropriation" said Marx): forms of perception, of action, of social and political practice, of the theoretical practice of the sciences, of art, of religion, etc. That autonomy of philosophy is expressed to us through the rejection of any "positivism," any "empiricism," any "psychologism," any "pragmatism." Because if the "truth" is this content, this thing or this formula of science, if truth is this "given" or this "object," in its opacity or in its transparency in fact, we do not know what can be done with philosophy. It suffices [that] with "studying reality" . . . philosophy will meet its natural death: it will be buried within existing sciences. (Althusser 1998, 28, my translation)

The Marxist notion of appropriation sets the problem of knowledge in the real terrain of practices *in* history and, consequently, also contaminates the philosophy that takes care of this problem with history. This is the sense in which a certain ambiguity or interchangeability that operates in the texts of the 1970s should be understood, where the *theory of theoretical practice* is also the "theory of practice in general—the materialist dialectic" (Althusser 2005, 169). It is not a mere rhetorical displacement, but a deep idea: a Theory of theoretical practice is already in itself a philosophy of the complex articulation of differentiated practices, a theory of a "social practice" that does not exist other than as a complexity of practices—which means, as an inconsistent generality:

> Thus, "social practice," the complex unity of the practices existing in a determinate society, contains a large number of distinct practices. . . . [T]his prior

condition is indispensable to an understanding of what theory itself, and its relation to "social practice" are for Marxism. (Althusser 2005, 167)

As the "Althusserian" Badiou deducted earlier, the "systematic organization" of the elemental notions of *historical materialism* through *dialectic materialism* produces the general concept of practice as an effect, understood as the process of transforming a given raw material. However,

> To say that the concept of practice is the most general concept of DM (its first regulated combination of notions) amounts to saying that in the "social whole" there exist only practices. . . . This also means that the generality of this concept does not belong to HM, but only to DM. The practice does not exist: "there is no practice in general, but only distinct practices." (Badiou 1967, 35)

History, as it is thought by historical materialism, only admits *concrete, determined, multiple practices*. It would seem that the radicality and potency of this thesis, which enable the placement of both ideological and theoretical practices (but also political practices) on the same terrain, have been insufficiently considered. And nevertheless, it is an altogether disruptive movement with regard to the traditionally described interplay of the pair *history* and *philosophy*.

Within this framework, Althusser's affirmation that "knowledge is concerned with the real world through its specific mode of appropriation of the real world" (Althusser and Balibar 1970, 54) should be considered. The question of knowledge will then be the question of the structure of that specific (and determined) mode of appropriation/transformation in which the *theoretical practices* consist of their difference (and therefore of their relationship) with regard to other practices.

This does not constitute a problem exclusive to the history of science, but engages philosophy itself—not only the region called "Philosophy of Science" but all of Philosophy (this means, a certain philosophical formation—of course not any philosophical formation, but the one that claims the name of *the* Philosophy) that develops from the standpoint of the question of knowledge and constitutes its function as the operator of a cognoscitive guarantee.

The materialist position disregards the question of an a priori guarantee of knowledge; it dissolves the philosophical (ideological) figure of the "epistemic drama" and, because of that, "staging the characters indispensable to this scenario . . . posing scientific consciousness the question of the conditions of possibility of its knowledge relation to its object" (Althusser and Balibar 1970, 54) loses its function. This confusion responds to the form in which philosophy has imagined the epistemic bond:

> a relation of interiority and contemporaneity between a mythical Subject and Object, required to take in charge, if need be by falsifying them, the real conditions, i.e., the real mechanism of the history of the production of knowledges, in order to subject them to religious, ethical and political ends (the preservation of the "faith," of "morality" or of "freedom," i.e., social values). (Althusser and Balibar 1970, 55)

Even if there still is a long road ahead before being able to speak about a fully materialist formulation of the problem of knowledge, the task of materialist philosophy with regard to this problem is indeed clear: to reflect on knowledge questioning its materials, without prefixing the answer with the "titles and rights" of other levels of social life (other concrete practices), morality, religion, and so on. Such is the double struggle supposed by formulating the problem of knowledge in materialist terms—that is to say, in an immanent relationship to concrete and determined theoretical practices, where their specificity lies—without subordinating them to the religious requisite of reading; but, then, without subordinating history to their purpose either.

The extent is remarkable to which the intervention on the "squares" occupied by the Philosophy of Knowledge constitutes a *political* strategy to deploy the new bond between philosophy and history. Surpassing this "turn of imagination"—which rests on the identification of *Logos* and history as the foundation of the "religious myth of reading"—demands placing the focus on the relationship proposed by Marx in terms of an "appropriation." This forbids resorting to the ideological solution that summons the characters Subject and Object in their *mirrored structure* of mutual recognition.

"Ideology is a process of redoubling, intrinsically . . . tied to the specular structure of fantasy. . . . If science is a process of transformation, ideology—insofar as the unconscious comes to constitute itself therein—is a process of repetition" (Badiou 1967, 37, my translation). There, it resorts to the *practices*, as modes of differential appropriation—what allows the reformulating of the relationship between *science* and *ideology*, in the terms of a *process*.

And precisely because it is a process of transformation, the cognoscitive relationship of appropriation is not configured around any kind of operator of warranties. It does not consist of a movement of closure; it supposes a singular and specific *structure*: a paradoxical *structure of aperture:*

> The paradox of the theoretical field is that it is an *infinite* because *definite* space, i.e., it has no limits, no external frontiers separating it from nothing, precisely because it is *defined* and limited within itself, carrying in itself the finitude of its definition, which, by excluding what it is not, makes it what it is. Its *definition* (a scientific operation *par excellence*), then, is what makes it both *infinite in its kind*, and marked inside itself, in all its determinations, by what is excluded from it *in it* by its very definition. (Althusser and Balibar 1970, 27)

This paradoxical condition of a space at once open and differentiated rests on what Althusser calls the "criterion of radical interiority" of knowledge in scientific practices. The structure of the theoretical field responds to the *paradoxical form* that supposes the coexistence of two premises, the *interior* condition of its definition and its *openness*, its lack of limits. In the aspects related to the problem of knowledge, the "criterion of radical interiority of the practices" establishes that *scientificity* is immanent to the theoretical practices, instead of constructing an a priori rationality or a prescriptive formula. But this is not all. The singularity of *immanent causality*, such as it is developed in the Althusserian problematic, is placed on the bond between the rationality of a formation and its *limits*, in that difficult-to-locate space where a *productive* mechanism is not merely *re-productive*.

That is the relationship between a formation and its limits because, in the case of theory, the "criterion of interiority" may not be uncoupled from the *open* condition of every science. As Étienne Balibar pointed out,

> Althusser, for his part, has not ceased to maintained that "the criteria of practice" for knowledge is internal to the theoretical practice, on condition that we remember that by definition a science is not a closed circle of ideas, but a practice opening on to other practices and on to its own development. (Balibar 1978, 211n5)

Althusser proposes his notions of theoretical problematic and symptomal reading in the framework of a rejection of the philosophical thesis that, by identifying truth with discourse, formulates the problem of knowledge as a problem about its guarantee, in a circular scheme tied to the specular structure of fantasy (Badiou 1967).

The *symptomal reading* is based on the consideration of a theoretical discourse that stems from "everything in it that 'sounds hollow' to an attentive ear, despite its fullness" (Althusser and Balibar 1970, 30). That is to say that reading, in order to be symptomal, must concentrate its attention on those zones where some imaginary formulas unavoidably weave into the theoretical texture, procuring to invest the spaces of *impasse*. And this is because it is there, in those extremely fragile spaces, where a science lives: a theory "depends less for its life on what it knows than on what it does not know" (Althusser and Balibar 1970, 30). It is those spaces alluded by the presence of ideological elements that indicate the *limits* of the theoretical discourse and constitute, for that same reason, its more vital points. That is why Althusser underlined the *paradoxical* movement he proposes as the matrix of theory: science is the science of ideology.

On other occasions, Althusser alluded to this thesis by evoking the Spinozian expression according to which:

> It is just because (*enim*) we possess (*habemus*) a true idea that . . . that we can also say: "*Verum index sui et falsi*"; what is true is the sign both of itself and of what is false, and the recognition of error (and of partial truths) depends on starting from what is true. (Althusser 1976, 185–86, ellipse in the original)

Truth is always uncovered in a process of secondary order; it is a retroactive reading of what was already there. But it may not be said that reading is itself what locates truth, each and every time it has the theoretical discourse she reads as a condition. Philosophical reading draws itself, therefore, as a transition between the gesture that reads and uncovers that which was already there without being uncovered. It is a *process without Subject, Origin, or End* where truth is not an attribute to be found, but the effect of a misadjustment.

UNCONSCIOUS-*SIVE* POLITICS: WORDS TO *(RE)COMMENCE*

The action of demarcation, profoundly bound to the problem of *reading*—and therefore of knowledge—places philosophy in a *liminal* space. The question we may ask, from then on, is whether a formula capable of defining *diagonal-philosophy* in the field of the materialist premise of *immanence*, which the development of the problem of knowledge deploys under the condition of the *criterion of radical interiority of practices*, may be thought of. We return, finally and on another road—which is, in its ultimate determination, the same—to the problem of *excess*. And with it, to the relationship between philosophy and *topique*.

Under diverse formulas we find the effort of Althusserian thinking to avoid closing the circle of complexity by attributing a supra-historical dimension to philosophy, even in the terms of a "practice" (a meta-*praxis*, practice of practices). On the contrary, with regard to the bond between philosophy and practices (always *concrete*, determined), Althusser insists on conceiving of philosophical materiality as the *reading of a topique* that is an *intervention*—a sort of abstract theoretical knowledge that is nonetheless heterogeneous to itself and that operates as a political intervention every time it assumes its own internal politicity.

This is how, early on in his well-known prologue to the second edition of *Pour Marx*, Althusser would explain the *philosophical* condition of his texts: "They are philosophical essays, with theoretical investigations as their objects, and as their aim an intervention in the present theoretico-ideological conjuncture in reaction to its dangerous tendencies. . . . They 'intervene' on two fronts, to trace, in Lenin's excellent expression, a 'line of demarcation' between Marxist theory on the one hand, and ideological tendencies . . . on the other" (Althusser 2005, 12).

That double condition—of being both a philosophical text and an intervention—would be translated years later into the paradoxical figure of the *eternity of philosophy*. "I will anticipate a tripe thesis: philosophy has no history = philosophy is 'eternal' = nothing happens in philosophy" (Althusser 1995, 333, my translation).

The "theory of the philosophy-effect" that consists of a repetition, of a nothingness that insists, and feeds back into an "eternal" causality, "in the sense in which Freud holds that the analytic unconscious is eternal" (Althusser 1995, 336, my translation) summons a structural causality that supposes a "system of instances between which the philosophical unconscious figures" (Althusser 1995, 337, my translation).

We arrive, thus, at the place of the (paradoxical) relationship between the *limit* and the *necessity* of overdetermination in the Althusserian problematic. This concept aims at an immanent, concrete, and decentered rationality that assumes the paradoxical bond of logics to the singular. *Paradoxical*, because singularity is itself a category of logic, but it is also a category on the *limits of logic*. In this sense, as a concept, overdetermination is placed at the limits of the conceptual; or to put it more controversially, it is the *limit-concept* of the bond between the conceptual and the nonconceptual.

Thus, *overdetermination* is an attempt to answer—perhaps an answer that still has not found its question, or that has not managed to formulate it in adequate terms—the problem of the *necessity in history*, a necessity that does not only coexist but also organizes itself *working as a limit*. It is not only about making history *thinkable*, but also about taking on the commitment to think about the historically concrete and singular while situated in its midst (without, thereby, as I have said, reducing it to a mere relativistic historicization of thought nor to a "history of ideas"). This sort of dialectic—if the term is still even fitting—is found in action and is more or less "visible" in the structure of *aperture* acknowledged by Althusserian thought to a theoretical *Gliederung*. And it advances producing a trench, a profound contradiction within philosophical discursivity itself, from which there is, however, no escape: "It is not a matter of 'suppressing philosophy' . . . any more than the Freudian cure would consist of suppressing the unconscious" (Althusser 1995, 340, my translation).[24]

As a specific principle of the materialist dialectic, overdetermination takes shape in the question of the *necessity that operates as scientific rationality* and enables the accounting of the complex and decentered condition of the Marxist historical totality. In this sense, overdetermination is proposed as a principle of intelligibility, a cypher of *rationality*. And yet—and this is essential to the question—in its logical development, it resorts to the *detour* and to exceptionality in order to think of the materialist commitment to necessity in *existence*—in other terms, in order to place the *singularity* of the concrete in history and the *real* and *processual* condition of its transformations, or the efficacy of political practice.

Conceptualizing overdetermination may be an impossible task or a paradoxical ambition, but it is precisely for that reason that we may affirm that it signals the *(re)beginning* of materialism in Althusserian philosophy.

Philosophy is in itself always a repetition (or better yet, *iteration*): a play of positions without development toward any single place—but with *real effects*. The introduction of this all but new term is the position of a difference within the philosophical field, and that is why its beginning is always a *(re)beginning*. Because of that, it is also more convenient to speak of a "materialist position *in* philosophy" rather than a "materialist philosophy."

An overdetermined weave may be accessed at any point from the theoretical perspective but not at any point from a political perspective. This dual disposition (theoretical and political) is not a dualism of thought (and thus, perhaps, what Badiou didn't get from Althusserian materialism), it is rather the effort to hold a space *between* both problematic planes and to make that space consistent as a "problematic"—as a *disjointed union*. It is therefore not capricious for Althusser to search for the operationality of the overdetermination principle in both fields—theoretical and political—simultaneously. On one side, the materialist dialectic is read as an immanent rationality of Marx's theoretical practices and as such, in Marx's scientific production, overdetermination is "torn away" from its practical performance. But that is not everything; the notion of overdetermination takes shape in Lenin's *political* strategy, in the thought of practical experience, in the field of its experience itself, which borders on the contemporaneity of the conjuncture.

> This is what is irreplaceable in Lenin's texts: the analysis of the structure of a conjuncture, the displacements and condensations of its contradictions and their paradoxical unity, all of which are the very existence of that "current situation" which political action was to transform, in the strongest sense of the word, between February and October, 1917. (Althusser 2005, 179)

Irreplaceable, Lenin's thought is a *political thought*, a thought that develops in the matter of politics. It is not the thought of a *theoretician* "who necessarily reflects on necessity's *fait accompli*" but the thought of political action, "on the necessity to be achieved" (Althusser 2005, 179).

Of course, it is not about finding Marx's "theory" in Lenin's "*praxis*"; nor about adding some theoretical practices to other political practices. It is about, on the contrary, thinking that a materialist problematic takes its consistency *between* theoretical practices and political practices and *between* scientific and political faces in a *topique*: therein lies the singularity of the materialist position in philosophy that the Althusserian enterprise procures.

It would be excessive to hurry onto conjectures regarding the multiple factors that assisted to the brutal silencing and mocking of Althusserian thought. We cannot, however, refrain from remembering the disquieting suggestion Étienne Balibar launched on friends and foes alike, at the end of the 1980s: "For almost twenty years, Althusser was, the controversial Marxist in France . . . . Wiping out the role of Althusser in this period is a typical aspect of a more general censorship, which has a very precise meaning: it means denying that Marxism in the post-war period (especially in the 60s and 70s) was not a simple repetition of dogmas" (Balibar 1993, 2).

NOTES

1. "The original Althusserian endeavor—with politics in the background—attempted to rescue Marxism by regenerating its theory; but this commitment brought—as Althusser himself

acknowledges—a grievous absence: that of political practice (class struggle). In his self-critical effort, he attempted to reintegrate practice, but relating it—and besides not through a necessary and essential bond—to theory. But, in this case, theory is not a science or knowledge, but a philosophy or a theoretical detachment of ideology. Theory as the sphere of truth remains autonomous and self-sufficient. In spite of his own rectifications and achievements in his hard self-criticism, Althusser has not been able to overcome his theoreticist "deviation" (Sánchez Vázquez 1975, 99, my translation).

2. After Althusser's death, in 1990, the edition of his unpublished writings was carried out tenaciously by the IMEC (Institut Mémoires de l' édition contemporaine) and the publishing house Stock and through the effort of many researchers who persisted in compiling, translating, and distributing a great number of his writings.

3. I refer both to his more or less direct disciples, such as Étienne Balibar, Jacques Rancière, Alain Badiou, Michel Pêcheux, and Pierre Macherey, as well as those who have critically recovered some of his problems or categories, such as Michel Foucault, Jacques Derrida, Slavoj Žižek, Ernesto Laclau, Judith Butler, and others.

4. Doubtlessly, in this sense, the Althusserian reading of Machiavelli can contribute to such an undertaking.

5. "Condensation is brought about by omission: that is, that the dream is not a faithful translation or a point-for-point projection of the dream-thoughts, but a highly incomplete and fragmentary version of them" (Freud 2010, 299).

6. "Unconscious thought constitutes a 'factory of thoughts' that produces 'nodal points' upon which a great number of the dream-thoughts converged, and because they had several meanings." (Freud 2010, 291)

7. "If it is true, as Leninist practice and reflection prove, that the revolutionary situation in Russia was precisely a result of the *intense overdetermination* of the basic class contradiction, we should perhaps ask what is *exceptional* about this 'exceptional *situation*,' and whether, like all exceptions, this one does not clarify its rule—is not, unbeknown to the rule, *the rule itself*. For, after all, *are we not always in exceptional situations?*" (Althusser 2005, 104).

8. "*Topique*" is used in this article in the sense of a "topographic representation of the psychic apparatus," following its psychoanalytic and later Althusserian use, rather than its more colloquial meaning.

9. That is why the whole lineage of critique formulated by diverse generations of *Cultural Studies* against this Althusserian problem is, from the beginning, poorly based. It could be said that, in some ways, Stuart Hall could be considered an exception, at least for his honest reading of Althusser's writtings: cf. Hall, 1985. Even though, it must be said, his approach contributed to crystallizing a consideration of the type of "Althusserian structuralism" that ignores its links to the concepts of plural temporality and class struggle, and an impoverished conception of ideology as a cultural theory of consciousness that dispenses with the concept of the unconscious (cf. among others, Hall 1977).

10. "Such is Marx's second reading: a reading which might well be called '*symptomatic*' (*symptomale*), insofar as it divulges the undivulged event in the text it reads, and in the same movement relates it to a *different text*, present as a necessary absence in the first. . . . Marx's second reading presupposes the existence of *two texts*, and the measurement of the first against the second. . . . [T]he *second text* is articulated with the lapses in the first text" (Althusser and Balibar 1970, 28).

11. Thus, Althusser demonstrates the relationship between the concentric *topique* of consciousness that the *Phenomenology of Spirit* prescribes and the conception of history as a teleological process: "*A circle of circles, consciousness has only one centre,* which solely determines it; it would need circles *with another centre than itself—decentered circles—*for it

to be affected at its centre by their effectivity, in short for its essence to be over-determined by them. But this is not the case. This truth emerges even more clearly from the Philosophy of History," according to which, *"the simplicity of Hegelian contradiction is never more than a reflection of the simplicity of this internal principle of a people, that is, not its material reality but its most abstract ideology"* (Althusser 2005, 102–3).

12. "If the Marxist dialectic is 'in principle' the opposite of the Hegelian dialectic, if it is *rational and not mystical-mystified-mystificatory*, this radical distinction must be manifest in its essence, that is, in its characteristic determinations and structures. . . .[T]hese structural differences can be demonstrated, described, determined and thought" (Althusser 2005, 93–94).

13. "Lenin gave this metaphor above all a practical meaning. A chain is as strong as its weakest link. . . . So far there is no revelation here for readers of Machiavelli" (Althusser 2005, 94).

14. One could even think, as Balibar seems to suggest (1978) that the history of Althusserian thought coincides with the movement of self-criticism. In that sense, in addition to the later prologue to the second edition of *Pour Marx* I have already mentioned, his *Éléments d'autocritique* (1974), *Lénine et la philosophie* (1971), *Marx dans ses limites* (1977) (cf. Althusser 1994), among many others could be mentioned, including, doubtlessly, his posthumously published last writings on aleatory materialism.

15. The suggestive essay "'Piccolo Teatro': Bertolazzi and Brecht: Notes on a Materialist Theatre," originally published in 1962 and later included in *For Marx* (Althusser 2005, 129–51), reveals this singular conception.

16. It may be suitable to open up a discussion about the total coincidence of overdetermination and politics that would lead us to establish some qualms with regard to thinking the key of a political ontology from an Althusserian perspective, in the sense that is proposed in the current framework of the so-called postfoundational thought.

17. Some interesting efforts of reading the connections between Althusser and Badiou have been done. (Cf. Farrán 2013)

18. This effort is, not fortuitously, what connects Althusser's philosophical intervention to the psychoanalytic stake of Lacan, who, on another order of problems, seems to develop a similar process: "In the course of his teaching, he explored different ways *jouissance* is captured by the signifier. Starting with the phallus, also designated as the signifier of *jouissance*, Lacan inaugurates an extraordinary series of terms that replace one another . . . . In fact, each of these terms may be considered a 'loose piece,' to use Jacques-Alain Miller's formulation, an element of the real that, through the operation of signification, is elevated to the dignity of the signifier, acting as a signifier, in order to stitch together what does not remain together." (Šumic 2011, 49, my translation)

19. Althusser puts this figure of *unity of disjunction* forth to account for the complexity of the Marxist problematic: "This attitude may be paradoxical, but Marx insists on it in categorical terms as the absolute condition of possibility of his theory of history; it reveals the existence of two problems, distinct in their disjoint unity. There is a theoretical problem which must be posed and resolved in order to explain the mechanism by which history has produced as its result the contemporary capitalist mode of production. But at the same time there is another absolutely distinct problem which must be posed and resolved, in order to understand that this result is indeed a social mode of production, that this result is precisely a form of social existence and not just any form of existence" (Althusser and Balibar 1970, 65).

20. A labor of research would be needed here, aimed at establishing the difference between the "union" employed by Althusser and the unity that could be derived from the Hegelian idealist dialectic, in order to specify to which extent a *dialectic* can be still spoken of. That is

not something I may develop here, but I cannot refrain from indicating the necessity of this task.

21. In contrast, ideology erases its own conditions of production and offers itself with the strength of tautological evidence, whose most accomplished form is still that of the discourse of the religious Subject "I am he who is."

22. This can be read in the prologue to the second edition of *Pour Marx* I already mentioned.

23. "As Spinoza has already put it, the concept *dog* cannot bark" (Althusser and Balibar 1970, 101).

24. "Il n'est pas question de 'supprimer la philosophie' . . . pas plus qu'il n'est question, dans la cure freudienne, de supprimer l'inconscient." (Althusser 1995, 340)

Chapter Five

Political Desire of the True

No Future without Marx

The question on how to address Marxist theory today in itself implies the rejection of simplified answers. For different reasons, Marxism could be considered—at the same time—extremely actual and almost dead, and while its conceptualization of *Capital*'s mechanism is unavoidable, the topic of "the crisis of Marxism" appears to be the current starting point for any productive approach to Marxism.

This contradiction has been captured by Étienne Balibar in this very suggestive idea: "There is no Marxist philosophy, and there never will be; on the other hand, Marx is more important for philosophy than ever before" (Balibar 1995, 1).

In a quite general way, one can understand this thesis in the sense of Derrida's position:

> It will be more and more a fault, a failing of theoretical, philosophical, political responsibility. When the dogma machine and the "Marxist" ideological apparatuses . . . are in the process of disappearing, we no longer have any excuse, only alibis, for turning away from this responsibility. There will be no future without this. Not without Marx, no future without Marx. (Derrida 1994, 14)

In a tense dialogue with this idea, I recall Balibar's question on why Marx will still be read in the twenty-first century "not only as a monument of the past but as a contemporary author" (Balibar 1995, 1). Besides sharing the aim, Balibar's development wouldn't entirely subscribe Derrida's thesis that "there must be more than one Marx," stated to produce his own call for a new reading of it in the twilight of the twentieth century. Balibar wouldn't subscribe to it because, in the trail of Lenin, his reading implies a *choice*, a side-taking in a *kampfplatz,* which certainly includes some criterion of the true—at least a practical or non-explicit one. Still, they both concur in the idea that it is the future, the very possibility of willing a future, that waits to be rediscovered in these spectral or "contemporary" writings. And it seems that, as in the darkest moments of twentieth century, heterodox philosophical thinking (such as Benjamin's, Adorno's, Lukacs's, Gramsci's, Althusser's) will be the one that actually will develop its critical potencies.

To search the *actual* Marx, this essay intends to follow the apparent contradiction of the dead and the future. In this sense, Louis Althusser would be the philosophical name of the kind of anachronism I aim to circumscribe: the one of the so-called *theoreticism*. In this sense, I will pose the thesis that the effort of giving rise to the very political power of Marxist theory today requires rigorous work on the precise status of theory itself. Far from speculative pleasure, this statement follows a strict urgency of current conjuncture: the menace of a joint venture between technocratic ideology and the worse kind of political spontaneism, the sort of *right-wing leftism* embodied in desperate or paranoid masses.

In this context governed by technocratic thinking, a paradoxical nonphilosophical practice of philosophy would arise as the most *actual* anachronism of Marx. As the most enigmatic, delicate, and powerful phrase of *The Eighteenth Brumaire of Luis Bonaparte* had suggested, there is an unwritten theory of time in the pulse of Marx's theory.

> The social revolution of the nineteenth century cannot take its poetry from the past but only from the future. It cannot begin with itself before it has stripped away all superstition about the past. The former revolutions required recollections of past world history in order to smother their own content. The revolution of the nineteenth century must let the dead bury their dead in order to arrive at its own content. There the phrase went beyond the content—here the content goes beyond the phrase. (Marx 1937, 6)

The enigma of the dislocation (*décalage*) between the phrase and the content opens the field of a theory of time that is both a practical defense of philosophy and a political call to assume the task that has to be done (cf. Catanzaro and Ipar 2003)—or, moreover, a defense of philosophy in its right

READING CAPITAL (AGAIN)

to existence, that can only be posed by means of a rigorous consideration of its inherent political core.

Many debates have been developed since Althusser's philosophical intervention. As Warren Montag has stated, "More had been written against him than about him . . . . [T]o denounce him as a Stalinist, as structuralist, or both, most of his critics, despite their often incompatible theoretical and political positions, unwittingly collaborate to produce an overwhelmingly negative judgment of his work" (Montag 2013, 1).

In this sense, the most significant concurrence is that one of Jacques Rancière and E. P. Thompson, who come together in an extremely dedicated struggle with Althusser, however for the opposite motives, but run into a similar conclusion: the rejection of theoreticism as a mostly conservative thought. While the latter considers the critique to historicism as a pure disregard of any political *praxis*, the former concedes that the most "theoreticist" thesis of Althusser *paradoxically* encouraged many young students to take part in political struggle, but nevertheless accuses his theory of furnishing a kind of solution "from above" to the revisionist crisis, which misconceives the power of the masses.[1] It is not my purpose to accurately discuss here these critiques,[2] but to notice that each of them embodies those specularly opposite ideological tendencies Althusser was fighting with, inside Marxist field: *historicism* as the blurring of the difference between the theory of history and the history of theory (and, consequently, the subordination of the real scientific practices to idealist philosophy's normative regulation) and *politicism* as the dilution of the difference between theoretical thought and political thought (and, consequently, the subordination of politics to an idealist, epistemological conception of *practice*). The Althusserian position resists *avant la lettre* both reductions of the overdetermined complex of concrete practices against the imaginary immediacy of an abstract, general, and pure *praxis*.

It might be difficult to understand, but it should be underlined, that it was for the purpose of conceiving the proper conception of the *concrete differences* of the most heterogeneous social practices that Althusser was driven to pose the problem of theory itself. In this regard, I suggest that the critical revision of idealist epistemology—to which Althusser was dedicated, during the early 1960s—was the prerequisite to consider concrete practices, in their different historical articulation and in the singular forms of their concrete existence. I propose, therefore, that the so-called "theoreticist" approach to Marx's *Capital* was organized by this aim, and it is this complex connection between politics and theory that happens to be misconstrued today when the worth of Marxist theory comes into debate (Althusser and Balibar 1970, 32).[3]

To explore *Capital* in order to look or find a genuine materialist approach is to demand that theory assume its own practical condition. And to pose the practical entity of theory is to problematize (recursively) the procedure of reading itself:

> I merely proposed a *"symptomatic" reading* of the works of Marx and of Marxism, one with another, i.e., the progressive and systematic production of a reflection of the problematic on its objects such as to make them *visible*, and the disinterment, the production of the deepest-lying problematic which will allow us to *see* what could otherwise only have existed allusively or practically. As a function of this demand, I can claim to have *read* the specific theoretical form of the Marxist dialectic in its directly political existence (and actively political: the policies of a revolutionary leader—Lenin—immersed in the revolution). . . . But this *reading* was not, nor could have been, a direct reading or the merely *"generalizing"* reading. . . . This reading was in principle a *dual* reading, the result of a different, "symptomatic" reading, which introduced into a *question* an answer given to its absent question. (Althusser and Balibar 1970, 33)

The *Reading Capital* enterprise is an appeal to produce the practical exercise of posing two questions at the same time: the question of the object of *Capital*, and the question of the specificity of the *relation* of theory with its object: "the question of the nature of the type of discourse set to work to handle this object, the question of scientific discourse" (Althusser and Balibar 1970, 14).

It is the question of theoretical discourse (a recursive interrogation about theoretical status) that is placed in the immanent space of existent and concrete theory. So, I may say that it is this meta-question what Althusser finds in a "practical state" in Marx's works: the immanency of a *practical criterion of the true*. The question about the specific status of theory, interrogated in its practical condition—in other words, *practice taken as the nature of theory* itself and not as any kind of "corruption," "expression," "application," "second instance," and so on—needs to be developed into two completely separated problematics, even though they exist together: the "epistemic" problem of the strictly scientific status of some determinate practices (therefore, the validation criteria "purely *internal* to the practice"[4]) and the problem of the material (historical) existence of scientific practices in a wider (extra-theoretical) conjuncture.

It must be underlined that there is a slight—but substantial—difference between the sort of critique Althusser discovers in Marx and a mere post-foundationalist critique to metaphysics, which is somehow implied in it. The difference lies in the exigency of deriving from the critique a new positive theory of knowledge production, which of course involves the question of how to discern a criterion of the true. There is no Marxist theory (neither as scientific discourse nor as political thought) if this requirement is abandoned to epistemological (or cultural) relativism.

This supposes an intellectual effort of stating theoretical specificity regarding other discursive formations and regarding other (nontheoretical) practices. Finally, this assumes a complex conception of *practice,* irreducible to a *simple or general relationship to real*—be that the notion of an immediate-corporeal contact with things or an immediate cognition of the truth (either in empiricist or idealist versions).

It was by means of a dual reading of *Capital* that Althusser was capable of identifying the complex bond that connects these two incommensurable (while quite imbricated) dimensions of a theoretical combination (*Verbindung*). It was by means of that practice of reading—which included the interrogation about reading procedures—that he was able to reach the singular dialectic that *conjoins and tenses* history and theory (as a double problem of the conjuncture as a result of historical process and as a structural mechanism).

> When we pose the question of the *mechanism* by which the *object* of knowledge produces the cognitive appropriation of the *real object*, we are posing a quite different question from that of the conditions of the *production* of knowledge. This latter question is derived from a theory of the history of theoretical practice, which, as we have seen, is only possible given the application of the concepts which enable us to think the structure of that practice and the history of its transformations. The question we are posing is a new one, one which is precisely passed over in silence in the other. The theory of the history of knowledge or theory of the history of theoretical practice enables us to understand *how* human knowledges are produced in the history of the succession of different modes of production, first in the form of ideology, then in the form of science. (Althusser and Balibar 1970, 70)

There, where superficial and precipitated readings have seen a dichotomy between "structure" and "genesis," and a subsequent choice for pure formalist standpoint, Althusser gives rise to a completely different question: the question of the singular (materialist) philosophical practice, capable of making room for the two problems *at the same time* (now renamed as the problem of a conjuncture as a "result" and the problem of a conjuncture as a "mechanism").

This is the question of dialectical materialism. Not dialectical materialism as a philosophical system, but dialectical materialism just as it is *in action*—working in a practical state—in Marx's writings.

OVERDETERMINATION: PRACTICE AND TIME

To pose the difference between Marx's and Hegelian dialectics, Althusser tried to name it with the Freudian notion of *overdetermination*. He followed the idea that the materialist conception of necessity may be developed in terms of the deep connection that bonds a *noncontemporary* concept of temporality with the complex structure of the social whole:

> *The structure of the social whole* must be strictly interrogated in order to find in it the secret of the conception of history in which the "development" of this social whole is thought . . . with the object of constructing *the Marxist concept of historical time* on the basis of the Marxist conception of the social totality." (Althusser and Balibar 1970, 96)

Whereas, in the idealist conception of social totality as a *spiritual whole*, real practices have no incidence but that one already presupposed by an essential philosophical principle (Althusser and Balibar 1970, 96).[5]

The question of effectivity is the question of philosophy, inasmuch as it is the question of the "laws of history." It must be considered, therefore, that Marxist intervention is emplaced in an already occupied field, by the Cartesian mechanistic system or the Leibnizian concept of expression—inasmuch as the scientific discovery of the theory of history developed in *Capital as a critical work* contained "in the practical state" (that is to say, without producing *the concept* of it in a philosophical opus) a "simple question" so new and unforeseen that "it contained enough to smash all the classical theories of causality":

> The mechanistic system, Cartesian in origin, which reduced causality to a *transitive* and analytical effectivity: it could not be made to think the effectivity of a whole on its elements, except at the cost of extra-ordinary distortions.... But a second system was available, one conceived precisely in order to deal with the effectivity of a whole on its elements: the Leibnizian concept of *expression*. This is the model that dominates all Hegel's thought. But it presupposes in principle that the whole in question be reducible to an *inner essence*, of which the elements of the whole are then no more than the phenomenal forms of expression, the inner principle of the essence being present at each point in the whole. (Althusser and Balibar 1970, 187)

As Balibar has posed (1993), both systems had been rejected by Marx in his *Thesis on Feuerbach*, but it had been especially from the rupture implied in *Thesis VI*, which rejects at the same time essential principle and phenomena attributes, that a new materialist causality can be shaped as a movement of a double struggle against idealism and empiricism (Marx 1976, 74).[6] Not without twists and turns, in a zigzagging way, with attempts and rectifications,[7] Althusser needs to go that far to reach the necessary space to pose a problem that has been so near all the time. What lies behind this ontological exploration is the belief that the proper statement of the *primacy of practice over theory* can only emerge from a proper critique of the ideological (idealist) notion of *practice*, insofar as it hides an unseen primacy of ideas (philosophy) over (historical determinated) practices. In this sense, a *dual reading* is the critical reading of that double movement, in which the foreclosure of the practical condition (and historical commitment) of *theory* accords with an ideological image of *practice* (finally constrained to *humanism*).

This critical procedure is implied in what Althusser, following Bachelard—in the peculiar way that Balibar has pointed out (Balibar 1978, 207–37), has called *rupture* (Althusser 2005, 277).[8] The Althusserian conception of *rupture* should be understood against the empiricist conception of time expressed in the image of an "essential section" (Althusser and Balibar 1970, 314)[9] : "the possibility of reading in the immediacy of a present (or of an instant) the whole system of determinations of a historical phenomenon" (Althusser and Balibar 1970, 314). And this takes us to a singular (almost paradoxical) conception of an *event that is a process* or a singular kind of break: the beginning of a process with no end (Balibar 1978, 207–37), where any reduction of the couple science/ideology to the philosophical dichotomy truth and error has no place.

In this sense, it should be underlined that the conception of a plural temporality is the core of materialism. And, if it is pursued as a *concept of time*, it is because it already worked in the very *practical process* in which Marxist materialism thought took place—a heterogeneous and contradictory process that conjoins theoretical and political practices: that of political men such as Lenin, who "meets Imperialism in his political practice in the modality of a current existence: in a concrete present" and that of the theoretician of history or the historian, who "meet it in another modality, the modality of non-currency and abstraction" (Althusser 2005, 178).

The aim to achieve a kind of thought capable of putting together what already resist being in touch—political practice and theoretical practice, conceived in their differential articulation—claims a deep consideration of the concept of time. For it is *in relation with temporality* that one of the main aspects of their difference can be found: theoretical practice as the thought of fait accompli, and political practice as reflection "on the present in the present, *on the necessity to be achieved*, on the means to produce it, on the strategic application points for these means; in short, on his own action" (Althusser 2005, 178).

Therefore, the opportunity of formulating in a theoretical form the singularity of this materialism lies in the "space" opened by the duplicity of reading that pursues "a variable relationship between two inseparable terms: the unity of practice and theory" (Althusser 2017, 66).[10] Once the epistemological dichotomy is discarded, one can start considering the difference between theory and politics, within the framework of a new kind of philosophical practice—that of a paradoxical *conjunctural theory*, or a revolutionary science:

> This is what is irreplaceable in Lenin's texts: the analysis of the structure of a *conjuncture*, the displacements and condensations of its contradictions and their paradoxical unity, all of which are the very existence of that "current situation" which political action was to transform, in the strongest sense of the word, between February and October, 1917. (Althusser 2005, 179)

THEORY *SIVE* PRACTICE

In his preface to *Reading Capital*, Althusser wonders,

> Need I add that once we have broken with the religious complicity between Logos and Being; between the Great Book that was, in its very being, the

> World, and the discourse of the knowledge of the world; between the essence of things and its reading—once we have broken those tacit pacts in which the men of a still fragile age secured themselves with magical alliances against the precariousness of history and the trembling of their own daring—need I add that, once we have broken these ties, a new conception of *discourse* at last becomes possible? (Althusser and Balibar 1970, 18)

Why could one say that the question of dialectics, as I have just developed in the previous part of this essay, is compelled in the gesture of posing the discursive status of theory? In *Philosophy for Non-Philosophers*, published in 2017 in English, Althusser develops an answer that might be understood in the sense I have stated: as a double-fronted battle against idealism of general practice, and empiricism of pure theory (which involves an illusion of transparency in language). This suppose two movements: (1) the critique of every image of practice, as an *imaginary immediate relationship to the real*, which Althusser recognizes as an element of the genealogy of the Myth of Eden; and (2) the effort of giving rise to a materialist conception of practice.

In the chapter, titled "The Myth of State of Nature," Althusser (2017) inscribes empiricism within the legacy of religious discourse, while suggesting that the epistemological *adequatio rei et intellectus* is deeply committed to an ideological notion of practice as an immediate relationship to the real, indebted to the "religious myth of reading":[11]

> Not only was it enough to stretch out one's hand to pick fruit that was always ripe in order to satisfy one's hunger and thirst; it was also enough for Adam to see something with his eyes or take it in his hand in order to know it completely. Contrary to what is all too often supposed, human beings had the right to know all things: this knowledge was provided by the senses, was identical to the understanding in man, was identical to the words designating it, and was perfectly *immediate and transparent*. Adam did not have to work, produce or seek in order to know. (Althusser 2017, 72)

Althusser is dealing with the idealist notion of practice as an immediate relationship to the real, to show that the most corporeal images, those of mechanic materialism, empiricism of direct pure action, are constitutive elements of the inner world profiled by idealist discourse structure, insofar as that notion of practice is the specular inverted partner of pure theory. From the Greek, *theory* means "to contemplate," which, in a direct allusion to the opposition between manual handling and vision, supposes that "one *does not handle what one sees*": "the hand [*main*], which 'handles' [*manie*] or 'manipulates' [*manipule*], which works, is contrasted to the eye, which sees at a distance, . . . commonly called *consciousness*" (Althusser 2017, 79, bracketed text in the original).

It is in the persistence of this dichotomy that separates pure theory as *vision* and pure practice as *manual labor* where idealist epistemology and different kinds of idealism of practices (from empiricism to phenomenology) work together. What both emphases lack is the inherent complexity of real human relations to the world, where neither the theory nor the practice could be found isolated one from the other. Inasmuch as the specificity of materialism is understood in terms of a simple inversion of primacy of pure theory over pure practice, it is still captured by the whole idealist problematic. It is at this point where the core of Marxist materialism is interrogated to develop a new concept of practice, capable of avoiding binary schemes.

In order to deal with this question, Althusser introduces, by means of the triadic approach that is involved in the concept of *social practice of production*, a dialectical problematization of the Aristotelian distinction between *praxis* and *poiesis*.

It is Étienne Balibar who has pointed out clearly the deepness of Marx's philosophical revolution in this singular rupture of the Aristotelian distribution of practices into the types of *poiesis* and *praxis*, where the former alludes to determined actions in the sort of natural (mechanical) necessity, the latter names the inner subjective transformation of a Subject. With the concept of *production*:

> Marx removed one of philosophy's most ancient taboos: the radical distinction between *praxis* and *poiesis* . . . .
>
> . . . [Marx's materialism is] not a mere inversion of the hierarchy—a "theoretical workerism" if I can put it thus . . .—but the identification of the two, the revolutionary thesis that *praxis* constantly passes over into *poiesis* and vice versa. There is never any effective freedom which is not also a material transformation, which is not registered historically in exteriority. But nor is there any work which is not a transformation of the self . . . .
>
> . . . [S]uch a thesis cannot but affect the third term of the classical triptych: *theôria*. (Balibar 1995, 41)

There, where positivist interpretations of the *Thesis XI* might find an invitation to abandon philosophy, instead, a revolutionary turn in the question of materialism, which gives shape to an interrogation about the type of apodicticity capable of conceiving the distance between historical objectivity and the true, can be found. In this sense, the problem of conceptualizing the specificity of different practices is a matter of furnishing the problem of an immanent and complex causality. It is there where dialectical materialism, insofar as it confronts at the same time the images of Cartesian mechanistic system and Leibnizian expressive causality, might open the path to a rigorous theory of history, while revolutionizing the philosophical field.

The challenge of defining a *non-immediate* conception of practice coincides with the interrogation of the Marxist whole in terms of the conception of the overdeterminated condition of human practices.[12] With the notion of *social production*, the whole triptych (*praxis-poiesis-theôria*) is disrupted. And it is at this point where the concept of *production* arises in its philosophical depth—that is to say, surpassing a mere sociological scope.

As a practice, *production* is irreducible to the image of an immediate relationship to the real because it is irreducible to a simple dyadic relation (hand and nature). It is both impossible to state production as a pure practice not mediated by cognition, ideas, abstractions of all sorts (be that "consciousness" or technical knowledge, physical theories inscribed in tools, cultural ideas involved in different kinds of works, etc.) and, what is more, it is impossible to consider it without stressing the social character of the relationship that overdetermines the dialectical bond between *praxis* and *poiesis*.

If, as Balibar has pointed out, Marx removed the distinction between *praxis* and *poiesis,* it is because the radically new category of practice that takes shape in his philosophical intervention is part of a new ontological thought. It might be considered a *transindividual* ontology, inasmuch as practices only can be considered "individual" inasmuch as they are social. As he pointed out, in relation to the *Theses on Feuerbach*, especially *Thesis IV*:

> It is significant that Marx (who spoke French almost as fluently as he did German) should have resorted to the foreign word *"ensemble"* here, clearly in order to avoid using the German "das ganze," the whole or totality.
>
> Perhaps things would be clearer formally [. . .] if we, in our turn, added a word to the text [. . .] to characterize the *constitutive relation* which displaces the question of the human essence, while, at the same time, providing a formal answer to it [. . .] . The word does in fact exist but is to be found in twentieth-century thinkers (Kojève, Simondon, Lacan . . .): we have, in fact, to think humanity as a transindividual reality. (Balibar 1995, 31, unbracketed ellipse in original)

Every practice is a social practice, and as such, brings into play a set of elements so complex that we are led to conceive them "not as acts or simple activities, but as *processes*: that is, *as a set of . . . elements sufficiently well adapted to each other for their reciprocal action to produce a result that modifies the initial givens*" (Althusser 2017, 82). *Overdetermination* is, in this sense, the kind of causality that can be figured as a *structure of structures*, where the material transformation of nature could only be considered as determined, by social relations: complex processes where both objectivity and subjectivity take shape.

> I have previously attempted to account for this phenomenon with the concept of *overdetermination*, which I borrowed from psycho-analysis; as one might suppose, this transfer of an analytical concept to Marxist theory was not an arbitrary borrowing but a necessary one, *for the same theoretical problem is at stake in both cases*: *with what concept are we to think the determination of either an element or a structure by a structure?* . . . The constant and real presence of this problem in Marx has been demonstrated by the rigorous analysis of his expressions and forms of reasoning in the preceding papers. It can be entirely summed up in the concept of "*Darstellung*," the key epistemological concept of the whole Marxist theory of value, the concept whose object is precisely to designate the mode of *presence* of the structure in its *effects*, and therefore to designate structural causality itself. (Althusser and Balibar 1970, 188)

Since *The German Ideology*, the category of division of labor introduces in the core of materialism a notion of practice that won't be any more redirected onto any simplified image. The relation that people have to their means of subsistence is governed by the relation of production, and is thus a social relation—"*a three-term abstraction*," Althusser emphasizes. Insofar as the practice of production includes this basic relation *as its condition*, "the relations governing the other practices can be *put into relation with* this first relation" (Althusser 2017, 82).

> And since this social relation is, in class societies, a conflictual, antagonistic relation, determination by production (the base) *is not mechanical, but includes a "play" that comes under the dialectic*. That is why this determination is said to be "in the last instance" . . . . To underscore this determination "in the last instance," Marx presented his general hypothesis on the nature of social formations and history in the form of a *topique* (Althusser 2017, 83).

If *production* can be considered, in this sense, a *term with a double function*—inasmuch as it determines the belonging of all terms to structure, while itself being excluded from it by the operation of posing a *"lieutenant,"* as many authors had posed—it is quite far from formalist tendencies of former structuralism. For the main problem of Marxist theory (what, as I have stated, implies the problem of apodicticity itself) is the problem of elaborating the concept of *time*. A proper approach to the question of production must furnish the problem of "invisible times," the concept of time as the principle on which is based the very possibility and necessity of a plurality of different histories, corresponding to different levels of a very complex topography. And to do it, without thereby evading, but on the contrary, necessarily accepting "the relative independence of each of these histories in the specific dependence which articulates each of the different levels of the social whole with the others" (Althusser and Balibar 1970, 101).

> I should say that we cannot restrict ourselves to reflecting the existence of *visible* and measurable times . . . ; we must, of absolute necessity, pose the question of the mode of existence of *invisible* times, of the invisible rhythms and punctuations concealed beneath the surface of each visible time. Merely reading *Capital* shows that Marx was highly sensitive to this requirement. It shows, for example, that the time of economic production is a specific time . . . , but also that, as a specific time, it is a complex and non-linear time— a time of times, a complex time that cannot be *read* in the continuity of the time of life or clocks, but has to be *constructed* out of the peculiar structures of production. (Althusser and Balibar 1970, 101)

It is at this point, where the singularity of the Althusserian reading of *Capital* resides, usually occluded by precipitated interpretations that directly assumed its belonging to Levi-Straussian structuralism or to barely non-Marxian post-structuralism: in the pursuing of a *materialism of overdetermination*, capable of conceiving the social whole as a hierarchical and unequal structured process, unified in its diversification by the type of articulation, displacement, and torsion that harmonizes different times with one another— in other words, a transindividual combination of practical processes, a *time of times:*

> We have known, since Freud, that the time of the unconscious cannot be confused with the time of biography. On the contrary, *the concept of the time of the unconscious must be constructed* in order to obtain an understanding of certain biographical traits. In exactly the same way, it is essential to construct

the concepts of the different historical times which are never given in the ideological obviousness of the continuity of time (which need only be suitably divided into a good periodization to obtain the time of history), but must be constructed out of the differential nature and differential articulation of their objects in the structure of the whole. (Althusser and Balibar 1970, 103)

The topography of overdetermination is not "an ontology of binarism"; it is not the mere problem of formal structures, not even the problem of structures as processes of variation, but the question of *structures as complex conjunctures*. This thesis poses itself the *void* of political practice in the very epistemological space of the materialist apodicticity.

POLITICAL PRACTICE/THEORETICAL PRACTICE

The question of materialism is, from then on, the question of pursuing a very peculiar kind of *necessity*, a necessity capable of inhabiting *at the same time*, the most heterogeneous practices. As Althusser himself, pointed out, "We shall start by considering *practices* in which the Marxist dialectic as such is *in action*: Marxist theoretical practice and Marxist political practice" (Althusser 2017, 66). It must be stressed that the sort of necessity capable of making room for political practice should be seriously considered with the paradoxical formula of a "rule of exception":

> If it is true, as Leninist practice and reflection prove, that the revolutionary situation in Russia was precisely a result of the *intense overdetermination* of the basic class contradiction, we should perhaps ask what is *exceptional* about this "exceptional *situation*," and whether, like all exceptions, this one does not clarify its rule—is not, unbeknown to the rule, *the rule itself.* (Althusser 2005, 104)

An accurate reading of this passage could note that the peculiar way in which Althusser understands this conjunction of theoretical and political practices—where dialectical materialism inhabits *in action*—is neither a kind of proper application of theory to politics, nor a complementation of the former by the latter. It is the whole rejection of any subsumption of the notions of politics and theory into the epistemological idealist schemes of pure Practice and pure Theory, the abstract and the concrete, the Subject and the Object:

I said that Marx left us no *Dialectics*. This is not quite accurate. He did leave us one first-rate methodological text, unfortunately without finishing it: the *Introduction to the Critique of Political Economy*, 1859. This text does not mention the "inversion" by name, but it does discuss its reality: the validating conditions for the scientific use of the concepts of Political Economy. A reflection on this use is enough to draw from it the basic elements of a Dialectics, since this use is nothing more nor less than the Dialectics in a practical state.

I said that Lenin left us no *Dialectics* . . . . This is not quite accurate. In his *Notebooks* Lenin did leave us some passages which are the sketch for a Dialectics. Mao Tse-tung developed these notes in the midst of a political struggle against dogmatic deviations inside the Chinese party in 1937, in an important text *On Contradiction*. (Althusser 2005, 182)

The aporetic trail that takes form in Althusser's writings on dialectical materialism in the 1960s, must be followed carefully to achieve the complex conjunction that makes Marxist theory not only the theory of history (or, of the class struggle), but also a singular formula of theoretical thought itself, the one that plunges into crises the whole epistemological tradition.

A (RE)COMMENCEMENT INSTEAD OF A CONCLUSION

If *Reading Capital* can be read as a call, it should be the call to develop the theoretical consequences of the most fruitful axiom of materialism: *the primacy of practice*. And one can find it a delicious paradox that the most accurate effort in giving rise to a theory based on this axiom, has been named *theoreticism*. In a footnote of *Reading Capital*, we can read this suggestive thesis:

For very profound reasons, it was often in fact *political* militants and leaders who, without being professional philosophers, were best able to read and understand *Capital* as philosophers. . . . [W]e can study *Marxist philosophy at work* in them, in the "practical" state, Marxist philosophy which has become politics, political action, analysis and decision. (Althusser and Balibar 1970, 76)

It is not just by chance, but for very "profound reasons"—that is, by means of a political practice—that dialectical materialism can be read in its philosophical depth. The question of dialectical materialism, in the scope of political leaders, is the question of the *conjunctural* nature of structures, and it is there where the claim of a proper concept of time takes place.

It is because political practice is, as I recall in previous pages, the practice that works on *the limits of the present,* that it can *practically* pursue the singular materialist thought that figures the *unrepresentable conjoint* between theory, that "necessarily reflects on necessity's *fait accompli,*" and political practice—the practice "of a revolutionary leader who reflects on the present in the present, on the necessity to be achieved, on the means to produce it, on the strategic application points for these means; in short, on his own action" (Althusser 2005, 179).

What Althusser had searched for in Lenin's or Mao's thought is neither mere illustration nor accurate interpretation of Marx's dialectical materialism, but the movement of a practical *detour* that indicates that political practice, far from being a complement to theory, introduces a *constitutive void*—a void that is an activity of opening an *inner distance*—in the decentered core of theoretical discourse's structure.

This inner distance that could only be reached by a big detour:

> One has to leave one's own world behind and make the Big Detour of the world to know one's own world. One can never venture too far afield in quest of the adventure of coming home.
> The same holds for philosophy. (Althusser 2017, 47)

A subtle paradox may indicate the worthiness of a renewed reading of *Capital* in the kind of symptomatic reading introduced by Althusser. It happens that, searching for the concept of time capable of suiting Marxist dialectical materialism, Althusser's anachronic theoreticism can expose one of today's weakest flanks of critical theory facing neoliberal ideology's force: the lack of a political desire for the true.

NOTES

1. "From the quarter of Louis Althusser and his numerous followers there has been launched an unmeasured assault upon 'historicism.' The advances of historical materialism, its supposed 'knowledge,' have rested—it turns out—upon one slender and rotten epistemological pillar ('empiricism'); when Althusser submitted this pillar to a stern interrogation it shuddered and crumbled to dust; and the whole enterprise of historical materialism collapsed in ruins around it. Not only does it turn out that men have never 'made their own history' at all (being only *träger* or vectors of ulterior structural determinations) but it is also revealed that the enterprise of historical materialism—the attainment of historical knowledge—has been misbegotten from the start, since 'real' history is unknowable and cannot be said to exist." (Thompson 1995, 2) And "The return to Marx, the autonomy of theoretical practice, the theory of the autonomy of instances: all of these are attempts to find a solution, from above, to the revisionist

crisis. The autonomy of instances, a substitute for the autonomy of the masses, was, in essence, a new figure of utopia. True, it was not a utopia populated by *phalansteries* or *Icarians* ready to welcome workers, but it still gave the thinker's solution there where the real movement seemed to come up short. If Marx describes utopian socialism as the infancy of the proletarian movement, a thought or idea from a moment when workers themselves had not yet developed solutions to their exploitation as workers, Althusser's theory of history can perhaps be described as a modern form of utopia, as the substitute for the self-emancipation we no longer believe in." (Rancière 2011, 33)

2. I've already discussed Thompson's theses (Romé 2011b) and for an Althusserian response to Rancière's critiques to Althusser, see Catanzaro 2016.

3. "When once before I claimed that it was necessary to give to this *practical* existence of Marxist philosophy, which exists in person in the practical state in that scientific practice of the analysis of the capitalist mode of production, *Capital*, and in the economic and political practice of the history of the workers' movement, the *form of theoretical existence indispensable* to its needs and our needs, I merely proposed a labour of investigation and critical elucidation, which would analyse one with another, according to the nature of their peculiar modalities, the different *degrees* of this existence, i.e., the different *works* which are the raw material of our reflection." (Althusser and Balibar 1970, 32)

4. "To speak of the criterion of practice where theory is concerned, and every other practice as well, then receives its full sense: for *theoretical practice* is indeed its own criterion, and contains in itself definite protocols with which to *validate* the quality of its product, i.e., the criteria of the scientificity of the products of scientific practice. This is exactly what happens in the real practice of the sciences: once they are truly constituted and developed they have no need for verification from *external practices* to declare the knowledges they produce to be 'true,' i.e., to be *knowledges*." (Althusser and Balibar 1970, 60)

5. "Because the Hegelian whole is a 'spiritual whole' . . . in which each part is a *pars totalis*, the unity of this double aspect of historical time (homogeneous continuity/contemporaneity) is possible and necessary" (Althusser and Balibar 1970, 96).

6. "Feuerbach dissolves the religious essence into the human essence. But the human essence is no abstraction inherent in each single individual. In its reality it is the ensemble of social relations. Feuerbach, who does not enter on a critique of this real essence, is consequently compelled: 1. To abstract from the historical process and to fix the religious sentiment [*Gemüt*] as something for itself and to presuppose an abstract—isolated—human individual. 2. Therefore, with him the human essence can be comprehended only as "genus," "as an internal, dumb generality which links the many individuals merely naturally." (Marx 1976, 64, bracketed text in the original)

7. As I have already posited, the Althusserian reading of *Thesis VI* is conflictive, as can be seen in *La querelle de l'humanisme*, 1967 (cf. Athusser 1995).

8. In 1845, Marx broke radically with every theory that based history and politics on an essence of man. This unique rupture contained three indissociable elements: (1) the formation of a theory of history and politics based on radically new concepts: the concepts of social formation, productive forces, relations of production, superstructure, ideologies—determination in the last instance by the economy, specific determination of the other levels, and so on; (2) a radical critique of the theoretical pretensions of every philosophical humanism; and (3) the definition of humanism as an ideology. This new conception is completely rigorous as well, but it is a new rigor: the essence criticized is defined as an ideology, a category belonging to the new theory of society and history. This rupture with every philosophical anthropology or humanism is no secondary detail; it is Marx's scientific discovery (Althusser 2005, 227).

9. "Essential section: (coupe d'essence). Ideological theories (empiricism, idealism, historicism) see the historical totality as analysable in a present, a contemporaneity, in which the relations between the parts can be seen and recorded. To see this present implies the possibility of cutting a section through the historical current, a section in which the essence of that current is visible. This essential section is impossible for Althusser and Balibar because there is no present for all the elements and structures at once in their conceptual system. The possibility of an essential section is one of the positive tests for an empiricist ideology of history." (B. Brewster, "Glossary," in Althusser and Balibar 1970, 314) "The Marxist thesis of the 'primacy of practice over theory' is nevertheless liable to misinterpretation, because of the little word 'primacy' and the sharp distinction between practice and theory. It is idealism which radically separates practice from theory and, in general, puts theory in power over practice. In fact, there is theory (knowledge) in all practice, as there is practice in all theory (all knowledge results from labour)" (Althusser 2017, 66).

10. "The Marxist thesis of the 'primacy of practice over theory' is nevertheless liable to misinterpretation, because of the little word 'primacy' and the sharp distinction between practice and theory. It is idealism which radically separates practice from theory and, in general, puts theory in power over practice. In fact, there is theory (knowledge) in all practice, as there is practice in all theory (all knowledge results from labour)" (Althusser 2017, 66).

11. "The yearning for a reading at sight, for Galileo's *Great Book of the World* itself, is older than all science, that it is still silently pondering the religious fantasies of epiphany and parousia, and the fascinating myth of the Scriptures, in which the body of truth, dressed in its words, is the Book: the Bible. This makes us suspect that to treat nature or reality as a Book, in which, according to Galileo, is spoken the silent discourse of a language whose 'characters are triangles, circles and other geometrical figures,' it was necessary to have a certain idea of reading which makes a written discourse the immediate transparency of the true, and the real the discourse of a voice.

"The first man ever to have posed the problem of reading, and in consequence, of writing, was Spinoza, and he was also the first man in the world to have proposed both a theory of history and a philosophy of the opacity of the immediate. With him, for the first time ever, a man linked together in this way the essence of reading and the essence of history in a theory of the difference between the imaginary and the true. This explains to us why Marx could not possibly have become Marx except by founding a theory of history and a philosophy of the historical distinction between ideology and science, and why in the last analysis this foundation was consummated in the dissipation of the religious myth of reading." (Althusser and Balibar 1970, 16–17)

12. "We know that the Marxist whole cannot possibly be confused with the Hegelian whole: it is a whole whose unity, far from being the expressive or 'spiritual' unity of Leibniz's or Hegel's whole, is constituted by a certain type of *complexity*, the unity of a *structured whole* containing what can be called levels or instances which are distinct and 'relatively autonomous,' and co-exist within this complex structural unity." (Althusser and Balibar 1970, 97)

References

Abós, Álvaro. 1984. *Las organizaciones sindicales y el poder militar*. Buenos Aires: CELA.
Agamben, Giorgio. 1998. *Homo Sacer. Sovereign Power and Bare Life*. Translated by Daniel Heller-Roazen. Stanford, CA: Stanford University Press.
Althusser, Louis. 1963. *Technocratism and Humanism*. MS 20 ALT/3/9 cote. IMEC Archives.
———. 1965. *Pour Marx*. Paris: Maspero.
———. 1967. *Sobre el trabajo teórico. Dificultades y recursos*. Barcelona: Anagrama.
———. 1969a. "Filosofía y Ciencias Humanas." In *La soledad de Maquiavelo*. Madrid: Akal.
———. 1969b. "Freud and Lacan." *New Left Review* 1, no. 55: 49–65.
———. 1969c. *Lénine et la philosophie*. Paris: Maspero.
———. 1971. *Lenin and Philosophy and Other Essays*. New York and London: Monthly Review Press.
———. 1973a. "Althusser replies to John Lewis." *Australian Left Review*, 23–36.
———. 1973b. *Résponse à John Lewis*. Paris: Maspero.
———. 1974. *Éléments d'autocritique*. Paris: Hachette.
———. 1976. *Essays in Self-Criticism*. London: NLB.
———. 1978a. *Ce qui ne peut plus durer dans le parti communiste*. Paris: Maspero.
———. 1978b. "Tinalmente qualcosa di vitale si libera dalla crisi e nella crisi del marxismo" (relazione al convegno di Venezia, Novembre 1977). In *Potere e opposizione nelle società post-rivoluzionarie. Il Manifesto (Quaderno no. 8)*, 220–44. Rome: Alfani.
———. 1988. "Machiavelli's Solitude." *Economy and Society* 17, no 4: 468–79.
———. 1990. *Philosophy and the Spontaneous Philosophy of the Scientists & Other Essays*. Translated by Gregory Elliot. New York-London: Verso.
———. 1991. "On Marx and Freud." Translated by Warren Montag. *Rethinking Marxism* 4, no. 1: 17–30.
———. (MS 1966) 1993. *Écrits sur la psychoanalyse: Freud et Lacan*. Paris: Stock-IMEC.
———. 1994a. *L'avenir dure longtemps*. Paris: Stock-IMEC.
———.1994b. *Écrits philosophiques et politiques, Tome I*. Edited by François Matheron. Paris: Stock-IMEC.
———. 1995. *Écrits philosophiques et politiques, Tome II*. Edited by François Matheron. Paris: Stock-IMEC.

———. 1997. "The Only Materialist Tradition, Part 1: Spinoza." In *The New Spinoza*, translated by Ted Stolze, edited by Warren Montag and Ted Stolze, 3–20. Minneapolis-London: University of Minnesota Press.

———. 1998a. *Lettres à Franca (1961–1973)*. Paris: Stock/Imec.

———. (1963) 1998b. "Philosophie et sciences humaines." In *Solitude de Machiavel*, 43–58. Paris: Presses Universitaires de France.

———. 2002. "Appendix: Louis Althusser 'On Marx and Brecht.'" In *Louis Althusser*, by Warren Montag, 136–49. London: Pallgrave.

———. 2003. "The Philosophical Conjuncture and Marxist Theoretical Research." In *The Humanist Controversy and Other Writings (1966–67)*, edited by François Matheron, translated by G. M. Goshgarian, 1–18. London: Verso.

———. 2004. *Maquiavelo y nosotros*. Translated by Beñat Baltza Álvarez. Madrid: Akal.

———. 2005. *For Marx*. Translated by Ben Brewster. New York-London: Verso.

———. 2006a. *Philosophy of the Encounter: Later Writings, 1978–1987*. Translated by G. M. Goshgarian. New York-London: Verso.

———. 2006b. *Politique et Historie, de Machiavel à Marx. Cours à l'École normale supérieure. 1955–1972*. Paris: Seuil.

———. 2010. *Machiavelli and Us*. Translated by Gregory Elliot. London-New York: Verso.

———. (MS 1969) 2011. *Sur la reproduction*. Paris: PUF.

———. (1972) 2012. *Cours sur Rousseau*. Paris: Le Temps de Cerises.

———. (MS 1969) 2014a. *Inititation à la philosophie pour les non-philosophes*. Paris: PUF.

———. 2014b. *On the Reproduction of Capitalism*. Translated by G. M. Goshgarian. London-New York: Verso.

———. 2017. *Philosophy for Non-Philosophers*. Translated by G. M. Goshgarian. New York-London: Bloomsbury.

———. 2018a. *History and Imperialism. Writings (1963–1986)* [*Écrits su L'Histoire*]. Translated G. M. Goshgarian. Cambridge: Polity Press.

———. (MS 1978) 2018b. *Que faire?* Paris: PUF.

Althusser, Louis, and Alain Badiou. 1969. *Materialismo histórico y materialismo dialéctico*. Córdoba: Pasado y Presente.

Althusser, Louis, and Étienne Balibar. 1968. *Lire le Capital*. Paris: Maspero.

———. 1970. *Reading Capital*. London-New York: NLB.

Althusser, Louis, Étienne Balibar, Pierre Macherey, Jacques Rancière, and Roger Establet. 1965. *Lire le Capital*. Paris: Maspero.

———. 2008. *Lire le Capital*. Paris: PUF.

Aricó, José. 1982. *Marx y América Latina*. Mexico D.F.: Alianza.

Arruzza, Cinzia. 2010. *Dangerous Liaisons: The Marriages and Divorces of Marxism and Feminism*. London-New York: Merlin Press.

———. 2015. "Gender as Social Temporality: Butler (and Marx)." *Historical Materialism* 23, no. 1: 28–52.

Arruzza, Cinzia, Tithi Bhattacharya, and Nancy Fraser. 2019. *Feminism for the 99%: A Manifesto*. London-New York: Verso.

Badiou, Alain. 1967. "The (Re)commencement of Dialectical Materialism." *Critique* 240: 438–67.

———. 1982. *Theorie Du Sujet*. Paris: Seuil.

———. 2005. *Metapolitics*. New York-London: Verso.

———. 2008. *Petit panthéon portatif. Althusser, Borreil, Canguilhem, Cavaillès, G. Châtelet, Deleuze, Derrida, Foucault, Hyppolite, Lacan, Lacoue-Labarthe, Lyotard, F. Proust, Sartre*. Paris: La Fabrique-Éditions.

Balibar, Étienne. 1978. "From Bachelard to Althusser. The Concept of 'Epistemological Break.'" Translated by Elizabeth Kingdom. *Economy and Society* 7, no. 3: 207–37.
———. 1991. *Écrits pour Althusser*. Paris: La Découverte.
———. 1993. "The Non-Contemporaneity of Althusser." In *The Althusserian Legacy*, edited by Anne Kaplan and Michael Sprinker, 1–16. New York: Verso.
———. 1995. *The Philosophy of Marx*. Translated by Chris Turner. London-New York: Verso.
———. 1997. *Droit de cite. Culture et politique en democratie*. Paris: PUF.
———. 2003. "Structuralism: A Destitution of the Subject?" Translated by James Swenson. *Differences* 14, no. 1: 2–21.
———. 2004. *Escritos por Althusser*. Buenos Aires: Nueva Visión.
———. 2012. *Cittadinanza*. Buenos Aires: Adriana Hidalgo.
———. 2016. "Notes sur la theorie du discours." *Decalages* 2, no. 1. http://scholar.oxy.edu/decalages/vol2/iss1/19.
———. 2018a. "Philosophies of the Transindividual: Spinoza, Marx, Freud." Translated by Mark G. E. Kelly. *Australasian Philosophical Review* 2, no. 1: 5–25.
———. 2018b. "Transindividuality in Dispute: A Response to My Readers." *Australasian Philosophical Review* 2, no. 1: 113–17. https://philpapers.org/asearch.pl?pub=89738.
Barret, Michele. 1980. *Women's Oppression Today: Problems in Marxist Feminist Analysis*. London-New York: Verso.
Baudrillard, Jean. 2000. *El espejo de la produccion*. Translated by Irene Agoff. Barcelona: Gedisa.
Bensaïd, Daniel. 1995. *La discordance des temps*. Paris: Les Éditions de la Passion.
Bhattacharya, Tithi. 2015. "How Not to Skip Class: Social Reproduction of Labor and the Global Working Class." *Viewpoint Magazine*. http:/viewpointmag.com/2015/10/31/how-not-to-skip-class-social-reproduction-of-labor-and-the-global-working-class.
———. 2017. *Social Reproduction Theory: Remapping Class, Recentering Oppression*. London: Pluto Press.
Bishop, Kyle. 2010. *American Zombie Gothic: The Rise and Fall (and Rise) of the Walking Dead in Popular Culture*. Jefferson, NC: McFarland.
Bohrer, Ashley. 2020. *Marxism and Intersectionality. Race, Gender, Class and Sexuality under Contemporary Capitalism*. New York: Columbia University Press.
Brenner, Johanna, and María Ramas. 1984. "Rethinking Women's Oppression." *New Left Review* 1, no. 144. http://newleftreview.org/issues/i144/articles/johanna-brenner-maria-ramas-rethinking-women-s-oppression.
Brown, Wendy. 2003. "Neo-Liberalism and the End of Liberal Democracy." *Theory & Event* 7, no. 1. 10.1353/tae.2003.0020.
Butler, Judith. 1997. *The Psychic Life of Power. Theories on Subjection*. Stanford, CA: Stanford University Press.|
———. 2006. *Gender Trouble: Feminism and the Subversion of Identity*. London-New York: Routledge.
———. 2011. *Bodies That Matter: On the Discursive Limits of Sex*. London-New York: Routledge.
Caletti, Sergio. 2001. *Sujeto, política, psicoanálisis. Discusiones althusserianas con Lacan, Foucault, Laclau, Butler y Žižek*. Buenos Aires: Prometeo.
———. 2006. "Decir, autorrepresentación, sujetos. Tres notas para un debate sobre política y comunicación." *Revista Versión* 17: 19–78.
Caletti, Sergio, and Natalia Romé. 2011. *La intervención de Althusser. Revisiones y debates*. Buenos Aires: Prometeo.

Caletti, Sergio, Natalia Romé, and Martina Sosa. 2011. *Lecturas de Althusser. Proyecciones de un campo problemático*. Buenos Aires: Imago Mundi.
Casullo, Nicolás. 2007. *Las cuestiones*. Mexico D.F.: Fondo de Cultura Económica.
Catanzaro, Gisela. 2016. "Aportes de la teoría crítica a una consideración materialista de las prácticas políticas." *Utopía y praxis latinoamericana* 21, no. 74: 13–28.
Catanzaro, Gisela, and Ezequiel Ipar. 2003. *Las aventuras del marxismo*. Buenos Aires: Gorla.
Chaui, Marilena de Souza. 2004. *Política en Spinoza*. Translated by Florencia Gómez. Buenos Aires: Gorla.
Collazo, Carolina. 2016. "Althusser y Derrida. La lectura como intervención política." *Decalages* 2, no. 1. https://scholar.oxy.edu/decalages/vol2/iss1/17.
Collazo, Carolina, and Natalia Romé, eds. 2020. *Asedio del tiempo*. Buenos Aires: CLACSO-IIGG.
Contadini, Didier. 2018. "Singulier/Pluriel. Temps et temporalités de(s) accumulation(s) initiale(s)." Unpublished manuscript.
Cortés, Martín. 2015. *Un nuevo Marxismo para América Latina*. Mexico D.F.: Siglo XXI.
Cosentino, Juan Carlos. 1998. *Angustia, fobia, despertar*. Buenos Aires: Eudeba.
Coulthard, Glen. 2014. *Red Skin, White Masks: Rejecting the Colonial Politics of Recognition*. Minneapolis: University of Minnesota.
Dalla Costa, Mariarosa, and Selma James. 1975. *The Power of Women and the Subversion of the Community*. Bristol, UK: Falling Wall Press.
Davies, William. 2016. "The New Neoliberalism." *New Left Review* 101. http://newleftreview.org/issues/ii101/articles/William-davies-the-new-neoliberalism.
Davis, Angela. 1983. *Women, Race and Class*. New York: Ballantine Books.
Delphi, Christine. 1999. *L'enemi principal. Tome I. Economie du patriarcat*. Paris: Syllepse.
Derrida, Jacques. 1993. *Spectres de Marx: l'état de la dette, le travail du deuil et la nouvelle Internationale*. Paris: Galilée.
———. 1994. *The Specters of Marx: The State of the Debt, the Work of Mourning and the New International*. Translated by Peggy Kamuf. London-New York: Routledge.
D'Hondt, Jacques. 1973. *Hegel y el pensamiento moderno. Seminario Dirigido por Jean Hyppolite*. Mexico D.F.: Siglo XXI.
Dolar, Mladen. 1993. "Beyond Interpellation." *Qui parle* 6, no. 2: 75–96.
———. 2018. "Eu estarei com vocee m sua noite de nupcias: Lacan e o Estranho." In *Esaios sobre Mortos-Vivos. The Walking Dead e outras metáforas*, by Diego Penha and Rodrigo Gonsalves, translated by Rodrigo Gonsalves, 167–204. São Paulo: Aller Editora.
Dussel, Enrique. 1990. *El ultimo Marx (1863–1882) y la liberación latinoamericana*. Mexico D.F.: Siglo XXI.
Echeverría, Bolivar. 1994. *Circulación capitalista y reproducción de la riqueza social. Apunte crítico sobre los esquemas de K. Marx*. Mexico D.F.: UNAM / Quito: Nariz del diablo.
Epstein, Jeffrey. 2016. *Democracy and Its Others*. New York-London: Bloomsbury.
Esposito, Roberto. 2015. *Persons and Things: From the Body's Point of View*. Translated by Z. Hanafi. Cambridge, UK: Polity Press.
Farrán, Roque. 2013. *Badiou y Lacan. El anudamiento del sujeto*. Buenos Aires: Prometeo.
Federici, Silvia. 2004. *Caliban and the Witch: Women, the Body and Primitive Accumulation*. New York: Autonomedia.
———. 2012. *Revolution at Point Zero: Housework, Reproduction, and Feminist Struggle*. London: Palgrave Macmillan.
———. 2018. *El patriarcado del salario. Críticas feministas al marxismo*. Buenos Aires: Tinta Limón and Traficantes de sueños.

———. 2019. "Feminism and Social Reproduction." In *Voices on the Left: Challenging Capitalist Hegemony*, by George Souvlis. Athens: Red Marks.
———. 2020. *Patriarchy of the Wage: Notes on Marx, Gender, and Feminism*. Oakland, CA: PM Press.
Firestone, Shulamith. (1970) 2003. *The Dialectic of the Sex: The Case for Feminist Revolution*. New York: Farrar, Straus and Giroux.
Fisher, Mark. 2016. *Capitalist Realism: Is There No Alternative?* London: Zero Books.
Foucault, Michel. 1969. *L'archéologie du savoir*. Paris: Gallimard.
———. 1971. *L'ordre du discours*. Paris: Gallimard.
———. 1972. *The Archaeology of Knowledge and the Discourse of Language*. New York: Pantheon Books.
———. (1977) 1979. *Discipline and Punish. The Birth of the Prison*. Translated by Alan Sheridan. New York: Pantheon Books.
———. 2001. *L'hermeneutique du Sujet*. Paris: Gallimard-Seuil.
———. 2010. *The Birth of Biopolitics: Lectures at the Collège de France 1978–1979*. Baringstoke-New York: Picadero.
Fouque, Antoinette. 1995. *Il y à deux sexes. Essais de feminologie*. Paris: Gallimard.
Fraser, Nancy. 2009. "Feminism, Capitalism and the Cunning of History." *New Left Review* 56: 97–117.
———. 2017. *The Old Is Dying and the New Cannot Be Born: From Progressive Neoliberalism to Trump and Beyond*. London-New York: Verso.
———. 2020. *Fortunes of Feminism: From State-Managed Capitalism to Neoliberal Crisis*. London: Verso.
Freud, Sigmund. (1921) 1960. *Group Psychology and the Analysis of the Ego* [*Massenpsychologie und Ich-Analyse*]. Translated by James Strachey. New York: Bantam Books.
———. (1901) 1965. *The Psychopatology of Everyday Life* [*Zur Psychopathologie des Alltagslebens*]. Translated by Alan Tyson. New York: Norton.
———. (1899) 2010. *The Interpretation of Dreams* [*Die Traumdeutung*]. Translated by James Strachey. New York: Basic Books.
———. (1909) 1914. *Family Romances. The Standard Edition of the Complete Psychological Works of Sigmund Freud*. Vol. 9. Translated by S. E. Jelliffe and F. Robbins. New York: Nervous and Mental Diseases Publishing.
Furtado, Celso. 1964. *Desarrollo y subdesarrollo*. Buenos Aires: Eudeba.
Gadet, Françoise, and Michel Pêcheux. 1981. *La langue introuvable*. Paris: La Decouverte.
Gainza, Mariana. 2011. "La actualidad de la lectura sintomáica." In Caletti and Romé, *La intervención de Althusser. Revisiones y debates*, 241–60..
García Linera, Álvaro. 1989. *Introducción al cuaderno Kovalevsky de Karl Marx*. La Paz: Ofensiva Roja.
———. 2009. *Forma valor y forma comunidad*. Quito, Ecuador: IAEN-Instituto de Altos Estudios Nacionales del Ecuador.
———. 2011. *El "Oenegismo," Enfermedad Infantil del Derechismo. O cómo la "reconducción" del Proceso de Cambio es la restauración neoliberal*. La Paz: Vicepresidencia del Estado Plurinacional; Presidencia de la Asamblea Legislativa Plurinacional.
Getachew, Adam. 2016. "Universalism after the Post-Colonial Turn: Interpreting the Haitian Revolution." *Political Theory* 44, no. 6: 821–45.
Glozman, Mara. 2016. "Lingüística, materialismo, (inter)discurso: elementos para una lectura de Las verdades evidentes." In *Las verdades evidentes. Lingüística, semántica, filosofía* by Michel Pêcheux, 7–17. Buenos Aires: Ediciones CCC.

———. 2020. "(Re)leer Pêcheux hoy el problema del décalage en la teoría materialista del discurso." *Pensamiento al margen* no. 12: 117–33.
Grüner, Eduardo. 2010. *La oscuridad y las luces. Capitalismo, cultura y revolución*. Buenos Aires: Edhasa.
Guattari, Félix, and Antonio Negri. 1999. *Las verdades nómadas & General Intellect, poder constuyente, comunismo*. Madrid: Akal.
Hall, Stuart. 1977. "Rethinking the 'Base-and-Superstructure' Metaphor." In *Papers on Class, Hegemony and Party :The Communist University of London*, edited by John Bloomfield, 43–72. London: Lawrence and Wishart.
———. 1985. "Signification, Representation, Ideology: Althusser and the Post-Structuralist Debates." *Critical Studies in Mass Communication* 2, no. 2 (June): 91–114.
———. 2016. *Cultural Studies 1983: A Theoretical History*. Durham, NC: Duke University Press.
Hamza, Agon. 2016. *Althusser and Pasolini: Philosophy, Marxim, and Film*. New York: Palgrave Macmillan.
Han, Byung-Chul. 2015. *The Transparency Society*. Stanford, CA: Stanford University Press.
Hartmann, Heidi. 1979. "The Unhappy Marriage of Marxism and Feminism: Towards a More Progressive Union." *Capital and Class* 3, no. 2: 1–33.
Harvey, David. 2005. *A Brief History of Neoliberalism*. Oxford: Oxford University Press.
Hayden, Dolores. 1985. *The Grand Domestic Revolution: A History of Feminist Designs for American Homes, Neighborhoods, and Cities*. Cambridge, MA: MIT Press.
Hegel, G. W. F. (1821) 1955. Grundlinien der Philosophie des Rechts (Mit Hegels eigenhändigen Randbemerkungen in seinem Handexemplar der Rechtsphilosophie) . Hamburg, Germany: Felix Meiner Verlag.
———. (1837) 1967. *Leçons sur la philosophie de l'historire* [*Vorlesungen über die Philosophie der Weltgeschichte*]. Translated by Annie Blanchet. Paris: Libraire Vrin.
Ípola, Emilio de. 2007. *Althusser, el infinito adiós*. Mexico D.F.: Siglo XXI.
James, C. R. L. 1989. *The Black Jacobins. Toussaint L'Ouverture and the Santo Domingo Revolution*. New York: Vintage Books–Random House.
Kelly, Mark, and Dimitris Vardoulakis. 2018. "Balibar and Transindividuality." *Australasian Philosophical Review* 2, no. 1: 1–114. https://philpapers.org/asearch.pl?pub=89738.
Lacan, Jacques. 1991. *Le séminaire, Livre XVII: L'envers de la psychanalyse*. Paris: Seuil.
———. 2004. *Le séminaire, Livre X: L'angoise. (1962–1963)*. Paris: Seuil.
Laclau, Ernesto, and Mouffe, Chantal. 1985. *Hegemony and Socialist Strategy: Towards a Radical Democratic Politics*. London: Verso.
Laplanche, Jean, and J. B. Pontalis. 1974. *The Language of Psychoanalysis*. Translated by Donald Nicholson-Smith and Daniel Lagache. New York: W. W. Norton.
Laslett , Barbara, and Johanna Brenner. 1989. " Gender and Social Reproduction: Historical Perspectives ." *Annual Review of Sociology* 15: 38 – 404.
Lauro, Sarah. 2015. *The Transatlantic Zombie: Slavery, Rebellion and Living Death*. New Brunswick, NJ: Rutgers University Press.
Laval, Christian, and Pierre Dardot. 2009. *La nouvelle raison du monde. Essai sur la société néolibérale*. Paris: La Découverte.
Lecourt, Dominique. 1970. "Sur *L'arqueologie du savoir*." *La Pensée* 152, no. 8: 68–87.
Lonzi, Carla. 2017. *Escupamos sobre Hegel. Y otros escritos*. Buenos Aires: Tinta Limón–Fundaciòn Rosa Luxemburgo.
Lordon, Frédéric. 2013. *La société des affects. Pour une structuralisme des passions*. Paris: Seuil.
Macherey, Pierre. 1965. "A propos de la rupture." *La Nouvelle Critique* 139 (May).

Machiavelli, Niccolò. 1964. *The Prince*. Translated by Mark Musa. New York: St. Martins Press.

Malamud, Mauricio. 2017. *Escritos (1969–1987)*. Edited by Marcelo Starcenbaum. Santiago de Chile: Doble Ciencia.

Marchart, Oliver. 2009. *El pensamiento político posfundacional. La diferencia política en Nancy, Lefort, Badiou y Laclau*, Buenos Aires: Fondo de Cultura Económica.

Marcuse, Herbert. (1964) 1991. *One-Dimensional Man. Studies in the Ideology of Advanced Industrial Society*. Boston: Beacon.

Mariátegui, José. 1928. *7 ensayos de interpretación de la Realidad Peruana*. Lima: Amauta.

Marini, Ruy. 1973. *Dialéctica de la dependencia*. Mexico D.F.: Era.

Martuscelli, Danilo, Jair Pinheiro, and Lúcio Flávio de Almeida. 2014. "Althusser: 50 anos depois." *Lutas Sociais* 18, no. 33. https://revistas.pucsp.br/ls/issue/view/1504/showToc.

Marx, Karl. 1906. *Capital: A Critique of Political Economy*. 3rd German ed. Translated by S. Moore and E. Aveling. New York: Untermann.

———. 1937. *The Eighteenth Brumaire of Luis Bonaparte*. Moscow: Progress Publishers.

———. 1976. "Theses on Feuerbach." In *Ludwig Feuerbach and the End of Classical German Philosophy*, by Friederich Engels. Peking: Foreign Languages Press.

Marx, Karl, and Friederich Engels. 1939. *The German Ideology*. Moscow: The Marx-Engels Institute.

———. 1964. *Einleitung zur Kritik der politischen Ökonomie, Tome 8*. Berlin: Dietz Verlag.

Mbembe, Achille. 2019. *Necropolis*. Durham, NC: Duke University Press.

McCallum, E. L., and Mikko Tuhkanen. 2011. *Queer Times, Queer Becomings*. Albany, NY State University of New York Press.

Merteuil, Morgane. 2017. "Le travail du sexe contre le sexe: pour un anayse materialiste du desir." In *Pour un féminisme de la totalité*, edited by Félix Boggio Éwajé-Épée, Stella Magliani-Belkacem, Morgane Merteuil, and Frédéric Monferrand. Paris: Periode–Editions Amsterdam.

Miller, Jacques-Alain. 2007. *La angustia lacaniana*, Buenos Aires: Paidós.

———. 2010. *Extimidad. Los cursos psicoanalíticos de Jacques-Alain Miller*. Buenos Aires: Paidós.

Milner, Jean-Claude. 2002. *Le périple structural: figures et paradigme*. Paris: Seuil.

Mintz, Sidney. (1966) 1971. "The Caribbean as a Socio-Cultural Area." In *Peoples and Cultures of the Caribbean*, edited by Michael Horowitz, 17–46. Garden City, NY: Natural History Press.

Montag, Warren. 2013. *Althusser and His Contemporaries: Philosophy's Perpetual War*. Durhan, NC: Duke University Press.

———. 2015. "Discourse and Decree: Spinoza, Althusser and Pêcheux." *Cahiers du GRM* 7. doi: 10.4000/grm.600.

———. 2017. "*Lire le Capital*: el teatro sin autor de Louis Althusser." In *Actas del Coloquio Internacional: 50 años de Lire le Capital*, coordinated by Pedro Karczmarczyk, Natalia Romé, and Marcelo Starcenbaum, 433–44. La Plata: Universidad Nacional de La Plata.

Moore, Jason. 2015. *Capitalism in the Web of Life. Ecology and Accumulation of Capital*. London-New York: Verso.

Morfino, Vittorio. 2014a. *El materialismo de Althusser*. Santiago de Chile: Palinodia.

———. 2014b. *Plural Temporality: Transindividuality and the Aleatory between Spinoza and Althusser*. New York: Brill.

———. 2017. "El concepto de causalidad estructural en Althusser." In Karczmarczyk, Romé, and Starcenbaum, *Actas del Coloquio Internacional: 50 años de Lire le Capital*, 445–65.

———. 2019a. "Althusser as Reader of Gramsci." *Revista de Filosofía de la Universidad Costa Rica* 58, no. 152 (September–December): 11–23.

———. 2019b. "On Étienne Balibar's 'Philosophies of the Transindividual.'" Translated by Dave Mesing. *Australasian Philosophical Review* 2, no. 1: 84–93.

Morfino, Vittorio, and Peter Thomas. 2017. *The Government of Time: Historical Materialism*. Leiden: Brill.

Murillo, Susana. 2008. *Colonizar el dolor. La interpelación ideológica del Banco Mundial en América Latina*. Buenos Aires: CLACSO.

———. 2012. "Hobbes, Kelsen, Schmitt, Foucault: ley y poder, una relación crítica." *Nuevo Itinerario* 7, no. 2. http://hum.unne.edu.ar/revistas/itinerario/revista7.htm.

Navarro, Fernanda. (1988) 1998. *Filosofía y Marxismo*. Mexico D.F.: Siglo XXI.

Ortega Reyna, Jaime, and V. Pacheco. 2019. *La incorregible imaginación. Itinerarios de Louis Althusser en América Latina y el Caribe*. Santiago de Chile: Doble Ciencia.

Pavón Cuellar, David. 2010. *From the Conscious Interior to an Exterior Unconscious: Lacan, Discourse Analysis and Social Psychology*. London: Karnac.

Pêcheux, Michel. 1975. *Les vérités de La Palice*. Paris: Maspero.

———. 1977. "Remontémonos de Foucault a Spinoza." In *El discurso político*, coordinated by Monforte Toledo, 181–97. Mexico D.F.: Nueva imagen.

———. 1978. "Münchhausen-Effekt. Von der Materialität." *Alternative*, no. 118.

———. 1982. *Language, Semantics and Ideology*. Translated by Harbans Nagpal. New York: St. Martin's Press.

———. 1983. "Anarchisme/Reformisme." MS PCH4. IMEC Archives.

———. 1984. "Sur les contextes épistémologiques de l'analyse de discours." *Mots*, no. 9, (October): 7–17.

———. 1990. "Il n'y a cause de ce qui cloche" (1978). In *L'inquietud du discours. Textes de Michel Pêcheux*, edited by D. Maldidier, 261–72. Paris: Editions des Cendres.

———. 2014. "Dare to Think and Dare to Rebel! Ideology, Marxism, Resistance, Class Struggle." *Décalages* 1, no. 4.

Penha, Diego, and Rodrigo Gonsalves, comp. 2018. *Ensaios sobre mortos-vivos. "The Walking Dead" e outras metáforas*. Translated by Rodrigo Gonsalves. São Paulo: Aller Editora.

Popovitch, Anna. 2017. *Althusser desde América Latina*. Buenos Aires: Biblos.

Pozzi, Pablo. 1988. *Oposición obrera a la dictadura (1976–1982)*. Buenos Aires: Contrapunto.

Rancière, Jacques. 1974. *La leçon d'Althusser*. Paris: Gallimard.

———. 1995. *La mésentente. Politique et philosophie*. Paris: Galilée.

———. 2009. *Moments politiques. Interventions 1977–2009*. Montreal: Lux Editeur.

———. 2011. *Althusser's Lesson*. Translated by Emiliano Battista. London: Bloomsbury Academic.

Rank, Otto. 1909. *The Myth of the Birth of the Hero*. Translated by S. E. Jelliffe and F. Robbins. New York: Nervous and Mental Diseases Publishing.

Ré, Carolina. 2011. "El lugar del sujeto. Abordaje crítico sobre la problemática de la identificación en la constitución del sujeto." In Caletti, *Sujeto, política, psicoanálisis. Discusiones althusserians con Lacan, Foucault, Laclau, Butler y Žižek*, 289–308.

———. 2020. "Sobre la temporalidad diferencial o el advenimiento del desajuste." In Collazo, Romé, and Ré, *Asedio del tiempo*, 19–34.

Read, Jason. 2015. *The Politics of Transindividuality, Historical Materialism*. Leiden: Brill.

Rivera Cusicanqui, Silvia. 2018. *Un mundo ch'ixi e posible: ensayos desde un presente en crisis*. Buenos Aires: Tinta Limón.

Rodríguez, Pablo. 2018. *Las palabras en las cosas*. Buenos Aires: Cebra.

Rodríguez Arraigada, Marcelo. 2016. *La tendencia materialista*. Santiago de Chile: Doble Ciencia.
Rodríguez Arraigada, Marcelo, and Zeto Borquez. 2010. *Louis Althusser. Filiación y (re)comienzo*. Santiago de Chile: Universidad de Chile, Facultad de Artes.
Romé, Natalia. 2011a. "En busca del materialismo. Filosofía, política e historia en la obra de Louis Althusser." In Caletti, *Sujeto, política, psicoanálisis. Discusiones althusserians con Lacan, Foucault, Laclau, Butler y Žižek*, 117–57.
———. 2011b. "Hacer filosofía para no contarse historias. Algunas notas sobre filosofía e historia." In Caletti and Romé, *La intervención de Althusser. Revisiones y debates*, 241–60.
———. 2015. *La posición materialista. El pensamiento de Louis Althusser entre la práctica teórica y práctica política*. La Plata: EDULP.
———. 2019. "Maquiavelo lector de Lacan. Notas sobre el vínculo entre discurso e inconsciente en la teoría althusseriana." *Revista Teoría y Crítica de la Psicología* 13: 241–63.
———. 2020. "El puro verde es tan gris. Althusser y la crítica del Tiempo Absoluto" In Collazo, Romé, and Ré, *Asedio del tiempo*, 35–54.
Romé, Natalia, and Carolina Collazo. 2017. *"Marseillaise Noire*. Pensar el estado de nuestro tiempo." *Actuel Marx/Intervenciones* no. 23: 83–106.
Sadin, Éric. 2013. *L'humanité augmenté. L'administration numerique du monde*. Paris: L'echapée.
Sánchez Vázquez, Adolfo. 1975. "El teoricismo de Althusser (Notas críticas sobre una autocrítica)." *Cuadernos políticos* no. 3: 82–99.
Santos, Theotonio dos. 1970. "Dependencia y cambio social." In *Cuadernos de Estudios Socioeconómicos*, vol. 1. Santiago de Chile: Universidad de Chile.
Schwarzböck, Silvia. 2015. *Los espantos. Estética y postdictadura*. Buenos Aires: Cuarenta Ríos.
Seabrook, William. (1929) 2016. *The Magic Island*. New York: Dover Publications.
Seccombe, Wally. 1995. *Weathering the Storm: Working-Class Families from the Industrial Revolution to the Fertility Decline*. London-New York: Verso.
Sotiris, Panagiotis. 2020. *A Philosophy for Communism: Rethinking Althusser*. Leiden: Brill.
Starcenbaum, Marcelo. 2011. "El marxismo incómodo: Althusser en la experiencia de *Pasado y Presente*." *Revista Izquierdas* no. 11 (December): 35–53. www.izquierdas.cl.
———. 2017. "El Althusser de los comunistas argentinos (1967–1976)." *Kavilando* 9, no. 2: 471–92.
Stavrakakis, Yannis. 2007. *The Lacanian Left. Essays on Psychoanalysis and Politics*. Albany: State University of New York Press.
Šumič, Jelica. 2011. "En el camino del semblante." *Debates y combates* no. 1: 41–74.
Terriles, Ricardo, and Silvia Hernández. 2014. "Algunas reflexiones sobre la concepción del sujeto y la epistemología en el Análisis del Discurso de Michel Pêcheux." *Décalages* 1, no. 4. https://scholar.oxy.edu/decalages/vol1/iss4/24.
Thompson, E. P. 1978. *The Poverty of Theory and Other Essays*. London: Monthly Review Press.
———. 1995. *The Poverty of Theory: Or an Orrery of Errors*. London: Merlin Press.
Tomba, Massimiliano. 2012. *Marx's Temporalities*. Translated by P. D. Thomas and S. R. Farris. Leiden: Brill, Historical Materialism Book Series.
Tombazos, Stavros. 1994. *Le Temps dans l'analyse économique. Les catégories du temps dans le Capital*. Paris: Cahiers des saisons.
Traverso, Enzo. 2017. *Left-Wing Melancholia: Marxism, History, and Memory*. New York: Columbia University Press.

Unzué, Martín. 2012. *El Estado Argentino (1976–2003). Ciclos de ajuste y cambios*. Buenos Aires: Imago Mundi.

Vogel, Lise. 1983. *Marxism and Oppression of Woman. Toward a Unitary Theory*. New Brunswick, NJ: Rutgers University Press.

———. 2017. Foreword to Bhattacharya, *Social Reproduction Theory: Remapping Class, Recentering Oppression*, x–xii.

Walsh, Rodolfo. 1977. "Open Letter from a Writer to the Military Junta." Ministerio de Justicia y Derechos Humanos, March 24, http://www.jus.gob.ar/media/2940455/carta_rw_ingles-espa_ol_web.pdf.

Young, Iris M. 2004. "Five Faces of Oppression." In *Oppression, Privilege, and Resistance: Theoretical Perspectives on Racism, Sexism, and Heterosexism*, edited by Lisa Maree Heldke and Peg O'Conor, 37–63. London: McGraw-Hill.

Zavaleta Mercado, René. 2009. *La autodeterminación de las masas*. Bogotá: Siglo del Hombre Editores.

Žižek, Slavoj. 1989. *The Sublime Object of Ideology*. London-New York: Verso.

———. 1997. *The Plague of Fantasies*. London-New York: Verso.

———. 2002. *Revolution at the Gates: Selected Writings of Lenin from 1917*. London-New York: Verso.

———. 2008. *Violence*. London: Profile Books.

Index

antihumanism, 19, 21
antihumanist, 100
apparatus, 15, 38, 49, 54, 58, 61n11, 137, 150n8, 153. *See also* ideology, Ideological State Apparatuses
alienation, concept of, 21, 22, 24, 25, 30, 67, 68, 69, 73, 78, 84, 113, 122n24
Arruzza, Cinzia, 5, 97, 103, 104, 105, 117, 119n8

Badiou, Alain, 5, 96, 133, 140, 141, 143, 144, 145, 148, 150n3, 151n17
Balibar, Étienne, xvi, 3, 19, 21, 22, 25, 36, 47, 62n20, 81, 83, 85, 86, 90n12, 134, 135, 145, 149, 151n14, 153, 159, 162, 163
Bhattacharya, Tithi, 5, 103, 104, 111, 113, 114, 116, 122n27
Brecht, Bertold, 25, 57, 87, 151n15
Butler, Judith, 5, 21, 24, 25, 26, 27, 29, 31, 33, 43, 61n12, 61n13, 62n17, 62n18, 64n30, 65n37, 104, 105, 117, 119n8, 150n4

Capital (book), xii, 38, 59n5, 63n28, 64n34, 75, 90n18, 101, 107, 133, 137, 155, 156, 157, 158, 160, 165, 167, 168
Case, theory of, 60n8, 145
causality, 16, 18, 24, 28, 35, 44, 48, 63n28, 75, 104, 147, 158, 159, 164; expressive, 16, 19, 49, 52, 59n5, 162; immanent, 29, 35, 49, 145; structural, 16, 21, 35, 69, 74, 75, 77, 87, 122n25, 147, 164
cause, 32, 34, 47, 48, 49, 53, 55, 57, 61n11, 63n28, 66n42, 81, 82, 90n16, 109, 113, 117. *See also* causality
chance, 48, 57, 85
class struggle, xvi, 3, 5, 9, 11, 12, 17, 18, 22, 24, 28, 35, 38, 39, 40, 42, 45, 46, 49, 57, 58, 59, 60n9, 62n21, 64n31, 65n39, 70, 84, 85, 86, 90n17, 100, 105, 117, 149n1, 167; antagonism, 9, 45, 46, 84, 88, 90n17; primacy of struggle, 22, 39, 58, 65n39, 101, 117
clinamen, 74. *See also* encounter
colonialism, 2, 71, 86; postcolonial studies, 67, 69, 93, 96, 109, 122n22
conjuncture, 3, 4, 5, 6, 10–11, 16, 17, 45, 46, 50, 51, 52, 52–54, 58, 65n40, 70, 80, 87, 88, 93, 94, 95, 95–96, 96, 100, 107, 112, 117, 118, 119n3, 121n18, 122n22, 128, 131, 134, 135, 137, 141, 149, 154, 160, 166
conjunction, 41, 64n35, 65n41, 75, 93, 101, 116, 117, 132, 166, 167; conjuncture/conjunction, 86
conjunctural thought, 22, 51, 58
conatus, 36. *See also* desire
consciousness, theatre of, 32, 34, 80
contingency, 49, 58, 64n35, 85, 107, 109
contradiction, xii, 32, 34, 36, 37, 42, 43, 44, 50, 74, 75, 77, 81, 84, 86, 90n18,

106, 107, 121n18, 121n20, 129, 132, 140, 147; overdetermined, 131

Darstellung, 35, 63n28, 107, 164. *See also* Vorstellung

décalage, 29, 32, 33, 34, 56, 63n26, 64n30, 67, 79, 129, 154; translated as *dislocation*, 32, 33, 36, 63n26, 71, 154; translated as *misadjustment*, 29, 34, 63n26, 69, 129, 130, 132, 146

Derrida, Jacques, 3, 81, 150n3, 153

desire, 4, 6, 24, 29, 31, 33, 36, 55, 58, 61n13, 63n23, 81, 88, 168

Diatkine, René, 75

discourse: concept of, 23, 38, 48, 49, 56, 74, 156; theory of, 32, 40, 42, 56

discursive processes, 39, 40, 47, 48, 49, 51, 52, 54, 58; discursive materiality, 38, 49, 52, 56, 57, 79; discursive formation, 34, 42, 43, 44, 50, 52, 63n25, 102

dispositive, 79, 81

encounter, x, xviii, 4, 24, 53, 60n8, 64n30, 65n41, 74, 94, 105, 133, 136

end, concept of, 146

ensemble, 21, 22, 25, 43, 45, 47, 49, 57, 58, 72, 163, 169n6. *See also* transindividual

essence, 19, 21–22, 35, 60n10, 73, 97, 110, 130, 159, 163, 169n8

Eurocentrism, 71, 72

Eurocommunism, 11

Eurocommunist, 9, 10–11

Federici, Silvia, 71, 105–106, 108, 109–111, 165

feminism, 5, 93, 95, 96, 97, 105, 117, 119n7

Feuerbach, Ludwig, ix, 19, 21, 60n10, 159, 163, 169n6. *See also* alienation

formation, 12, 16, 19, 21, 44, 51, 80, 81, 85, 87, 105, 129, 131; social formation, 12, 18, 19, 25, 44, 46, 51, 53, 67, 73, 78, 104, 106, 107, 109, 115, 141, 164, 169n8; discursive formation, 34, 42, 43, 44, 49, 50, 52, 54, 56, 65n41, 83, 86, 123n30, 157

Foucault, Michel, xiii, xvii, 3, 18, 21, 24, 37, 37–38, 40, 41, 41–43, 48, 60n9, 61n15, 62n17, 64n29–64n31, 67, 86, 150n3

Freud, Sigmund, 14, 15, 16, 28, 30, 31, 32, 36, 39, 48, 55, 85, 86, 129, 130, 147, 165

Genesis, 24, 29, 69, 73, 74, 75, 77, 81, 112, 114

Gliederung, 35, 107, 147

Gramsci, Antonio, 3, 10, 11, 17, 18, 24, 58, 59n5, 153

Haitian revolution, 72, 73, 79, 90n13

Hegel, G. W. F., xii, 11, 13, 34, 35, 64n35, 77, 97, 109, 119n6, 119n7, 119n9, 131, 135, 137, 159. *See also* dialectics

historicism, ix, 13, 14, 18, 45, 59n5, 69, 72, 80, 105, 116, 155, 168n1, 170n9

historical materialism, 39, 47, 94, 95, 105, 108, 109, 143, 168n1

history, theory of, 10, 13, 15, 16, 21, 29, 38, 42, 49, 65n40, 130, 134, 158, 162, 167, 168n1, 169n8, 170n11

Hobbes, Thomas, 23, 60n10, 81, 85, 90n16; Hobbesian pact, 81, 82

humanism, 19, 21, 65n41, 69, 72, 80, 84, 85, 87, 96, 97, 101, 110, 169n8

idealism, 6, 10, 21, 22, 30, 42, 48, 60n10, 80, 90n11, 159, 161, 170n9, 170n10; idealist dialectics, 151n20

identification, theory of, 13, 14, 17, 19, 19–20, 26, 32, 48. *See also* Freud

ideological struggle, 31, 87, 99, 100, 101

ideology: concept of, x, 14, 18, 20, 21, 22, 23, 24, 27, 35, 61n11, 61n15, 62n19, 90n9, 100, 144, 150n9, 152n21; dominant, 3, 6, 53, 65n41, 69, 99, 101, 102, 119n3; existence of, xiii, 21, 23; Ideological State Apparatuses, x, xiii, 13, 23, 27, 53, 61n16; ideology in epistemological critique, 22, 65n41, 159; state, 18, 38, 53; theory of, xiii, 13, 14, 26, 27, 28, 31, 47, 48, 53, 58, 65n41, 84, 112

interior, 25, 62n19, 145; interiority, 18, 21, 22, 23, 23–24, 25, 34, 44, 45, 79, 140, 144, 146

Index

interior/exterior, 28, 56, 62n19, 86; vs. extimacy, 62n19, 86. *See also* alienation; phenomenology; Hegel

imaginary, Althusser's concept of, 12, 18, 29, 54, 56, 155; materialism of the imaginary, 21, 37

immanence, xvii, 37, 49, 62n22, 63n28, 146. *See also* causality, immanent

immediacy, illusion of, 52, 73–74, 75, 155, 159. *See also* imaginary

imperialism, 9, 11, 19, 70, 71, 77, 87, 89n1, 115, 117, 121n20, 122n22, 160

interpellation, concept of, 15, 19, 21, 24, 26, 34, 54, 62n18

jouissance, 29, 31, 33, 58

Lacan, Jacques, ix, 27, 29, 30, 31, 32, 33, 34, 35, 36, 48, 56, 63n23, 63n28, 65n41, 86, 151n18, 163

langue, 49, 52

linguistics, 27, 37, 40, 49, 61n13, 64n31, 73, 119n8

Machiavelli, Niccolò, xiv, 16–17, 17–18, 25, 28, 29, 30, 31, 33, 35, 36, 37, 51, 52, 57, 61n15, 63n27, 150n4, 151n13

Marx, Karl, ix, 4, 11, 14, 15, 16, 19, 21, 35, 38, 60n6, 64n30, 64n35, 75, 77, 95, 113, 136, 159, 169n8

Marxism, ix, x, 3, 15, 17, 71, 99, 109

Marxist theory, xiii, 3, 22, 29, 46, 48, 64n31, 69, 86, 93, 100, 103, 107, 128, 130, 132, 138, 153, 154, 164, 165

materialism, xii, 21, 24, 37, 39, 47, 74, 78, 94–95, 115, 132, 141, 164, 166, 167

material dialectics, 95; Marxist dialectics, xvii, 16, 128; materialist dialectics, 6, 16, 132, 133, 138

materialist position, 16, 17, 28, 72, 84, 87, 129, 133, 143, 148, 149; aleatory materialism, xii, 74, 151n14

Montag, Warren, 5, 6n1, 21, 23, 24, 48, 52, 56, 155

Morfino, Vittorio, 5, 59n5, 63n28, 107, 122n25

myth, 31, 33, 53, 55, 57, 67, 71, 73–74, 76, 78, 161. *See also* state of nature; reading

necessity, 27, 49, 64n35, 65n38, 66n42, 90n12, 132, 147, 148, 160, 166

neo-anarchism, 102

neoliberalism, 3, 19, 67, 70, 81, 96, 98, 99, 117; neoliberalization, 2, 9, 69, 96, 98; origin, concept of, 31, 33, 55, 68, 70–71, 74, 146

overdetermination, xvii, 6, 16, 22, 26, 29, 35, 48, 51, 65n40, 106, 109, 112, 128, 129, 131, 132, 133, 139, 140, 147, 158, 164, 165

Pêcheux, Michel, 32, 33, 34–35, 37, 39, 40–42, 43–52, 52–53, 54, 56, 59, 65n41, 115

phenomenology, phenomenological, 45, 54, 55, 97, 102, 162

philosophy: Althusser's conception of, xvii, 74, 76, 87, 127, 128, 133, 140, 142, 148; materialist, xvii, 133, 135, 136, 140, 144, 148

political thought, 10, 16, 29, 110, 117, 128, 149, 155, 157; politicism, 102, 115, 117, 155. *See also* Machiavelli; political practice; state power

practice, ix, x, xv, 12, 137, 139, 142, 143, 157, 158, 159, 160, 164; ideological concept of, 12; political practice, xvii, 14, 16, 17, 52, 59n5, 65n41, 81, 93, 94, 95, 97, 117, 127, 128, 133, 166; theoretical practice, xvii, 65n40, 95, 127, 128, 131, 132, 133, 139, 142, 166

praxis and *poiesis*, 12, 84, 90n11, 139, 162, 163

present, 13, 33, 52; presentism, 94, 99; absolute present, 12, 13, 52, 54. *See also* temporality

primitive accumulation, 58, 67, 75, 77, 78, 90n10, 106, 109, 111, 112

power, xvii, 17, 18, 23, 24–25, 26, 27, 31, 33, 34, 37, 38, 43, 46, 62n17, 70, 72, 75, 82, 83, 86, 120n11, 137, 155, 170n9, 170n10; state power, 14, 17–18, 18, 19, 24, 28, 30, 36, 43, 44, 81, 112

psychoanalysis, 15, 17, 24, 26, 30, 31, 49, 51, 64n31, 65n41, 119n8, 136; and ideology, 15; and politics, 26, 27, 30, 136; and philosophy, 26

reading, theory of, xii, 75; Edenic myth of reading, 57, 75; symptomatical reading, 64n34, 68; symptomatic reading, xii, xviii, 14, 168
real subsumption, 67, 86
reformism, theoretical, 10, 44, 52
reproduction, 5, 16, 22, 24, 46, 51, 69, 70, 77, 93, 102–104, 109, 115. *See also* social reproduction theory
Revolution, 12, 23, 73, 79, 154, 162

singular, 3, 16, 17, 60n8, 65n40, 122n22, 147; singularity, 60n8, 65n41, 148. *See also* case
science, 42, 49, 59n5, 64n30, 64n35, 65n38, 90n12, 95, 101, 118n1, 128, 129, 134, 135, 137, 138, 140, 141, 143, 144, 145, 169n4. *See also* ideology; theory
Spinoza, Baruch, 36, 37, 41, 43, 61n11, 130, 141
Spirit, 40, 100, 138, 150n11
spiritual, 12, 13, 14, 16, 22, 23, 47, 77, 109, 158, 169n5, 170n12
state of nature, 57, 67, 73, 77, 79, 81, 106, 161
structuralism, 64n35, 105, 107, 150n9, 165
structure, 6, 13, 16, 19–20, 22, 33, 35, 42, 47, 49, 51, 52, 62n20, 75, 76, 97, 107, 109, 113, 119n9, 121n20, 130, 132, 135, 143, 144, 149, 157, 158, 164. *See also* structural causality
subject, 18, 19–20, 22, 24, 27, 31, 33, 55, 56, 60n10, 61n16, 64n29, 67, 73, 79, 81, 84, 118n1, 130, 136, 137, 144, 146, 162, 164; subjection, xiv, 19, 26, 27, 32, 36, 48, 62n19, 79; subjectivation, 19, 27, 105
subjectivity, 24, 62n19, 81, 85, 164. *See also* interpellation; ideology; alienation

technocratism, 96, 100, 101, 102, 115, 117, 121n15
teleology, 70, 107, 141. *See also* Hegel
theatre, 32, 34, 52, 63n28, 80, 87, 90n18; materialist theatre, 151n15

theological, 21, 43, 61n13, 64n35, 73, 77, 80, 84, 114
theology, 57
theory, Althusser's conception of, ix–xviii, 6, 13, 34, 51, 95, 127, 129, 133, 139, 160. *See also* theoretical practice
time, concept of, 10, 11, 12, 13, 14, 15, 16, 26, 30, 38, 59, 71, 72, 74, 107, 130, 160, 165
temporality, 12, 14, 25, 26, 38, 49, 53, 55, 59, 78, 94, 105, 106, 158, 160; noncontemporary time, 36, 71, 72, 107, 158; plural temporality, 5, 29, 104, 107, 150n9, 160
topique, 14, 18, 22, 24, 26, 29, 31, 35, 36, 49, 54, 86, 102, 129, 130, 136, 139; topography, 55, 117, 165, 166
totality, materialist concept of, 10, 11, 22, 26, 100, 113, 148, 158; complex totality, 22, 113; spiritual totality, 47, 77, 109. *See also* idealism; Hegel; overdetermination; phenomenology
transindividual, 5, 18, 19, 21, 24–25, 44, 47, 58, 117, 122n27, 163, 165

unconscious, 15, 17, 18, 22, 24, 25, 26, 28, 29, 31, 33, 35, 37, 38, 39, 43, 44, 45, 48, 60n9, 62n20, 65n36, 65n41, 79, 85, 86, 90n9, 129, 144, 146, 147, 150n6, 150n9, 165
unconsciousness, 44
universality, 67, 71, 86; universalization, 16, 47
Unheimlich, 31, 86. *See also* Freud

Vorstellung, 63n28, 138

whole, x, xiv, 9, 13, 14, 15, 16, 22, 24, 37, 42, 45, 60n7, 60n10, 64n32, 87, 90n14, 107, 109, 114, 143, 150n9, 158, 159, 163, 166, 167, 168n1, 170n12

Žižek, Slavoj, 27–30, 33, 34, 35, 62n18, 62n19, 121n17, 150n3
zombies, 67, 72, 80, 81, 84, 86, 88

About the Author

Natalia Romé is chair professor in social sciences at the Universidad de Buenos Aires, where she directs the Master in Communication and Culture Studies program and co-coordinates the Program of Critical Studies "Between Marxism and the National-Popular." She is Senior Researcher in Instituto de Investigaciones Gino Germani, Universidad de Buenos Aires and also teaches at the Universidad Nacional de La Plata. Romé is one of the founding members of the *Red Latinoamericana de Estudios Althusserianos*, a member of the editorial board of *Demarcaciones*, and since 2009 is a part of the organizing committee of Althusserian Studies Conferences. She has published many papers on Ideology and Discourse Studies, Political Philosophy, Marxism, and Psychoanalysis, in Argentina, Chile, México, Brazil, Germany, Italy, New Zealand, and the United States. Romé is the author of *La posición materialista. El pensamiento de Louis Althusser entre la práctica teórica y la práctica política* (2015) and coeditor of *La intervención de Althusser* (2011) and *Lecturas de Altusser* (2011), among other books.

www.ingramcontent.com/pod-product-compliance
Lightning Source LLC
Chambersburg PA
CBHW021849300426
44115CB00005B/82